Shadow of the Rain

A Collection

By Raushan Burkitbayeva - Nukenova

HERTFORDSHIRE PRESS

A raven black horse amid the vast steppe,
Time is going by inevitably!
No solid space can slow it down.
Oh, wormwood wind –
The shadow of the rain,
Is blown through limbs of lightning!

A Shamelessly Ethno-focussed Preface

A Divine Psyche has many spirits. An esoteric intuition we Wiccans have taught from times immemorial. Although, in due season, Sufi songsmiths and perfumed gallants equally pondered on the implications of this very same truth. So, as a self-confessed ugly poet, or in other words, an ethno-focussed, squat, overweight, gnome delighted to find beauty through the three original Muses worshiped on Mount Helicon in Boeotia, namely, **Aoidē** ("song"), **Meletē** ("occasion" or "practice"), and **Mnēmē** ("memory"), the privilege of writing this preface for Raushan Burkit Bayeva-Nukenova's second work has fallen to me. An undeserved and unexpected blessing, even though one foretold, perhaps, by ancient runes to the gifted Dutch Seeress, Freya Aswynn, many years ago. Albeit, that recalled, an undertaking only recently made manifest in the manner of a sudden, sanctified, benedicite. To contextualize, my first approach to Freya seemed to induce her clearly prophetic tongue to foretell of my increasing involvement with "ethnic mysteries". A previously unprecedented prediction, delivered amid evocative inscriptions penned by our English summer sunshine on the surrounding environment. Certainly, back then, I interpreted these dual omens as signs that this remarkable woman would prove highly instrumental in my life - way before she agreed to ordain me as a priest of the Goddess Nerthus. Or, for that matter, effortlessly demonstrate she was much more than a mere celebrity. On the contrary, Freya – rather like Raushan - is a woman revealing the sensible intelligence necessary to champion a re-emergent Art. And as such, both of these women easily rise above the momentary caprice of fame into a genuinely spiritual sensibility. Yet, with hindsight, each one of us appears to have been anointed by powers celestial to represent the recovery of a truly Expressionist paradigm.

Hence, in this bold and insightful second collection of Expressionistic literatures, Raushan Burkit Bayeva-Nukenova invites her readers to revel in the cogitations of a Kazakh Radical

Traditionalist. A literary position provoking the exploration of Eurasian motives, Central Asian reactions to London, nomadic love, and the contours of ethnic memory. Every one of which is lyrically scrutinized - along with the dissonant place of women in our postmodern world. However, unlike her highly successful (and probing) first volume **The Wormwood Wind**, the author of this present book seeks to extend her poetic analysis of perennial affairs, before taking her first tentative footsteps into prose. This may be why pundits are already saying **Shadow of the Rain** portrays diverse strains of shamelessly autobiographical material throughout its fresh and innovative pages. All explaining, of course, the obvious value of such a tome as a rarefied contribution to those literary discernments mapping contemporary Woman's exact boundaries.

Overall, Raushan Burkit Bayeva-Nukenova's examination of nationality, colour, religion, and Kazakh cultural customs, will blatantly challenge the assumptions of Western readers, while opening the doors of their perception into a uniquely Central Asian perspective. Therefore, I have no hesitation, yet again, in heartily recommending this text to our English speaking audiences.

London 2017
David Parry

HERTFORDSHIRE PRESS

Published in United Kingdom
Hertfordshire Press Ltd © 2016

9 Cherry Bank, Chapel Street
Hemel Hempstead, Herts.
HP2 5DE, United Kingdom
e-mail: *publisher@hertfordshirepress.com*
www.hertfordshirepress.com

Shadow of the Rain
by Raushan Burkitbayeva-Nukenova ©

English

Translated by Vassiliy Lakhonin
Edited by David Parry
Design by Aleksandra Vlasova & Allwell Solutions
Project manager Anna Lari

....

ISBN 978-1-910886-31-1

Shadow of the Rain

Table of Content

Chapter 1

Nomadic love

Shadow of the Rain

Taraz Mulberry

What a dreamlike mulberry,
With a carved crown-like canopy,
Having stretched out its heavy branches,
To the darkest of skies.
Oh, this undying mulberry,
A witness to hearty japes,
Whereby young gatecrashers
Wept: ever sheltered by its falling shadow.
Oh, Oh, this old mulberry,
It is like a steppingstone for reckless dates,
Wherein agitated voices rushed
Toward silently sleeping stars.
Ah, this sweet mulberry!
You gave your shelter with open hands,
While your juicy wine berries,
Poured like blood in malted waves.
Eh, this miserable mulberry:
Witness of too many secrets.
You stand as a punished culprit,
Although, never having betrayed anyone.
Let your branches strive to the sky again,
While old scars blur from our memories.
And again, let children frolic here about,
Even though they might not let the berries grow.
And every time, I focus my thoughtful eyes,
As if I were a child once more
Recalling past times as if anew,
I will embrace your solid trunk.

The Shadow of Genghis Khan

Rain, snow,
And a bitterly cold mist -
It seems to sleet all the livelong day.
Perhaps the ravine will fill to its brim,
Ironically illuminated by rampant shadows:
Each conqueror being a kister in legend!
And as such, leads these cloud-hordes skyward
Forcing poets to beg forgiveness for fabled plots.
Yet see – those broken smoke trails in the air,
On the border of roofs and centuries,
Wherein blurry lines, like joyous tidings,
Suggest chilled Kaisak regiments.
Boncuks, flags, Horsemen afloat.
All wailing into the snowstorms snarl,
While their shadows shine on our windowsills -
Each analogous to deep prints in heavy snow.
Somewhere there is a hill of holy relics
Its shadow guarding these drifting guardians.
Simultaneously, Cumans sing like a blizzard
As Genghis Khan brings back fear.

Shadow of the Rain

***

Doubtful grapes swelled with tears,
As rain perpetually pattered outside.
Air castles also broke apart,
Albeit forgotten within languishing berths.
Where are the ships and valorous captains?
Where do the talking parrots sleep?
Only groomed and formidable figures
Ask for locations, or search hidden runes.
Who will revive these stones with prayers?
Who can decipher old arcane words?
Only after admiring such terrible battles
Did the prairie grass start to weep -
While surrounding feathers turned gray
                                    from grief.
Yet, poppies still burn brighter than flame
So, who will voluntarily release their reins?
Or saddle the loosened horses?
How like an arrow directed at God,
Do those minarets fade into desert light.
Our battle cries demanding this journey
                                    starts
With a ring of shabby coins.

Almaty

At the foothill of mottled Alatau,
Where snow remains all summer,
Where deeds and dreams are audacious,
Do Almaty houses strive skyward.
A city of beautiful stones and gardens,
Embraced by delightful apple trees in bloom.
Fountains are murmuring in the cool shade
As friends rest together in the afternoon.
Babies are sleeping in strollers in the parks.
Lanterns shine through the lace of foliage.
Tender Ladies look like flowers.
My Almaty-City is a Garden of Eden!

Night in Khiva

Unopened bud, shy and gentle -
Covered by veils from a stranger's eye,
I can feel you …..
Like the jingle of jewelry (so familiar to me)
But sounding quiet, while feeling tactile.
Listen ….. the echoes of these tumbril bracelets
                                    jingle,
As necklaces rising through diaphanous breaths.
Allowing you to hide your excitement,
Even though my heart grasped wordless truths:
Each making a relentless shadow.
Silently, you slid behind me in the darkness.
Oh let this fire burn: enflaming both heart and soul!
Times of rendezvous… a gratitude to destiny...
I beg for mercy on your behalf.

Raushan Burkitbayeva - Nukenova

Once upon a time

I will light a slow fire
And my fire will burn every sadness.
Each thought intensely occurring,
Across violet horizons.
Watching from Heaven
Old lunar ball, twisted by dreams,
Will break the barrier of night.
And captured by this fancy,
Will jingle amid crystal hailstones.
As stars fall into my hand -
Unexpectedly balancing opposites.
And through this long separation
A dashing vagrant will wink,
By intangible campfires, wherein sparking swords
Are swallowed by unfathomable whirlwinds.
I need such a necklace,
Before this dazed court falls silent.
And dropped coins glance on sands,
To reveal this mystic side-face.
Oh, refined vignette ...

Shadow of the Rain

In inshore Tugai

Daily, I run to you as an arrow,
Choked by sweat and dust ...
Witnessing sparks and stars near the moon.
We froze with laughter,
While over the cool river
Your voice sounded sonant.
Meanwhile, branches bent over the water,
Just like your thin figure.
As quiet jingles flowed behind the back
Of tight plaits ...
And you are so soft with me,
My dearest.
The night unwinds our dreams,
Similarly to your plaits.
While stars melt in their altitude
Under morning-drenched dews.
Yet, our moon pours its gentle light,
On everyone near and far,
As fervent horses wait for me,
Champing at their bits.
Let the wind once again bring jingling bracelets,
Where tender songs live
In summer grasses.

Raushan Burkitbayeva - Nukenova

Gobelin

Never yielding as a prisoner of nomads,
Your Gobelin home has charmed me.
Its threads stretching from olden days,
In a fashion similar to dusty paths
Through an endless swish of flags.
Here is a cloud of wool,
Twined by the hands of steppe-dwellers,
Like a train of troublesome thoughts
Allowing our Moon to roll it into a thorny ball.
And a sad song whirls like a bird,
While a swift-footed horse runs across a field.
Leaving footprints soaked through with bitter tears:
"I believe you will come back with the sunrise" -
As arrows fly through the rings of centuries.
My beloved ones are waiting on settled shores.
Awaiting a reunion hidden from public glances,
That sparkle like stars in a painting of the river.

Shadow of the Rain

***

The vastness of the steppes is so plangent,
Reminiscent of Kobyz Korkyt Ata's
                              weeping.
Similarly, that horseshoe (an arba) when
                              put in harness,
Is like a string path to eternal places.
Lets listen to the winds as they stir dreams
Among ever silent constellations.
Although, dumping your ladle allows noisy
                              rain to squelch.
Perhaps he was right. Retaliation is
                              inevitable,
Meaning everyone waits for an end: for
                              rescue.
It is said an old fugitive while playing at
                              night,
Lost a necklace of stars in the river.
He wanted to escape from declining
                              consequences,
Whilst the kobyz sings in a divine hand.

Raushan Burkitbayeva - Nukenova

***

Soul – is a wild nomad...
Intoxicated by fairy tales,
While covered with bars of night,
To allure without music or words.
Yet, full of wondrous expectations,
As fragrant oleaster smells scent a dusty
                                    garden,
Wherein bitter suffering,
Flamed purple – like a mature
                                    pomegranate.
Oh, you night beauties,
Twisting like an emerald vine,
Cause headstrong youngsters lose their
                                    minds!
It seems they are seduced by your brown
                                    eyes.
Explaining why I fly like a bird,
And wander along sunny riverbanks.
Where I stroll like a stringy light,
With a pearl thread in my hand.

Berel barrow

Whose dream is guarded by steppe balbals
On these silent landscapes?
Who sleeps for so long?
What does this tired face   want to tell?
Apart from mouthing a mountain rivers kui*
As it flies above this valley and wills in silver lettering
Sounds similar to a message from the depths of the
                                    ages.
You, however, are blinded to sacrificial connections
And greet racehorses with delight
While their jewelry sparkles with gold.
But, chiefs announce their ancient decree.
And vultures shine with no deterrence,
As we open our diamond supplies.

Kui- music piece for dombra (kaz.)*

Raushan Burkitbayeva - Nukenova

***

Where are you, my childhood?
Are you next door?
Water hardens in backwaters.
As blurry eyes and flecks of insomnia
Spoon fatal memories into a pond.
I remember our revelations
And the fragrance of night gardens,
Allied to the assurances of naïve love,
Colliding on sleepy trains.
As the clatter of wheels, villages,
And landscapes, flash outside the window.
Over there, screams, things, altering faces.
And Old Moon's lantern, like a silent
                              guardian,
Beckon night as a quiet cloud.
Similar, therefore, to a rainstorm from
                              oblivion,
The Soul flies outwards - a sacred event:
Or the personal gift of being free!

Shadow of the Rain

***

The inscription is deciphered
On a silver bowl of Saks barrow
Issyk town
The boring circle of a table lamp
Knock against heartless hours.
As star-flies meet the sundown,
To disregard time and ignore us.
Another day gets cold like tea in a mug!
Yet, a secret was uncovered by chance.

A truth kept for hundreds of years -
It gave us the name of an ancestor!
Through the thickness of years...

Raushan Burkitbayeva - Nukenova

In alpine meadows

I will give you a flowery meadow
Among rainbow Alpine fields.
Although, don't be deceived by the violets glance.
But watch, instead, the spleeny chamomile
As it sings of Eternity.
Or bell-flowers sonorously jingling,
Amid a bemused lunar blindness.
Certainly, blue skies crown floral carpets,
As beauteous marigolds burn like fire.
Each akin to a golden arrow in hunter's quiver
And making my heart tremble,
While the heady spirit of mint-grass
Must be taken by unseeing July rains.
Each staking this meadow of lengthy bliss,
Like a boncuk of sedge among living breezes,
Repeating the song of the heavenly Oriole.
Herein, we will lie. Sleeping in a blossomed embrace,
As the bushes of briar mature,
And mountain onions pour out their bitterness -
Similar to unsuspected culprits
Long estranged from abundance.
Albeit, already transcribed at the roadside:
A place where green lights provide an elastic sheet.
Yet, the most painful of open wounds can be healed
                        by plantain.
And horizons in the sky remain innocently pure.

Shadow of the Rain

Oriental bazaar

Oriental bazaar,
Exquisite diversity.
Sultriness and rumpus,
And the voices of barkers.
Coolness of silk,
Rewarding glances,
Ginger and saffron,
Sinuous figures under the veil.
Here are the halva and sherbet.
Your playful answer.
Here are figs and persimmons,
I wish I could not lose my mind.
Grapes and pomegranates,
Your violet eyes.
I do not want dinars,
You are as slim as sycamore.
And the master is a chump
Proudly wearing his turban,
And enfolding our bazaar in silence -

Raushan Burkitbayeva - Nukenova

At night - it is like Mazar.
Sleeping - tired fellah,
Merciful Allah!
Clouded by thoughts like a turban,
With garments of darkness.
I wish I could see your figure,
Oh, the devil tempts me.
I will kindle a fire,
And you will come to my tent -
Then, let the flutes play.
You are as graceful as a gazelle.
And your figure sways,
Like red tulips a-play.
Precious stones -
The sparkle of beautiful eyes.
Glowing as the starlight.
To the thrill of the gentle shadows.
Purple light fades away,
Love allows no judgment.
From love, I will be drunk,
And you will disappear like mist.

Courier

A rider races on a horse,
The rider is racing.
As the Sun squinting in the saddle
He is scared.
What message will he bring?
Joy or sorrow?
Our village waits in silence,
There on the hillside.

Raushan Burkitbayeva - Nukenova

***

Shades are playing on a bench...
In spring, an elder sleeps in a garden,
In the coloured, embroidered, skullcap,
Mantled by carved greenery.
Crowds of lovebirds in the alleys –
They fly to see each other,
And echoing their bloomy thoughts,
A flurried day trembles.
I hear the silken whisper,
And fly each sonorous rhyme.
Repulsing every noise and laugh,
The Muses want to wield again.

At the bus stop

Piles of melons and watermelons huddled at each
stop.
It seems local farmers did a great job.
It is hard to go past these
Genuinely miraculous things
Tormented by thirst and midday heat -
Like a fever.
Those girls, lovely maidens...
Stripped to the succulent core.
As men gaze at their young bodies
Devouringly…

Raushan Burkitbayeva - Nukenova

"Kyz-Kuu" - "Catch the young girl"

My days fly away
Like clouds.
I cannot strap them
To the saddle.
…
Thoughts fly forward like an arrow,
I will catch them as they float
And place them in a prison of fortune.
I will clap spurs to my horse
While at full tilt.
I will challenge my rival.
I will catch up and finally embrace,
My dream.
And until the time when I get old,
I will not part from Tulpar.
Instead, I will snatch a kiss from unprepared lips.
You will blush like a nocturnal red sky,
While you will tame temper with a whip …..
But there are no hurdles for brave Dzhigits

Shadow of the Rain

***

A cold wind freezes unbidden tears.
While time breaks hope into pieces.
Yet, rosy dreams sweep doubts away,
Although, these daydreams collapse in
melancholy.
I cannot believe that autumn is at my door.
But I will try to trick it stealthily.
I will paint in red those silver streaks of
gray.
And gift my love with renewed vigor!

***

At the bottom of a clear glass,
Like the petals of a tea rose,
Ever forgetful of the terrible cold,
Tea leaves are waiting for new songs.

As their secrets are uncovered,
They dance, recalling the summer.
The fever of fierce deliberated glances,
Playing against the smoke of an elastic
cigarette.

A game of shadows in Jasmine bushes,
Reflect motives inside a forgotten romance.
While the rustle of crumpled muslin,
Recalls an afternoon in a state of trance.

Raushan Burkitbayeva - Nukenova

And passionate whispers by the fountain,
Unease of short, but shaded, light.

It has the hue of hidden deceptions,
Amid a heady scent of lilacs.

These ups and downs -
Like a ritual dance in the night,
Allow tea leaves to crave for Sunday.
When everyone wants to be back in
                              summertime ...

*Kabardino-Balkaria,
Chegem, July 2003*

Shadow of the Rain

***

The light of an autumn garden
Is speckled with gold.
The smoke of farewell fires
Echoes over a silent river.
The ash of feelings – with silver
Sloughed live leafs,
Ripening at night
With golden dome lines,
Do you hear the serenade sung by rain?
Outside this door?
The fear of solitude
Will descent as a windstorm.
In her dreams and nights,
During a hot summer.
Cold – with bitter phrases

Resounds within
mountain snow.

Raushan Burkitbayeva - Nukenova

***

Last summer disappeared
With the last sunset:
With ripe pears
That bent branches to the ground.
All causing my flock of birds to fly
With majestic verse,
While praising,
Fresh bread on the table!

Eurasia

Stitches ache – invisible – dull.
We live at the crossroads
Of thoughtless pain.
Being neither settled Europe, nor hot Asia,
But a land of changing winds - Eurasia.
Frivolously, we venerate God and Tradition.
We even occasionally go to the Mosque.
Restless, we look and wait for something,
While sinking into cussing and fussing.
Yet, we are not hypocritical. We are simply two-faced.
Partly believing in Khayyam's presages,
We are godless and Muslims both -
Half-sinners in half self-deceptive,
We rush to the precipice, in fear and trembling
Of losing our faith to a legendary happiness:
While imbibing each strangers' fantasy.
A polygon of ideas, my antithetical Eurasia.

Raushan Burkitbayeva - Nukenova

Foremothers!

With one hand, one lulls a child to sleep.
With the other – one protects the world: its silence.
You walk into night like the moon, twinkling with
heartfelt light.
You give to the stars, creator of the universe!
Oh, the embodiment of wisdom, patience,
You are the underflow of love in the form of a river.
You are the song that pulses in newborn children,
You are the inspiration of lovers and poets!
Foremothers – heroes of battle!
As fearless warriors, you fought in bloody war.
Thus, I bow my head in the honor of your names.
You shield us from perpetual troubles.
From the darkness of belligerent distress.

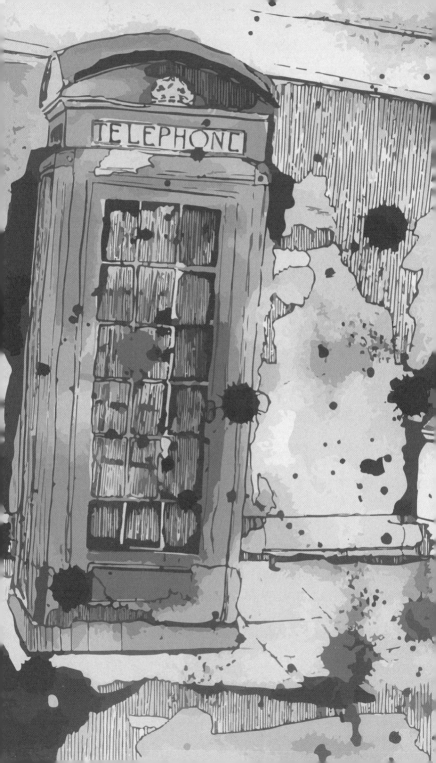

Chapter 2

It is raining in London…

Shadow of the Rain

In London

Invisible gaps breach space,
As rain moves along each sodden cloud.
It captures the British capital,
And all its islands,
Like a whip beating disobedient captives:
Threatening to throw them into prison.
Yet, useless winds are positioned as a guard,
Against issues necessitating wrapped whisky bottles,
While, in an old theater, performances reach a full
house.
Shakespeare has not abandoning his stage,
Although, the rain raises an albescent flag.
Along a new theater in an old corner,
Across from Piccadilly shop-windows,
Where music plunges into a secret gloom:
In this realm of aging tunes and idylls.
Each reminiscent of a faded dress -
Once the work of fashionable designers -
But, nowadays in far less demand.
Like moth-eaten velvet on a rusting chair,
Or ever-silent lace curtains,
Hiding viewers, but never drying them from rainfall.

***

The noise and crowd of Piccadilly!
What is the reason? Innovation and
                          fashion?
A new camp for Hippies?
No – the filming of an advertisement for
                          Cristiano Ronaldo.
Unsurprisingly, pretty girls shine like bulbs
                  and garlands,
Smiling as fame shoots his bolt.
They say he kicked a goal directly into
                  young girls' hearts.

***

Twilight narrows in street quarters,
On a night untied by a transport hub.
Soon this city will be plunged into
                    moonlight,
And snow will cover every stair: every gate.
Yet, Henry the Eighth still stands spit-and-
                  polished.
While adolescents miserably fail their
                  exams.
Enough is never enough, it seems.
Therefore, each needs to learn about –
                  kings or daughters.
The Tower of London (that keeper of
                  secrets),

Shadow of the Rain

Ghosts, a flock of crows, and tributes to
                                    etiquette.
Oh, the shadows of rain hang over Big Ben.
Oh, those silent thoughts washed away
                                    with the Thames

                    ***

Each year we greet the autumn,
With its apple pie Sunshine.
All shining inside the red body,
Of a bus on the threshold
Of a two-storey whatnot,
With piles of sheets and books interring
Long forgotten corpses.
It's rays curl each doll's hair -
Those repulsive simulacra of humanity -
Disguising indigestible secrets.
So, the Talmud sits unopened in a library:
The Tom Talmud library.
Yet, where else do men learn in these
                                    exaggerated times,
Such top-secret etiquettes?
Some say the light goes out in the morning
As a sparkling of mercurial stars
Benights the way for youth,
Only interested in the clarities of a
                                    mundane science.

Raushan Burkitbayeva - Nukenova

Cambridge

Silver eyes – like spawning eggs,
Or traffic lights blinding the road-river ahead
While plumose clouds over every roof,
Sharing fragments of a sentence by a newspaper
                              kiosk.
The fleeting glances of passers-by
Form silhouettes against sliding houses.
Cambridge is a student-like city:
A pier of dreams in nouveau riche minds.
Stirring faces and dialects -
Along escalators transporting shadows to a subway.
Yet, meeting the rain with its gusty winds,
We will free the Prince! We will become lucky!
As streams of sunshine shake their hair
Over the titmice of Cambridge square.
Facts proving not even the gossip of tabloids,
Can model as the old faith once did.
Oh, hand over history to Don Esquire
And exhale on the Bridge of Sighs,
With each lung of an inflated chest
Full of DNA helix codes.
All composing a hit in the studio,
Against stretching body-sides in kayak
Reminiscent of picturesque shores off Kema.
Only eminent hearts remember,
Petrified books with forgotten theorems.
Truly, a son continues the glory of his father

Shadow of the Rain

As raised glasses toast for good luck in surrounding
pubs.
Rusting foliage sticks to the soles
Of an autumnal outburst
Loudly announced by rumors!
These difficult days leaned into the sunset.
Although bicycle spokes no longer tinkle.
Cambridge – is a smithy of Nobel laureates.
The sun is shining – guaranteeing victory!
The sun is ever shining – guaranteeing victory!

Raushan Burkitbayeva - Nukenova

To William Blake

To see a World in a Grain of Sand
And a Heaven in a Wild Flower,
Hold Infinity in the palm of your hand
And Eternity in an hour.
William Blake

Shadow of the Rain

Across sky palms shimmer the radiance of truth.
A gift of poetry from loving eternities.
A light from the centuries wherein distance fades
nothing.
His creations are attractive sympathies,
Like grains of magnetism on a painter's palette.
As viewers, we are ever kept in sight,
Imprisoned in our cages of mundane perspective.
Of beams refracted through the prism of decades,
Crushed onto a wooden board of color, sound, and
light.
Overall, he left his engraving on our hearts.
As narrations of innocence, sketches of phantoms,
All decoded nowadays.
Messages – the whimsy of madness.
Bothersome rain in a thunderstorms chord.
In powerless, but textured etchings.
Yet, we are haunted by the ghost of a flea,
By books illustrations, portraits and poems.

Raushan Burkitbayeva - Nukenova

Winston Churchill

Create your own universe
Along the path you yourself engineer!
There are no perfect ways in War,
Apart from going down in history riding a tank!
Overall, a fat man with a Cuban cigar,
And lover of Armenian cognac.
A descendant of the Duke of Marlborough,
The conqueror of global Evil:
An inventor and survivor.
Once a boy wallowing through a quagmire,
With no fear or doubt –
They say …..
Until, the bog opened like a jaw,
Dragging him into the abyss.
He begged for help so desperately –
They say …..
Fortunately, help came -

Shadow of the Rain

In the form of a passing farmer
Who cut a thick branch from a tree
And rescued the poor fellow.
I know anyone would have done it,
Of course
Without considering it bravery.
Yet, the father of the rescued boy
Reciprocated with gramercy.
He paid for his tuition and books
And revealed Fleming to the world
(Penicillin being discovered by him),
Saving, thenceforth, a lot of lives in an asclepian
                                    process,
While the one who escaped death,
Becamea Tory Prime Minister.

---

* Tory - British monarchist party

Raushan Burkitbayeva - Nukenova

A Visit by Captain Flint

After opening one's door,
The night often breaks in with a censer -
Shattering plans: making sleep unreliable.
Yet, the moon landed in the core of his ship,
Turning the entire house upside down.
His pirates having been left behind
Inside a hostile storm. And these storms
Have all the seeming of ferocity
Accompanied, as they are, by ever-raising waves.
Look - the hold is full of skim gold.
All treasures gained at the cost of a fragile life:
Akin to ships and eggshells.
Look – human blood streams as it playfully splashes
Into the Void -
Wherein men fight for women!
Of course, glittering garnets are usually burdened
                    with wickedness.
Oh, Captain Flint ….. surely, you had a hand in this?
When all said and done, your pirates feast at that
                    table.
However, they are disregarded in my papers
And my piastres! Wait, where are those piastres?
Each one translucent like a bouquet of asters
                    trembling in a glass.
Although, by morning the storm subsides as
                    Bullfinches sing.
I will do coffee with them. Would you like cream,
                    sugar, or ginger?

Shadow of the Rain

Following the conflagration, he sealed his letter with
wax.
He was kind - albeit declared as a brigand by his
executioner.
In the end, Captain Flint lined out a rout and sailed
away,
Having made a dent in the universe.

A leaf, circled with yellow spots.
Will fall from finery
As a sign - the shadow of impermanence,
Yet, this fall is spilling over me
And wraps me in a rainy blanket.
Oh, the Sovereign Square empties again
Like a lethargic moon with upturned eyebrows,
Which repeatedly asks the same question.
Hence, I watch the guard changing
At their Royal Palace.
Allowing the chilled moon to fall asleep.
Before motions on the porch
Suddenly escort the solemn entrance
Of soldiers under the gaze of a tin eye,
That delights the crowd of screams masses.
This family is adored by the whole of London
They say …..

Raushan Burkitbayeva - Nukenova

***

The Queen has waved to us!
Amid a pandemonium of police officers.
Curiously, she appears to impersonate gloss
While wearing the crown of a lost Empire -
Decked, as she is, with the diamonds of
                              Cullinan:
Grand seigneurs,
Black crows,
And the fog of history.
Rain subtly murmurs outside my window,
Making me fearful of asking questions
                              aloud.
Boats are overturned,
While the vagabond-wind appears in my
                              dreams.
Like misty distances and fading light.
Life is so short, so instantaneous!
Only smoking stars offer comforting
                              answers
That slowly melt in the morning.

***

Were you waiting for the last fearful gasp?
Wondering if you will make it till morning?
Or will the axe, with a single stroke
Cut through the thread of life?

***

Shadow of the Rain

Centuries decay, but legends remain fresh.
Similar to the signs of shadows growing
                              white along a wall.
Perhaps you will even hear sinister shouts
                              with a shudder,
As the agony of prisoners from obliterated
                              antiquity,
Turns the moon pale with drained passions.
In this maze, someone's screams after seeing
                              a ghost.
And one cannot help feeling complicit
                              oneself,
Although, the executioner still begs
                              forgiveness from
                              his victim.
Are ghosts afraid of emptiness?
Above the tower – waifs of mist continually
                              waft,
While our souls cannot recognize quietude.
Once, stillness was caught in a trap,
As night listened and then moving the
                              other way round.
Possibly, inmates will forget their past,
Amid hopes threatened by the darkness.
Tourists will leave! Everything will be as it
                              was before.
Each face getting paler in a lattice frame.
Maybe, another life is watching us!
Rain languishes on the fly,
As it tries to fill both ditch and emptiness.
I can even see a Maple leaf floating towards
                              me,

Raushan Burkitbayeva - Nukenova

(Slightly inked with yellowness)
At the same time as a bird flies away from
                                the Tower,
To enjoy a serene afternoon.
But, the wind will throw a handful of snow,
In its due season.
Thereafter, I will give up on sleep and rest.
Within thick walls and icy sadness.
Indeed, I feel better on the steppe with its
                                blurry distances.
Whereon I found a friend-dragoman.
Over there, people will hide and tiptoe
                                behind every yurt.
Also, labourers, like stars in the night,
Openly performing magic and singing at
                                their stoves,
In regions faraway.
Astoundingly, I have guest from overseas -
                                a messenger from
                                God,
And conversation creeps through long
                                pathways.
A generous dastarkhan* will be offered.
Surly, Genghis Khan himself would
                                appreciate such
                                hostility!

---

* Dastarkhan - feast with treats (Kaz.)

53

Shadow of the Rain

Mary Stuart

The revelation of a Queen-sinner,
Under the cover of royal dresses.
Knowing the secrets of the darkest deep,
Where hidden places obscure passion and duty.

France and Scotland got married!
But, heaven stood against this union,
Even though their faith could have changed destiny.
Albeit, sterile marriages become a heavy burden.

Our homelands can be mean stepmothers,
So, it greeted the queen with cold indifference.
Nevertheless, she followed the voice of her heart,
And faced death in front of an angry crowd.

Her dress was mounted like a red flag!
On a grey scaffold – warm with a fountain of blood.
Remembered ... as red ink is spilled -
Over books stained with stories.

Raushan Burkitbayeva - Nukenova

***

Passions glow for centuries.
Like crimson trains stretching across a red
dress.
Truly, Zweig is lost in conjecture and
Schiller is a master
dramaturge.
Yet, Mary Stuart remains the passion of
their oeuvres,
Their feelings being beyond the Queen's
control.
Look - her flaming heart is laid on a
chopping block.
Oh, how marvelous in joy and anger,
Although, a devoted love is never allowed!
Instead, embittered by the venom of
complexity,
The tongues of traitors make insidious
claims.
Nowadays, the path to a throne is perilous

Shadow of the Rain

And follows an arduous bureaucracy:
Caught in an eternity of anticipation and
                                    distress.
Brodsky noticed this twist of fate,
In sonnets written for Mary Stuart.
Yet, with hindsight, her scaffolding had
                            no reasonable
                            grounds,
While hysteria always means the end of a
                            world!
Of course, history perpetually looks for a
                            pretext,
And filmmakers are lost in its mysteries.
But, anticipation is not eclipsed by
                            evidence
Nor censured by fierce debates.

Ann Bolein

She took to the stage as to the scaffold.
Her silks merging with each green lawn.
So airily, with no heaviness of soul,
Above the Tower a dull seagull flew.
He had long tried to conquer her,
But, fog crept over the Thames like a threat.
Omened by flashing star fall into oblivion.
There were only thorns from the one he called a rose,
They claimed.
But, now she is taken to the scaffold,
The thread of her pulse severed at the wrist.
Blinking away a tear with green sleeves,
She took solace from other women of surging
                              passions.
From the darkness of those times, along black
                              corridors,
The ghost of an executed monarch turns white.
Scaring the guards and looking reproachfully
Back through the long train of bloody history.
There is an explanation in rain and misty distances.
Under the canopy of heaven - boiling magma.
No titles, no throne, rescued you.
Rather, a stamp of desolation had imprinted you.

Shadow of the Rain

***

Will you knock the window with a nib?
Be aware of what we are not supposed to
                                    do.
"Vivat! Vivat, vivat!"
"Oh my God! It is not my fault!"
Yet, there is no point in arguing with them.
Indeed, Holy Fear is inspired by Thor,
Hugin, Munin, Baldrick,
Brenvin, Gvillum,
They walk in flowerbeds so pompously,
Finding their nests too frightening for
                                    relaxation.
Long live the kingdom!
It is guarded beside the castle faithfully.
While the time of its collapse is blurred by
                                    clouds.

Audrey Hepburn

It is daylight outside the window.
However, throughout the night snow will have piled,
By a house both quiet and dark.
The hosts had gone a long time ago.
Explaining why this forest sleeps covered in a warm
blanket.
The moon also left, as did the stars.
As a burden of velvet curtains.
Years – those gray hairs of insomnia,
Breath burning frost
Like an open-ended message
Laid before a window in the manner of a white rose:
Each coming after a great delay.
She waited for it obstinately,
Diverging from the portrait in a yellowed frame,
To a life like a snow globe glimpsed
Across the ruinous raid of daytime.
Draughts roamed in the house.
Gloves – moulded her hands.
And ball gowns laying around,
With neither use nor purpose
Complimenting this graceful, fragile, figurine:
In films - a naughty brunette.
Her eyes, nonetheless, sparkled as two agates,
Enlarged under a florid bonnet.
Her waist, it was said, the size of two girths,
Mirroring her gentle and apologetic smile.
Oh, Audrey - the muse of Givenchy,
Are you still in a hurry for "Breakfast at Tiffany's"!

Jack the Ripper

The quiet and peaceful streets of London torn apart,
By hissing sounds and bloody mail.
By a letter sent from a crimson point.
Stirring up the beehive of Scotland Yard.
As another nocturnal blade on the throat of a poor
victim,
Shows Jack the Ripper as a bold, cold-blooded,
human monster.
Mentioned in blacklists and to joined the ranks of
villainy,
Could even Holmes stop him?
A surgeon acts under the shadow of night.
Where are the lights to uncover this sinister
treatment?
Yet, sacrificial daughters lay on his devilish altar.
Amid a squall of guesswork flying like a storm
In the constables cabin.
All the woes from Pandora's box
Showered across city and suburb,
While anxiety walked outside everyone's house,
Reaching into the home of a disgraced love.
Meanwhile, shadows sneaked beside empurpled
stones,
And the blade in hand is not blunted by time.
Maybe luck will favour these Ladies of leisure?
As they meander across cobblestones with moral
burdens.

Yet, the rain studiously washes those murderous
                              spots,
Whereon, fog equally wanders over the Thames into
                              alleys
And archives cherishing these memories.
Some say, fear strangles the lonesome with booming
                              echoes.
Others add that the moon plays with a spirit-lamp.
"Do not sleep, do not sleep!" – the Spirit of
                              spiritualism whispers.
But, the temptation of nights' mysteries –
Are as a crystal of alexandrite.
Perhaps a chaplet of sonnets and a divination prism
Will encourage Shakespeare into a feast of poetry?
Nevertheless, tables twirl as apprehension prevents
                              every pond
From being approached in a reservoir of darkness.
Listen - mermaids weave a network of songs in the
                              shadowlands.
Where does this pain come from? Possibly, only poets
                              know.
They name it unmerciful blues.
But we have faith in the Eucharist,
In what we had and what we will be in the future.
Each moment of life being similar to an inhalation of
                              happiness,
Whilst exhalation passes on immortality.

Shadow of the Rain

***

Fog grows stronger above London,
But, a cup of tea will ease the spleen.
Shakespeare shines again like Mont Blanc.
His crown of sonnets never being
                          surpassed,
While Othello and Hamlet ask questions.
Romeo is waiting for his advice,
So is beautiful Juliet.
The range of tragedy is not degenerating,
Yet, Old Father Thames does not notice it.
Immortal light of the Renaissance,
You justly glorify the throne of any king.
Marking marks in centuries like a myriad
                          of treasures,
Without causing disputes, disagreements.

Princess Diana

How fragile is the scape, oh my Hortensia!
That fluffy hat will turn blue in the wind.
As a fog of divergent claims flies in equipage.
Hence, she moans: "I will die without love!"

How heavy the burden of a crown and moisture
                              soaked train.
When glances, like needles, prove more ruthless than
                              tailors.
She fought for her dreams with courage,
Although, most merely look from a side mirror.

Blushed cheeks: heavy blossom trusses,
Bending through heat to the thorny grass.
With the sincerest thought for many centuries
You caught my heart: you reign by right!

Shadow of the Rain

***

Oh God! I am not guilty,
For the loss of love.
That snow flies full flowery,
With a swan fan at dawn.
The frost comes into play like a nobleman.
Beethoven is tormented by fugues.
The thrill of a premiere often sounds like
                                an alarm,
Perhaps, the draught of wings is
                                unbearable.
He put his clothes on,
And goes to the scene of a blizzard,
As an orchestra directs his destiny.
Curiously, his foot is strained by melodious
                                arcs.
Ah, life is no longer than a snowfall,
While each sunset sails slowly away.
Crescendo. Goddaughter-Monad -
Then came the call that will not go away!

The capital

Rome is like Apollo: the marble whitens.
The Spanish Grand welcomes Madrid.
Berlin blows an organ fanfare.
And Lisbon and Amsterdam are in a hurry:
Blushing like lanterns out of shyness.
Yet, Budapest leaned near a refreshing pond,
While Dublin laid its plaid in a cage.
Fastidiously, Brussels calling for a picnic,
(this giant had cut the "Cabbage")*,
As the Vatican bowed its head.
Of course, Copenhagen is a carousel of tales.
Although, Reykjavik blew a large volcano.
But, Luxembourg – is neither cheerful nor gloomy.
Oh, mon Amour! Oh, mon Amour!
They are all worthy of fame and love.
Thank God you exist and always will!

—————————

Cabbage – money (slang)

Shadow of the Rain

***

I am amazed by the firmness
Of the British Empire.
As another batch, probably,
Join their Major League classes.
Yet, each ice cube soaks
In premium whiskey.
Oh, those sharpened skates -
At the stadium of phrases.
Pompously reigning -
Within a merciless dressage.
Will Cambridge beat
Oxford in its riverboat rivalry*?
Either way, Shakespeare stands immortal
Over dead filmmakers.
Of course, the Beatles were left by landing
                                    troops,
While Tungus came to life in a forest.
Yet, the old world dilapidates,
As an oak cut by constant feuding.
Its exorbitant ambitions
Grew unrestrained -
Like an electrical arch.
Is there a melody playing over the Thames?
And was the Hoopoe struck by
                                    imagination,
When he clambered among the rocks?
Overall, sleep has become a phantasm,
Torn apart like a beehive,

Raushan Burkitbayeva - Nukenova

Since, even the Sun stings
With a cancerous stigma.
One day – as a carefree Mowgli -
In the manner of Kipling in his jungle
                              Book,
We will all take a puzzled look,
Into a world that has lost its mind...

Shadow of the Rain

To Vladimir Nabokov

> *And in this age of fire and anger*
> *We shall live in other centuries -*
> *In the coolness of my tune,*
> *In thy lily valleys.*
> *V. Nabokov*

Raushan Burkitbayeva - Nukenova

Footprints on the threshold of a monogram.
On roughly fallen snow.
Porcelain painted with a delightful garden freeze,
While from the shadows a magic moon shines.

Here, cold and boring evenings hold sway.
As chilly and harsh winds blow from the north.
Look – a saffron ball has rolled into an ice-hole,
Simultaneously, a grey dove swaggered at the window.

Those signatures from the steppe blind us with their
                              whiteness.
Sending shivers across an icy fowl.
Even when it beats and crawls under a shirt.
Wait, do not be in a rush my friend.

This countryside snoozes with a prosaic sleep,
Each attracted to the other with magnetic force.
Oh, the silence of holy reticence.
Oh, the passion of love as it refuses to fade away.

The shimmer of stars eased our numbness -
While sparkling snow reflected from crystal to crystal.
This is a day of mysterious gifts!

Chapter 3.

Motives of Eurasia

Shadow of the Rain

Late date

To S. Seifullin
I am afraid to look in the mirror,
And be drowned as if in an abyss...
Here is a handsome man: slick, a dandy.
Touching up his mustache, collar, bow-knot.
His hair has a velvet tint.
Taken together, his look is cheerful and inquisitive.
- Oh, it is hot in here! Quick, get out of the room! -
His name is Sake ..... and he wears a twisted scarf.
I noticed he pacified his step and then sat down,
Afterwards, quietly singing a song on a chair:
- Oh, that thick wave of hair
Oh, my black-eyed beauty!
You are so mellifluous...
You are the one whom I knew would come!
Indeed, throwing away his cloak and fiddling with his
cane,

Allowed time to disappear. Where are you my guest?
Our cups of tea are getting cold.
He will come, but I will die....
The bell of his mechanical watch fell silent.
And he too avoided looking in the mirror.
How often do these personal inks dry?
He could dedicate so many poems to me!
Human envy – what a shame it has a bitter taste!
But, a poet cannot be revived.
Herein are exhibits under glass.
This house now looks like a tomb.
I was late for a date,
He stood like a statue.
Sadly, I have not met you,
Leaving a chasm of hours full of tears.

Shadow of the Rain

Olzhas

Great Steppe, he chants in praise of you,
While your peaceful rest he heroically protects.
Truly, the conscience of a poet is a claxon in the
                              world.
Officials may merciless count their liras.
And officers are often beaten by the merciless lyre.
- Close to a testing range! We do not need rockets?
Yet, pickets boil with vivid waves.
As open hands and hearts demand to sing.
There is a right to life. We will defend it together!
And, hand in hand, we will march,
Planting a garden, so our land can became more
                              beautiful.
You did a great thing, Olzhas -
You saved our ancestral home from destruction!

Raushan Burkitbayeva - Nukenova

Masters

Love can be a curse,
And a fatal torment.
But, once arms open to an embrace,
The soul proves impossible to burn.
Two luminaries cannot shine as bright
When close to each other.
It seems one always gives way,
While the other flies like a Phoenix.
Yet, troubles may still lie in wait,
To throw us into another abyss,
Although, the Muse will never leaving us,
Since, love smolders inside our hearts.

Shadow of the Rain

To Batyrkhan Shukenov

As an arrow clearly passes,
This news arrived in a flash.
And with burning pain,
> Pierced the hearts of our
> fellows.

Overwhelmed like a wave,
It knocked us out of storm-filled mountains.
May your path be paved,
With flowers on the steps of a Palace,
Since even men,
> Were grieving without
> hiding their tears,

With the dream of girls.
> So seeing you leave, we said
> farewell.

While poppies mourned,
> On the slopes: shivering and
> trembling,

With songs like birds,
Returning to their homeland again.
Suddenly all places,
Turned into lakes of sadness.

Raushan Burkitbayeva - Nukenova

On a sole impulse,
People echoed your songs.
In the fog of despair,
Common grief united us.
Your voice like a banner,

Floating quietly over the
steppe!

Again May thunderstorms,
Resound outside our windows.
The city was cleaned,

From black smoke by the
wings of soul.

Glorified roses,

Shed your smile.

From a bear hug,
You never run away…
And the night was lit up,

With illuminated hits from
mobile phones.

The magic power of love,

- In thousands of choruses!

All sang live,

While confessions were made to
microphones.

The echo reverberated us,
Like the eternal light of stars in the numb vastness.
18.05.2015

Shadow of the Rain

To Batyrkhan Shukenov

I know you will not come back again.
To a house that once echoed your steps.
A place fallen silent amid gloomy rain:
Trying to catch rays of laughter through a sieve.

The cool silk of white roses,
Emphasizes the darkness of separation.
You left immediately after the downpour,
To a place where the night gives birth to sounds.

Vainly, we searched for you in May,
As lilacs exploded on the boulevard.
You lived in songs: you loved us all,
While each and every house adored you …

Forever in our hearts you will live,
As a guest of the sad tea rose.
And we will cherish every glance,
You shine from the sky like a bright star.

Additional petals of heartening roses
Paves the long road heavenward.
A "Soldier of Love" left his post...
But we dare not beg for another date.

Raushan Burkitbayeva - Nukenova

***

Silver threads of love –
Pulled over the stave,
Can reign by a guitar.

Day in, day out, waiting tirelessly,
Through the weeping of rain and moaning
                                        winds,
He will hear the melody.
You are like a poet, always in love:
Breathing in unison with our planet.

***

This evening again,
We will recall a jingling song.
May the winds blow,
Since he feels cramped in the city.

The "unloved" will
Henceforth be beloved.
So, let sadness fade away,
And be chased by the clouds.
He was a "Soldier of Love…..
Now he has become a general.
You can call us,
We will all support you!
18.04.2015

Shadow of the Rain

***

A route in life,
Is traced for each of us –
The stone house,
Or timber crib, is on its way.
And planets give their signs,
To save us from trouble.
Each day flies towards the sky,
Of glorious victories.
And what is written in the heavens,
Will endure for your generation.
What is inevitable,
Will be predicted in detail.
But thoughts snake,
Around a rebellious soul.
And the horses of treason,

Rush to a ford,

To throw off the yoke,

Of a desperate fate.

And we all change,

Routes and paths,

While stars in the night,

Change our
destinies,

With fiery flourishes,
Written across history.
Dreams and love,

Should illuminate
our century.

Making us happy,
To be men of the world!

Raushan Burkitbayeva - Nukenova

On the edge

A burning essence you will surely behold,
In your flight over the gorge.
When clouds clench your chest so tightly
(And lightning dances in amusement),
That they all trace a path of life.

By fracturing true destiny
The chasm of boring years still stares at you.
Until a lens of tears allows
A vision of the afterworlds light...

The light of passion in my fiery dreams,
And in the wriggling of mountain rivers,
Build alpine tracks from a height,
Wherein we are carried away to the wilds.

To the Professor Beata Pastve Wojciechowski

Shadow of the Rain

Our lives are stretched along a rigorous thread,
Which is sewn into a living notebook.
Suddenly, a concise word is cut,
Declaring a temporal dissonance!
Wherein a hell of rising pressure
Loops - ripping the snarl.
I will fall into a healing laziness
Chopin – a current in the bloodstream!
Yet, needles of memory will again string,
The harmony of life's lessons.
This nocturne will fill every page
Even if the diagnosis is cruel...
Since, in the eyes of Holy Sky Father,
I will be seen winking insignificantly.
But, no matter how thorny my path will becomes,
The outcome is painfully familiar to me.

Raushan Burkitbayeva - Nukenova

Lisa – Zhengey

Young Muscovite,
Wondrous bird:
She flew across the steppe like a breeze,
Although, there are no electric trains here!
Instead, I will give her a ride: my sister!
A local chap offered his help, of course,
But her eyebrows curved -
She was specialist with diploma!
As such, she will train local sheep breeders
And innocent lambs -
Curly and lovely.
She will meticulously study the ancient sciences.
Delicate nature -
A curl of caracul: a sparkle of astrakhan.
She controls these living colours -
Of unlucky fellows.
Then, handing the keys of that ancient knowledge,
To local tribesmen,
She seductively plays as a lovely girl.
Leading an obedient daughter-in-law to eldcıly
                              kinsfolk,
She, our Liza, takes a deep breathe.
After all, Moscow is so far away!
And she will find her happiness in children.

Long distance trucker

The evening is stretching,
                    Like cherry jam,
Sweet and chewy,
On splendid lilacs.
He will stop in the guesthouse,
Having driven all day.
He has seen his landlady,
                    And decided to rest.
He will take the children in his arms,
                    To a neighboring house.
The hostile villagers,
Will lay the table.
With melodious laughter,
They will feed and wash him…
With steaming laziness,
                    He will show his languor.
With smile on his face,
He will hand his key to the driver.
He fluffs,
          The pillows with two swans.
The cherry liqueur,
          Muddles his mind.
Brown cherries,
          Hot summer.
The white moon,
          Warms him with kindness.

The night stretches,
Like molasses.
Wet asphalt,
            Sands along the border.
The thread of rain,
Linen hair.
The summer again,
With roads and cherries.
The children's look is severe,
And his is guilty.
Familiar from childhood,
                        Trusting eyes.
Unwittingly returning back,
                        The past years.
So generous was his host,
                        To the children!

Shadow of the Rain

The road of a trucker

Not obscured by time,
The river runs changing its course.
Over there is childhood – with puffy stacks,
Although, it is empty on the outskirts.

Father's truck collects dust.
The track pit - potholes everywhere,
That time will never come back to us.
Other cities and countries lure us.

Waves cut through the shore,
As that river breaks stones in its water.
But, I abide to strict mandates
I bear my father fate.

Captured spirit strays in the wilds of buildings,
The grids of each street – an imprisoned freedom.

Raushan Burkitbayeva - Nukenova

I will chase the poets out of their warm beds,
While a swarm of thoughts sweeps away old junk and
rubbish.
In the steppes are mountains and scorched deserts.
Over there, free winds dance, jump, and roar.
And he is breathing smoky wormwood,
And sails in the eternal sky: the happy man.
Oh tell me, where are the nomad tents, camps,
Bonfires, - where did the caravans go?
Nowadays, dried up trees with fallen leafs,
Shade rock paintings on the river Ili.
Yet, our ancestral land is bestowed to us forever!
Oh, how can we save this fragile sphere -
With all its rivers filled with life with moisture?
Perhaps it is best to not interrupt this time of
shaking!
A trembling time when the weave of fate will not be
severed.

Loona Park

This season Loona Park is closed,
And only a prodigal wind plays therein.
A bleak guard sniffs inside his booth,
Like a wood spirit in a thick forest.
Being abandoned by all the crows nearby,
He surrounds himself with a surly clique.
Yet, the leaves alone now circle around him,
In a place where the hubbub of children once
                                sounded.
Currently, the moon can ride for free:
Recklessly swaying as it swings on the slide,
Whilst a naughty wind whispers softly,
About wandering in presently silent spaces.
Each explaining the sly guards edgy look,
As he keenly keeps someone's secrets.
Indeed, it is not the swings that he guards -
But, cradles of hope and an anchors of fear.

Raushan Burkitbayeva - Nukenova

Balbals*

With the burden of grievous years,
A fine light glazed in the eyes.
You were blessed with a release from pain.
Inspired, therefore, by shivery dawn...
And the dust of time, and the ashes of my fears,
My shadow was covered with a smothering wave.
Perhaps, a stubborn spirit lifted and scattered
                              sentiments over the ashes
Of bygone days: in the abyss on an edge.
And the heart, was already ready for a heart attack.
Yet suddenly, a joyous melody started to play.
Although, I was not ready for such a fact,
But felt a surge of powerful energy...
Oh, please do not get in my coach,
Fly away to heights beyond the clouds -
My way is through the desert to Nazareth,
While you ascend to heaven with your dreams.
Possibly, the time of your feast has come,
And many people will celebrate it with you.
But alas, I am tired; these festivities will not awaken me.
They will only muddle me through instant joy,
Since thereafter, I may fall on evil days.
Instead, I will lock myself in a holt.
And insensitive therein, I will petrify - deaf and dumb,
Like a stone balbal – a steppe totem:
Two roads then converge at this point ...

_____

* Balbal - stone statue, comes from the Turkic word "baba" - ancestor, the
father

"Once Again About Love"

I watch an old movie -
While a lump forms in my throat,
Along with tears at this long episode.
The cloak of this city is now sodden.

As a signal specimen,
Wherein fraud is excluded,
From genuine leather
This is still a shabby suitcase.

Guileless and pure -
Frames in the solid sky.
Artists that have passed away
Play at unmanned flight...

Flattering our tired gazes
At the airport, Alma-Ata.
Doronina sang a familiar song
About a black cat.

Coral sand dunes -
The drifting colors.
Is it funny that the Sun and Moon
Wander in our dreams.
02.11.2014

Raushan Burkitbayeva - Nukenova

***

The truth was shimmering,
At the bottom of a wine glass.
A game with crystals,
Was reflected dreamily...
And prints on the glass,
                              Evidenced an
                              invisible fate,
Washed away by tears in silence.

***

The howl of an Emergency,
                              Will wake the
                              quarter.
With the branches of lilac,
The portal is veiled.
And buildings will shiver,
Frightening the crows.
The sleeve of a bathrobe,
Is wrapped with fog.
Taraz, 16.10.2014

***

How many takeoff runways are there in the
                              sky?
How many people got to the moon?

Shadow of the Rain

He saw a UFO in the night –
It seems that the fellow completely flipped
out.

***

Someone draws, someone sings...
Time mercilessly grinds everything to dust.
What a pity, we lose all our dreams.
But, stones of desires still shine on the
bottom.

Raushan Burkitbayeva - Nukenova

Summer Nights

Night breathes with hot sands,
Whilst mud yearns and sleeps in the river.
With sweaty hands, the fishermen
Untangles and clutches his net:
Sweat corroding the folds of his skin,
As a gant itches like a nightmare.
Clocks worsen insomnia, they say,
While the body can ache from tedious fevers.
Grass shriveled beneath the snag,
Accompanied by a frog weeping plaintively.
This poor fellow has desires in his lonely house,
And grumbles at the moon.
Ah, that cauldron is filled with sadness.
Clogged, as it is, by stardust from heaven.
And the old plaintive,
Leaned over a tired river.
Since, even the rain - white and fine -
Leaked from that bucket.
On a forgotten and crazy world,
Where little flies to a high rise building.

Shadow of the Rain

In the park

Heavy clusters of tender lilacs -
Like lovers hiding in the cool and shade.
The smell of jasmine intoxicates and bemuses,
Beware of him, sweetie, he we will betray you.
Yet, in the bliss and foam of a boule de neige -
My honey, you would comfort my heart.
Ah, candles and flowers were alight near that
                              chestnut:
But, I am so tired. I will sat down by the fountain.
The smell of wine permeates the air,
Only a narcissus proudly shines.

Raushan Burkitbayeva - Nukenova

***

As if after a long winter!
The tired river froze.
But somewhere the spring riots,
Albeit here, again, the blizzard howls.

So sedate and pompous is everything
                                    around.
Or monotonous and dull ….. depending.
One's life goes by,
Yet, suddenly –
Breaking the ice and each of the obstacles,
One thrives,
                            Soul empowered.
As the solemn chimes of spring
Cheer without hiding joy.
Then, the river rages and the sun shines,
And blood boils,
                            and cascades,
As a bird song,

laughing again.
Only then does a zenith ignite -
As a stubborn, bold, and fresh wind,
Gathering my dreams,
Of serene and quiet destiny,
Across a silent steppe.

Landing

Under the wing of an aircraft
Garlands of lights -
From an unknown city
Appear amidst the steppes.

Light in the night, as a signal.
Here, someone is waiting for someone.
The lights of love,
Which magnetize.

The jetliner prepares for landing,
As if leaping.
So I will go in obscurity,
I will go "light handed".

Lighted landmarks
Those signaling lights.
I, however, will come with good intentions,
I will find friends here.

Raushan Burkitbayeva - Nukenova

***

It is not the branch, or the line, that broke
                    down...
So, my hand hung like a whip.
That shadow slid like swarthy seal,
As my path was crossed by grief.
And the wind that hysterically screamed
                    over the river,
Carried his pain behind those barriers...
While a yellow leaf stuck to the glass
                    throughout skin.
To live without you - is probably
                    impossible.
But there's no strength to chase you in my
                    soul,
Rather, my heart wants to fly like snow
                    in the space of a
                    night.

***

Autumn, you came to me uninvited.
You dropped a yellow envelope at my
                    window,
Whilst the Ashberry, like reddish peas,
Tasted as bitter as the sorrows of forgotten
                    days.
The flights of cranes carried away summer,
And reintroduced cold dawns.

Shadow of the Rain

Yet, tender dreams will offer warmth.
- Slow down, winter - they shout.
Warm days are still to come.
And nights often breaks into fire:
As song lines,
Amid solemn, but heavenly, flotillas.
Thereafter, autumn knocked timidly on my
                                        door.
I would take off my wet coat and go to
                              meet her.
Truly, cold beaches still hide behind the
                            mist,
But, we sit and take tea together.

Cobbler

A cobbler's booth at a crossroads.
Some fresh news from a philosopher.
Maybe he will clue you to find happiness?
Thousands of destinies, hundreds of roads,
Amid tired shoes reposing on a shelf.
He will cheer us up with a joke -
He heals our souls like a doctor.
A tossy heel broke the shank,
And there the boot's zipper broke,
While taps flew off from those boots:
All laying on beds like patients.
Explaining why the cobbler grins again,
At all the tricks of capricious fashion.
Squeezing small nails, until after the checkup,
He hammers away with a gnarled brow.
From where do you wend your way?
How big is your wallet today? -
Looking at shoes, he will understand.
When necessary, he will even sue on a small patch.
Our wiseman and philosopher   a local cobbler,
At the crossroads of fate and roads...

Chapter 4.

A jar of melody

Aether

From the sonorous strings of lyres,
                    The aether is woven,
From moonlight,
                    And seaside quietude,
From a mountain echo,
                    Happy laughter,
Water splashes,
                    Against wood ...
From the shine of every star,
                    Poetic dreams arise.
The anxiety of dawn,
Groans at the door ...
From the first knocks,
Of tiny fists,
From patches of sunlight,
On newborn cries...
From the warbles of all birds,
And the flicker of eyelashes,
From a whisper, a rustle,
                    Paper piles,
In pictures and words,
Amid poems without words,
From tunes all around,
                    That you hear...

To the Muse

In the silence of the night when sounds fall
                              asleep,
And you feel the hidden pulses of mind,
Suddenly the muse leads us by the hand so
                              easily.
Oh, words will be thrown in a river, like
                              pearls...
Rather, we must find a way to catch them
                    on invisible
                    threads,
And string these precious things into a
                    necklace,
With needles of feeling.
Following which you must bring your
                    necklace to me.

***

As a guiding star,
Will lead us through the desert -
Through heat and wind and cold -
So, I hope the Muse will not leave us!
Instead, drawing apart from mountain
                    ranges,
And keeping us safe from the abyss...
(Through snow and fog), she will shine,
Like a star of love: a star of hope!

Melancholy

This million-plus city,
Is empty without you.
It is not foliage underfoot -
It is the crunch of the first snow.

You flew away to Lisbon -
The bell of silky nights.
The sweetest jingle in the world -
The jingle of your keys!

Raushan Burkitbayeva - Nukenova

Groves

Amidst the gloomy steppes,
Groves tower high.
As islands of hope and love.
Thence, the chill will retreat
In icy fragments,
As blade of grass break into the light.
May the tender, friendly, foliage of the Birch,
Hide us from the looks of strangers.
And may the time of rendez vous,
Calm you down,
And may words-of-mouth skirt you.

An Invasion of Starlings

The fog is soaked with coniferous coolness,
While in the morning, fresh foliage is clean.
And bunches of grapes are getting sweet,
As the fence bows down with their weight,
Barely holding this heaviness.

Afghan starlings as hooligans -
Tear and chatter with no shame!
Emptying bunches like glasses.
Vinous, stuffed with figs.
That bogie will not frighten them.

And the faithful dog - hoarse from the strain,
Helplessly tries to startle them.
If he only had our feet, our hands!
But, he scratches the solid trunks with canine paws.
As the Starlings have fun and do not care...

And the poor dog has realized it is useless.
He cannot chase away these uninvited guests.
Already exhausted from the heat of a long summer,
He knows there are no rules for birds.
They fly where they want and do not need sugar bones.

Still ..... duty calls!
He is the owner of his garden.
And once again comes into the fight -
For grapes!
23.01.2015

Raushan Burkitbayeva - Nukenova

***

My thoughts,
Are like clouds,
Taking away my hope
For eternity.
Bright stars,
In quite melancholy,
Have drowned again,

                    In a muddy river.

The ice of indifference

                    Chained each
wave,

That lunar oval,

                    Is like a splinter.

A cold wind,

                    Versifies the
streets:

The slow verse,
Was inspired by sadness,
While morning ice,
Will crack in sorrow,
At a farewell dance,

                    Like a flight of
snowflakes.

Shadow of the Rain

***

Round backed shadows glide along the
river,
All puddles and holes being glazed.
Yet, the elderly are wrapped in thick
clothes.
Indeed, big city Ladies swank around in
furs.
But the tired grin of clumsy cars,
Saw sand clogged in frozen tires.
As mad Horseman ride past you,
Perhaps there is a reason for their haste?
Certainly, cold shivers run down the skin,
Like a frost on glass,
While the slow rhythm of thoughts,
Reminds hope that passions remain warm:
Although an abort light is on.
Oh, that stubborn sun illuminates the day.
And rigid fisherman break the ice.
And a smile still signifies the warmth and
spring.
And each encounter is a mysterious sign.

In the Museum

In reverent silence,
Amid ancient artifacts -
Steeped in legends,
We met once.
It seemed like a gilded moment.
Your dark face glowed,
With tremulous attention.
You listened to the fables,
With splendid insights.
To stories and plots,
All coming with questions
And always waiting for serious answers...

Awakening

Why it is sad this morning? -
The Sun curtained by a cloud...
Our house veiled with dusk.
Yesterday was so bright.
But, now everything is full of sadness.
However, this will go no further.
No, we will not let the blues in!
We will turn the horses in the morning
To the light, joy, and love!
We will celebrate this day with singing.
So, be of good cheer.
Each moment of happiness must be caught!

Eternal Illusion

Running like a cold, thin, slice of orange,
Our Moon is a proud beauty.
As a harpsichord spreads its sounds
Like the silence of a tender Actress.
Oh, the curtain has drooped: lost in the folds,
Secrets hide somewhere in their depths.
A diva, full of mysteries,
Dissolved by a cloud in the window.
The stars - your nightly audience,
Those, critics of soundless subjects.
Where are they, your young partners?
Where is the merger of souls and hot bodies?
That candle on the table flickered out,
But, bright oranges are still shining.
She waited for him vainly at the New Year,
Although, her mirrors looked empty.
Some curtains are like shields in a home.
They shield the soul from anguish.
They promise yesterday will fade away,
Through eternal lamentations across the river.

Shadow of the Rain

It is near Midnight...

Midnight approaches: dreams slowly fade away.
They smell like orange peel.
Or someone's tears frozen on the glass,
Flashing like black pearls, behind a curtain.
The century passes. A new century begins.
The crystal jingle will catch this edge.
While your twin smiles at you in a mirror,
And your sadness inexplicably disappears ...

Raushan Burkitbayeva - Nukenova

An Autumn Story

From the smoky garden,
Wrapped in a warm evening -
Through the cast-iron fence,
Autumn is moving forward.
Mincing after her obediently,
Is Rain: exhausted by the cold.
Yet, after waiting for a call in a stuffy apartment
(all day with short amplitude),
He will finally disappear in curls of willow,
Like descending wind:
Singing a farewell tune.
Oh, my quiet and empty evening,
Impressed on the glass like a fingerprint
And flattened as a leaf of maple.
Look - a pair of kid gloves,
Forgotten by your new admirer...
26.11.2008

Night fantasies

Violet shades,
And crimson sunsets...
A bouquet of lilacs on the table.
A poster hangs on the wall.
This modest housing
Is full of a bachelor's desolation.
Sour jam in a pot
And scattered clothes.
Turquoise glints
From the window glass.
And with waves of blossoming plum,
A curtain has recently been draped.
Pancakes on the table,
A carpet hung across the wall.
As girls have a sweet dream,

Their conversation getting quit excited.
Previously washed and spotted stains ...
A Bulldog asleep on the carpet.
Bones ache in bad weather,
While flowers wither on the windowsill.
On the table – pills and bottles.
A clock rings on the wall.
As the smell of valerian throughout the house,
Tellingly fingers a Rosary.
Purple shadows.
Anxieties of sunrise.
Predawn apparitions.
All silently wandering around the room.
A candle flickers out on the table,
As a mosquito sits on the wall.
But, day will dispel groundless fears,
And every nightmare will be over.

The Fire of Love

On the fire of love,
How many souls were burned!
Through the fire of love,
Innumerable songs were composed!
But, tears are like rain,
Although, unable to choke this fire.
Cupid, our leader, runs after you,
We are all in a hurry!
Somewhere, warm hands,
Try to hold souls before they fly away.
Someone sang softly,
Peering into the horizon.

Our Dates

We see each other rarely,
You left me, my friend.
Oh, those Juniper branches,
Are like dark circles of sadness.
So, wrapping both trembling shoulders in a scarf,
I will come to our staircase.
How can I dispel these doubts?
A shadow falls on your face,
And fog embraces each street.
But, only the Juniper shivers.
We were happy some time ago...
Yet, you are gone.
How can I live without you?

On a Swarthy Face

The shadow of embarrassment,
Fell on your swarthy face.
Yet, my apparition
Still excited you.
As for you, my little boy -
Flying full of love
And so passionately girded,
You keep singing and talking.
It is amusing to observe!
But, I am scared to show my feelings,
As I know this excitement will only last for a minute,
And when you leave,
It will be both empty and fearful.

Snowstorm

Oh, this crazy blizzard
Is so natural to me!
The infidelity of a spouse
Freezes a soul!

Oh, the heat from those thoughts,
Still burns my soul!
While their current hits like a ton of bricks.
Meanwhile, obvious tears break loose.

I want to tear you apart,
And break myself like a vase,
And punish all the villains...
Oh, my God, where is my mind!

Shadow of the Rain

***

Through the fabric of heavenly longings,
Is sewn with the thread of rain,
People still crave for inspiration:
When entering and parting from this life.

In the maelstrom of love, an Alchemist
Will blend a list of names.
Then, wrapping fates and lines,
The moon is secretly roped into this
                                    process.

The steppe mumbles with a creaking cart.
But, why do these steep gapes appear - as
                                    scars.
Like an incursion of vagrant clouds,
Moulding the edge of a thunderstorm.

Transforming this surge of energy,
Into a creative new blast -
From dots of stars and elegies
The rush of melodies will soon frame
                                   everything.

Someone unstrings each thread,
While snow crochets the laces.
"Sketches", "a Labyrinth", Schnittke.
As Claude Monet paints "Haystacks" -

Being opposed to the flights of Degas
                                   ballerinas!

26.11.2014

Shadow of the Rain

The Day Dropped with Fatigue

The day dropped with fatigue,
                    Bows towards the west.
And the cool night flies,
                    Like as invisible cavalry.
Continual insomnia,
Knocks on my dark window.
And sonorous thoughts thunder,
                    Over there, on the outskirts...
Why don't you sleep,
Rebellious soul?
All dreams are swept along,
                    By a snowy road.
But, you are looking through this darkness,

        At the distances - as before.
As if you hear the call of love,
                    Distant, gentle...
Yet, morning again we will flee,
                    From the crossroads.
And the wind of time whistles,
With sounds like a biting whip.
An autumn frost,
Goes grey on temples.

And the cry of farewell, will,
                    Open a blue expanse of us.
The blue vastness will bring us,
A farewell cry.

Elegy

If you could become a wind,
A light-winged wind,
You would reach here quickly,
                    Across desert and sea.
On stellar road,
Raising snow dust.
Calming those on edge,
And infuriated,
From sudden jealously,
Or overwhelmed with madness.
You will send a serene calmness,
                    Out of trickery.
So let the clouds that glide,
                    Dissolving and melting,
And carry away my fears and doubts,
Without a trace.
As a sudden rain, sparse,
                    Like the tears of a man,
With rare drops, touching the ground,
                    Barely, evaporating,
But, scared of disquieting,
                    Blissful arrangements!
In luxurious palace chambers,
                    And dark alleys,
Stare at the starry sky,
For hours.
Indulge in sweet,
Although agonizing reveries.
Shamefacedly she denuded dainty,

Shadow of the Rain

White arms and shoulders.
While the pliant neck leaned toward,
                    As spring water.
It seemed that no water,
                    Was in crystal jar,
Albeit tenderness and the caress of distant,
                    And trembling hands,
Held for a brief moment,
                    Fingers swooning blissfully.
The coolness of silk, or the purple glow of wine,
                    Enliven the whole body.
Falling invitingly into languor,
                    And unconsciousness.
Whispered passionately with cherry lips,
                    The precious holy name.
It replaced her hymns,

                    Her prayers,
Caressing her ears,

                    Her tired body.
And, like lilac,

                    That bended under the
                    weight,
Of a lush snow white

                    Inflorescences,
All stooped lower,

                    And lower,
And almost broke,
From feebleness and bliss.

Suddenly, she woke up,
And straightened.
A dark shadow passed over,
Her pale face.
Maybe he indulges in pleasures with the other,
                              Forgetting her.
While this prolonged absence,
And deadly separation,
Made short news,
Like a sip of solace.
No, I would rather endure death,
Than be in doubt!
Oh, she touched the rosehip,
                              With her hand.
I wish I could fall asleep and become,
A sleeping beauty,
So, everything would be,
In the land of nod,
And grow cold,
In the coolness of porcelain.

In the serene ethereal,
                              Dream,
Without sadness,
And wait until,
Your lips,
Wake me up!

Shadow of the Rain

***

Candle melts,
       From the warmth of your hands,
It melts slowly…
The lips,
Snatch your hot kisses.

And melting with joy.
My tender angel,
       Do not fly away.
Be a kind friend.
Here, we were promised,
       To have a true paradise,
Beyond this circle.
Do not tighten your wings.
       Do not let go,
Quivering bird,
Do not disappear,
       As a dream.
Am I dreaming?

Chapter 5.

City of apples

Bazaar

Frosty air is fatal to the ligaments,
But, tempers both spirit and frays the nerves.
Yet, busy days are relentless and swampy,
While someone will always be the first in this race.
Flying snow will vanish in Azan*
As will sleepless minarets with droning pipes.
Every Bazaar relishes such news like a cauldron.
As sun-dried apricots remind one of summer.
Oh, the Orient cannot be imagined without a
                              Bazaar's hustle:
Without turbans everywhere around,
Without exotic goods, market stalls, colourful cloth.
All veiled with melodies from the east.
As long as this sly humour is alive,
(A worn wind in a crowd of bathrobes),
The world is still blessed. People are not dead.
And a peace of mind is sewed through a rainbow.

---

* Azan - an appeal to the obligatory prayer

Raushan Burkitbayeva - Nukenova

Alma-Ata

Poor city,
In the fume of smog.
A smoke-dried in a pit…
Amid flattened winds – needing rescue.
The rain on windows – as bird droppings.
Yet, by tectonic efforts,
Those dim lights are striving to be stars.
Simultaneously filling glacial leaves with glitter-snow.
A lovely city aspiring above the smog,
Abandoning its enormous traffic jams.
Your dense range of skyscrapers,
Lie above a winding canyon.
With the peaks of spruces, which pirouette -
Overturning every sunset
And whirling within a duet.
Oh, a polygon of deutschemarks
And Japanese progression.
But, a flourish of rivers (given to us as a gift),
Drive the press into fighting for salvation.
Against the grind of a pursuit-flight
And never-ending Oporto.
So, a man runs away from his neighborhood,
Into the realm of a protected mountain:
A spotted leopard -
A city of apples.
Decorated by dowdy
Apricots, their colour among the beams -
Like a thin stream of clean images.

Shadow of the Rain

***

The entrance hall smells,
Of smoked meat (beshbarmak at Bay's*),
Of western seas (brought from Dubai),
Of fresh pastries.
Indeed, there is a fine aroma of coffee in
                                    the morning,
Although, the panels are speckled like a
                                    cave,
With images, inscriptions,
Barcodes,
And painted stains.
But, every hall entrance is also a silent
                                    witnesses,
To weddings, ages, and losses.
A facade of treasures,
As a corpse in a mausoleum.
Yet, the inhabitants of the house
Gain strengths, give birth, grow old.
Change their furniture,
Appliances, decoration.
As spring flows into autumn blues -
As the Moon and Sun give salvage,
While irregular changes have no mercy.
Those writers, of course, did not use all
                                    their starry ink.
Since, our souls are still vulnerable,
And want to be loved.
Where are the flocks of sparrows?
They still swear in parks,

Raushan Burkitbayeva - Nukenova

Even though fed as pigeons.
Winter spreads.
Like the wings of a blizzard swan.
Ah, even gold melts,
In the fire of ordeals within our hearths.
Now, the heart of haunted birds,
Beats in our chests.

_____

Beshbarmak – a traditional starchy meal from meat. From the Turk language – five fingers, eaten with the fingers. Bay - a wealthy landowner

Shadow of the Rain

***

In a barrel of melt-water,
A kid tries to catch.
The two-horned moon.
Oh, come to the yurt of this shepherd,
And you will be offered a steppe drink -
With a foamy cloud.
Coltsfoot, Helichrysum,
Wormwood and lemon balm -
Will be added for flavor:
To dispel fatigue and anxiety.

***

What appears in dreams of melting snow?
A sigh of relief at dawn?
Listen instead to the heavy steps of a
                              missing answer.
Time slips through our fingers,
As hands keep the warmth of a shake.
Therein, friends become closer:
Replacing brothers vanished in the winter.
Oh, the gate creaks plaintively,
Waiting for us. Welcome back!
Yet, mum is still busy at the stove.
Ah, "Frost and the Sun" on a Sunday!

The Dynasty

Night fragmented in a window frame,
While reflecting the notebooks of school writing.
Yet, mother helps with homework,
Until the morning sun.
Ah, red ink without remorse.
Corrected errors.
Then life gives its lessons,
Allotting marks to little kids.
As a father – a rigorous mathematician,
Doing sums brilliantly.
Afterwards, tying a ribbon into a knot,
And teaching labour in the countryside,
Our sisters bend over these notebooks,
Like school teachers themselves.
One day, our grandchildren will mature like grapes.
They will bake potatoes amid the ashes of time.
Ah, these four volumes of Ushakov,
I got them as a rarity,
Like the fortunate shine as a horseshoe -
Blessing our parents.

Outrage

The quietest snow goes down like an avalanche,
Silencing glaciers broken off without an echo.
Maybe that cloud of smog is guilty,
Since, there are more evil and less of laughter.
Indeed, the traffic in never-ending road,
Like a skyscraper reaches the sky and stars.
Then, our Universe is seized with dismay.
Amid the heartless outrage of advanced ideas.

The Light of Blood

That is all…the agony and pain are finished.
The horizon is raining: then whitens with
                                        snow:
Each a process uncovering terra firma.
This body is like an empty nest,
Since, both the soul and body dash against
                                        eons,
Like February after long blizzards,
Yielding, as it does, to the expanse of
                                        droplets.
Thereafter, children and grandchildren
                                        stand in a
                                        semicircle.
She will be next to her beloved husband.
As spring flies to us like a starling!

                    ***

On the branch – a bunch of bullfinches,
In the captivity of an agonizing slumber:
All merging with the colours of dawn.
Long since petrified in song and stance.
Similar to shards of ice sliding down from
                                        our roofs,
But, only dawn draws the branch of an
                                        Ashberry.
Oh, the cries of those birds scares the
                                        silence,
And chases away sweet sleep.

Patrol

Ringing silence, as the sting of a wasp -
Barbed wire along a borderline.
A prickly hedgehog, like a tumbleweed,
Became a transgressor, willy-nilly.
His chin growing a prickly beard overnight,
As a flask with drinking water slowly emptied.
This outpost is always tense in the dark,
While a barely sleeping young mother,
Rips a swollen horizon apart each dawn.
Governed by the charter of a vigilant garrison.
Look – the shell of these quail eggs has cracked.
Amid a flicker of burnt eyelashes.

Raushan Burkitbayeva - Nukenova

Mudflow

Through a magnifier of the moraine,
From eternal captivity,
To the cries of sirens,
These blocks of stone, clay, and sand,
Glide gently,
Down to the foot,
Of each grinding effort.
Overwhelming, threatening,
Between every terrible mudflow:
They sweeps things mercilessly,
Every which way.
Sticking out like masts
Amid pines and spruces,
These flows of mud then carry all away.
Mother Nature, you do not mess with Her!

Indian Summer

Roses scattered like small beads.
Amber honey coloured foliage.
Do not confuse that Lady with questions,
The one called out by night flutes.

With cobwebs of sadness wrapped in a scarf,
And languid eyes holding each shadow of hope,
She sinks into a deep, albeit unexpected, delight:
Exposing the garden to a new fall of leaves.

Let the days thaw in every short instance.
Be mellowed by the fog.
Allow the fear of loneliness to run away
As whiteness and blushing colour the night.

Oh, those waves of feeling besotting eternity.
With a haze of coffee cream and temptation.
Yet, each day streams with tenderness.
An Indian summer has no limits ... they say.

So, immersing a brush in livid paint: like leaves,
And draw a sketch for us, like a painter,
The autumn arrives with questions -
Although leaning creepily on its palette.

Hill Folks

Sea foams,
With splendid lilacs.
Sunrise and sunset,
Cannot stop arguing.
Soul and age are disparate.
Herds of clouds,
Blown away by the wind.
And where is the Heaven,
And the edge of Earth?
On those massive rocks,
Flowers have bloomed,
Look into the face of the abyss,
From the heugh -
Where a small village wreathes in the gorge,
Like a lunar disc in the bottle,
Even though blurring like Chacha.
The whole family sings,
You have saved it.
Yet, an abrek can sharpen its thin dagger,
In moonlight.
It can cook some meat pasties,
A juicy Khinkal.
Oh, centenarian sage,
Raise your glass of wine.
Both bitterness and sweetness
Have blended in that glass,
While fogs
And an aul put their hats on a fog -
Wherein a tipsy guest,
Fell asleep in a hut.

Shadow of the Rain

Peasant Girl

Aren't mindful stars bored,
By a defilement of the moon?
Perhaps, they got a catalog of dresses,
With recipes concerning different diets.
Ah, the Sun will fall into a barn,
Melting the manure.
As a drunken colonel at his bath,
Jokes with naive girls,
While everyone and everywhere
Is thirsty for happiness and love.
Oh, the slide of galloping days -
Do not grimace in the face of fate!
After all, an Ashberry bitters on the lips,
Offering its bare branches on a walkway,
Before we reach home ..... sweet home!
Indeed, the stars never get cold!

***

A stringy and viscous sunset,
Is in a languor of honey:
While the lunar disc is washed by the sea.
Run up of the patient wave.
Over there, poppies grow crimson on hills,
Since, everyone is waiting for the sails.
Of an old legend. Although, love does not
age.
Indeed, the heart neither shivers, nor withers.

Kamyzyak – Reed Beach

It is bursting with pride – in a "box!"
As a driver on the Astrakhan steppe,
You become a real star,
Azamat, Kamyzyak – go ahead!
Talking the clay of a jug,
And a batch of wit - put in in fire,
Then hauling your load to the top,
While avoiding burns and chases,
Made labour a flashing joke: like fire.
And Moscow has not rejected this raid.
(like migratory birds).
Indeed, this folk is of Asian origin.
They feel the smell of nomadic bonfires,
Where shubat* merges with a Volga wave.
Oh, the bitterness of smoky wormwood.
Look- ancestral spirits are behind you!
Their laughter, as sharp arrows in a quiver,
Are reminiscent of verbal and daring attacks.
Certainly, your squad is reliable and courageous.
It will protect and support you.
They say Stepan Razin - your noble friend,
Shattered the royal calm.
Offering inspiration thereby - a good sign:
Even conquering the Ostankino spire!
Yet, the label he pinned on that tower -
Was also for us here below. Joking and drinking,
The KVN is a conqueror,
So, we Kazakhs remain proud!

---

* Astra - Star (lat.)
* Shubat - fermented drink made from camel's milk

Night Butterflies

The lantern creaks -
A witness to disgrace.
Night butterflies gather as a crowd.
He did not set this up,
Though he was tortured.
Indeed, his kist is veiled by shattered
dreams:
All hurting him, but letting him stand.
So, he shivers in the crossfire,
And envies the white Cadillac,
That fiercely hates white light -
As a damned and fallen soul.
Night lasts on the slow road, they say,
While muddy rains offer solace to mistakes.
Indeed, he earned his asthma from the
smog.
And tossed petals at the doorstep.
Allowing Jasmine to bloom as a wedding
suit.

***

The day quickly faded,
With random pictures.
And in the extraordinary silence

Raushan Burkitbayeva - Nukenova

The thumbed porn magazine in a subway.
Betrayed his eagerness: erased his shame.
He was trying to descry something.
Oh God, tomorrow is Sunday,
What if children look!
He threw his magazine on the rails,
As a cutie-pie stared at him in fear.
In response, he looked sober:
Although, enjoying a sweaty sleep on the
                                    Metro.

Shadow of the Rain

Windowsill

Shadows are playing and dancing,
Trees stand still along the road.
Windowsills look at bypassers:
Pleased to see a magpie.

Day will sail away and night shines.
Music gets louder in a distant window.
His experience ... will it be useful?
He counts the dates of a fornicating Moon.

Rains refresh his memory,
And a lilac heavily presses his chest.
And limping, dry on a rock,
He collects dew like mercury.

Lanterns like night watchmen,
Keep strict watch with no rest.
He wants to fly in the sky like a bird
Like a flock of quarrelsome jackdaws.

Nearby, the oak has grown so quickly.
It protects as a son protects his old father.
In the bitter cold, and hot summer -
Shadows get slightly thicker.

Dragonfly

A dragonfly hovers like a shadow -
Shooting in slow motion,
Like Selfie photo:
With facets in its eyes.
It will fly over the fence,
To admire views around a nearby house.
It settles on someone's courtyard.
She is familiar with private secrets -
With the careless flight of other insects,
Who are speedily prevented from prying,
While the wings of an unborn song,
Hide a garden in the path of love.
Itself obscuring rows of chamomile fields,
All doomed to die.
Albeit keen to stream words,
Across a hunters deadly web -
Each swallowed by a mud river.

Shadow of the Rain

Chapter 6.

Lightning Branch

Nocturne

A youth saw his lightening branch sparkle.
Then, fell into a long autumn with a deep groan.
Simultaneously, a ripe apple curled in shadows,
Leaving verses as mementos.

Lightweight and easy,
Snow falls and the fog gets thicker,
While clouds with layers of sadness,
Rest on a singing, windy, dune.

Oh, winter evening - an insomniac night.
A time whiled away by a cooling stove.
These days of bad weather are not welcomed,
Since a frosty separation knocks at the door.

An inevitable fate is coming.
Taking the form of an instant twilight.
Carelessly, candles burn out like old stars:
Openly talking about love.

Do not spare or give an excess,
Of kind words and coloured smiles.
Sadness flies through the alley,
Like leaves across youth and love!

A spring waltz around birdsong.
Days flock and shower with foliage.
Rays play in a sandpit.
As cups are in love with their saucers.

Raushan Burkitbayeva - Nukenova

Oh, eternally cold stars,
Watch the Moon behind the wagon.
"Make way!" - And a formidable rider,
Puts time in stirrups.

Through the cinder of thaw holes -
A stalk from under the snow,
Patiently waits for warmth,
Since, its winter visa has expired.

Rime, ice, and silver,
All loaded on a crystal kist.
A necklace of Georgian wines,
Touched by the print of a ray.

Veins swell on leaves.
The smoke of a lilac fence.
All bird boxes came to life,
As an old telegraph.

Interest

I wander what keeps those slow stars,
From scattering?
This question is distressful.
And swaying in the wind,
Their light is so shrill.
They will wipe away each whisper,
And all trickery.
Their performance lasts forever.
Oh, abysmal pit of stars.
We fly to meet the end,
Where the truth is visible.

Leap Year

Two days - heat annoyed February.
Then, rain washed the sticky sweat away.
A view of unsightly, scrubby, steppes.
As even a bissextile did not resolve conflict.

Leap years menace like a scythe.
So armed, they are reputed to be the
                                culprit.
Dense shades lay with ribbons, they say:
Yet, hold a pistol of fiction to one's head.

Moon pupils blur their glass vision,
While snow tissues lay as linen.
All making snow stutter and murmur.
As a loving snowdrop flashed by a window!

***

Sister-insomnia plays,
With long-playing record,
And shamelessly with stars,
A visiting Gentleman flirts.

The dawn is coming. Metamorphosis -
Transforms a dull landscape.
The forecasts will not be justified.
The moon suddenly put on weight.

And curvy distant shores,

Shadow of the Rain

Fatefully foresee our hopes.
Doomed, as they are, with sadness,
The clouds weep with tears of relief.

***

Your name is like an echo in the
                              mountains.
Reckless as is snow flying from fear.
As a strict ban: a rigid taboo.
Yet, our herd broke down into the abyss.

In the clouds,
Life is rain.
It thunders,
As the smirk of chief.

Branches of lightning,
As the roots of love,
Burns wood,
And catch the streams.

A short wink,
Fills a thunderstorm,
With hugs -
Although, it startles the osier.

Breaking through a dam of separations,
A bow merges with its bowstring.
The wind brought me your name -
From a valley of mists and dreams.

Reminiscences

May dawns and rainbows of delight,
Sparkle with a golden pollen.
Bumblebees hassle their chasers,
Like a big bunches of Lilacs.

Each day fades and evening languishes,
Like gardens under lacy clouds.
Old Moon is reflected in the surface of a
lake.
Daisies read their fortune in stacks.

Breathing cool air - a harsh potion,
Albeit muddled from the bliss of fresh rain,
Couples sit on benches again:
As a honey-night is ahead.

The smoke of obsession melts slowly.
The wind often picks up flowers.
Through a net of rain and the gloom of
oblivion,
Moonlight flows onto the lake.

***

The ponds freeze,
From cold water.
A cone of light until snug,
Without consulting one's eyes.
Saws ice for the March

Shadow of the Rain

Igniting the fire of gusto.

***

Steppe roads breathe dust.
Scratchy air in a dried throat.
An eagle's shadow is the last hope.
Not a drop of rain with callus thoughts.

***

Timid light from a covert star,
Melts in the depths of a cloud.
I hear this quiet voice often:
Shattering broken sleep.
Gloom edges out of a corner,
By the whiteness of a curtain,
Following a pale Moon.
Why do shadows creep across a table -
Scolding my handwriting?
I will knock for Selena again,
And bury my inspiration.
They say that the winged Pegasus,
Flew to a house,
Wherein wine was poured in squares,
Like precious metals.
Nowadays, I do not sleep, but absently
                                    look,
Into the darkness.
He does not like marriage.
Thank you for the flight!

Raushan Burkitbayeva - Nukenova

***

A snake crawled out from the depths,
Of Asian heat.
The night took off its turban,
Oh, mature wisdom:
Silence, peace.

***

The Sun, frozen in the cool of a cave,
Warms that snake on the sand dune.
Its threat has been poured into a critical
                                    glance,
As a tortoise crawls plowing the land.

Shadow of the Rain

Kaleidoscope

A spinning vista of days and nights,
Change the colour foliage and hair.
Childhood cannot be rewound,
As a newspaper peppered with events.

Bright colours are often toxic.
Toys are dangerous for children's minds.
Advertising forgery - so damaging,
And promises as reliable as a fume.

Kaleidoscope was a favorite game
For us kids in soviet times.
The world was limited at the borderline:
Our yards were magic wells.

A glass with coloured ornaments,
A wonderful mosaic to delight the eye.
A train takes us out of the house,
The world is outside. Mum's strict orders.

I collect toys in a box -
Bricks, dolls, cars, a whirligig.
At night, the Moon will give us a kiss:
A silhouette blinks through the tulle on the floor...

Raushan Burkitbayeva - Nukenova

***

In the mud of May warm rain -
And petals are mixed with hail.
A sparrow pecks at these balls so naively,
Confusing them with grapes.

***

A lullaby tune at the bedside.
Dreams as butterflies - shadow of colours.
A young mother caresses with love.
One is ready to fly with her as a hero,
And conquer all space and time,
Thereby, giving her our treasures.
Then, mother gives a loving kiss.
A bliss that cannot be repeated.
But, we grew up and our house got empty.
Now, crowds of cares and waves of
                              separation,
Echo like our mums old songs.
However, her hand remains warm and
                              tender.
Albeit, only in dreams does she come to a
                              bedside,
And caress us with her tender hands.
Indeed, filial duty will always remain.
"Do not worry, I will be with you!"
As outside, rain pours into puddles.
Perhaps, we have forgotten how to cry in
                              pain.

Shadow of the Rain

Yet, the wind whispers, "Cry, my dear!"
As boys play their war games.
Our mothers were against violence and war.
Possibly, their prayers will still save us.

***

Scorching summer,
With night respites.
On a pier of spiffed fashions,
By a beach without needless details.
Those scorching nights,
Wait for revelatory rains.
Yet, the Sun is shining with red sparks,
Through pear branches,
Behind the darkness of a glass,
Murmuring underneath bulky seagulls.

***

Rails. Rails. A time-bill.
Meetings. Farewell. Railway station.
And a nerdy taxi,
Knowing all the answers.
You ordered tickets.
Expectations. Distance.
Short instances in a house.
Rivers. Mountains. Cities.
Trains stretching through time.
P.S. I do not sleep at home anymore,
I wander around the world like a cloud!

Raushan Burkitbayeva - Nukenova

***

Above those cloudy country roads,
A stubborn motor roars.
The student froze – poor fellow.
Life is so tough, so be ready!
Watch as a clockwork bomb,
Ticks and threatens – the bastard.
A mother sleeps at home.
She is loaded with housework.
Life is like a dog race,
As the landfill of Betpak Dala*.
This house will bear chains:
The debts and sorrows of tomorrow.
Professors will teach you.
But there are places where your knowledge

Tunnels like a mine of books.
Indeed, those stars are sparks of the
universe!

* Betpak Dala – steppe, desert. – ill-fated flatland

Shadow of the Rain

The rain returns from wandering,
Making foliage dance along a road.
Those tears of love and forgiveness -
Fall between every line at times.
Although, they enlightening apologetic
                                words.
In an endless rustle of water.
Truly, the young Moon hurries to a date,
Neglecting orders.

Bog Willow

The blushing sunset fell,
On reeds riverside,
While leaves covered a bog willow,
Waiting impatiently for its misfire.
Oh, that goose is resting on a beam,
His stomach stuffed with grains,
Almost like a tacky flag, or Falstaff.
Look, the last leaf is signaling through knocks,
Like stars twinkled above the waves.
This is why the goose flew like an arrow,
With dusty feathers on a shadowy wall,
As the bog willow burned to say goodbye.
Each event missed by those hounds -
Whose victory cries wedged in the sky!
Let the stars illuminate mysterious signs,
Amid the modest beauty of the Savannah.

Shadow of the Rain

***

The excited whispers of rowans,
In September - what should we expect?
The ruins of an air castle -
Or clouds pouring rain,
While, swallows leave their nests,
After the advent of a cold-spell.
That sunset will wrap its webs,
Around a spoken goodbye in a shaded garden.
Yet, slow snow always gathers pace,
Hovering above a silent field.
Do not be afraid of winter, I repeat.
Stars shine to give us hope!

Raushan Burkitbayeva - Nukenova

Moon Serenade

The Moon's face in an oval frame,
Perched at a window,
Looks intently, stubbornly,
Snatching sleep from the night.
As a flute plays quiet music,
Above a carousel of sleepy stars.
Each one watches lunar curls messed by the
                                wind.
Ah, the air is gilded with dust,
While shadows sway in the garden.
Fish plash in a pond,
By the dark foliage of plums,
On grass keeping their imprints.

***

From habit, night strikes at the stars.
Forging them into a velvet curtain.
As waves of vanity flood across stations,
Where a coquettish Moon proves late
                                again.
She was choosing an outfit.

***

Clouds glide on the sky.
As a mesmerizing river.

Shadow of the Rain

That star, unable to withstand heat,
Becomes a pearl droplet.

***

Hot winds from the mane of centuries,
Rush at the smell of spring rains,
While, the jingle of starry inflorescences,
Raises music above the birds.

Raushan Burkitbayeva - Nukenova

On the Edge

Between sleeping and waking,
Between faith and doubt,
A line is not thinner than the glaive.
Flame cuts slowly.
Illuminating the light of insight,
Into a fuzzy vision,
Wherein meaning is sometimes lost,
Like clouds over the mountain.
Staves grumble under our feet -
As seven alarms.
Old Moon face – as parts of a tune,
Makes harmony of tedious passages.
Two palms, two wings.
Night raised all bridges.
Look – a paper kite in the sky.
Sleep, sleep, my beauty!
Cherries ripens outside my window,
As thoughts maturing in a flash.
The morning turns into day,
While time closes this circle.

Shadow of the Rain

***

The sun reaches for the glass -
Light and shade on the floor.
The fire of heaven,
Burns my hand.

***

December sews lace
With frosty incisors.
Those filigree pictures,
Deserve success,

Raushan Burkitbayeva - Nukenova

As the keeper of a star.

Ah, the keeper of stars,
Is on duty tonight.
A figure whose silhouette, like a shadow,
Looms at our windows
It moans like a vagrant,
Wanting to warm.
Oh, those treasured grams:
All prayers are alike.
Tears on glass,
Or drops on a lens.
Each will remind of us of verses -
Look, this miserable heron,
Has stretched out on the floor,
Whilst, through a slit in the balcony,
Stories unfold,
About criminal dramas.

Tight leather bottles,
Filled with mists,
On the edge of a star
Will blow winds around.
The rains will then start -
All a Mamayev horde of dreams,
Broken until the morning.

Rubber hardens
With a tearful Hevea.
And the red chief
Gets sober for a meeting.

Shadow of the Rain

A swaying horsetail.
As crimson holy rain,
Comes down to Kalahari.
There, the sharp-sighted Sun breaks,
M,elted sealing wax

From letter which was
Brought by a moonbeam,
When darkness retreats.
Captive stars tremble,
In a magic expanse,
While their hot tears -
Bring snow and rain again.

Throughout the night I look,
At those slow-motion frames,
Reflected in mirrors.
Without getting a wink of sleep,
In a blackened window -
I can see the sharp circle of our Moon,
Among scattered constellations.
And frolic at the sharp edge
Of its day-by-day diminution.
Indeed, as a stargazer, I wait for news about comets:
Taking only a mosquito peep -
At the same time as information gets annoying and
louder.
Things are full of anger,
Thirsty for blood.
They head Middle Age -
And rush to bedsides:
And as an X-Ray agent,

Raushan Burkitbayeva - Nukenova

Drilling near nominated victims,
With his drowsy, vampiric, eyes.
They truly, fatigue our overwhelmed brains -
Similarly to bags of snowy cotton.
But, the Moon burns Her threads and bridges.
On the splendid road
Of someone's life:
And with a guilty smile,
Till dawn,
She tells fortunes -
Until disappearing unnoticed,
Like a demonized traveler.
Yet, we continue to live!
Although, the Moon, like a loaf of bread,
Soaked by rain.
Is remembered among the stars.

Etude

I like it when wet leaves fly.
Seeing me off at the road.
What should I expect? No one forbids,
These poems and letters' ripening as a harvest.
As independent strangers,
Coming to help a city of rainbows.
Ah, the trouble bypasses.
And light in a window delights our senses.

Sakura Blossom

A city smothered in a lilac mist.
Its branches groan with grapes.
Pink mists cover this quarter,
As a wind rushed into its parks.
Yes, the dome of heaven shines,
With a handful of bright lights.
Admiring the play of shadows,
Someone is missing in a subway.
Ah, an organza veil of lush blossoms -
Surrounded by ancient Sakura flowers,
Will let this storm pass by:
Like an obsessive moment in my life ...

***

A shower of ripe grapes,
Bubbles in a cherry river,
As lush colours are blurred,
By light clouds fling away.
Look, those Housewives merely fluster,
Without asking what a harvest brings?
Where are we getting the jam from?
All they can do is observe those blooms
                              wistfully.

***

A ray falls on a window -
Playful, sulky.

Shadow of the Rain

A hieroglyph of silence -
Both intricate and citrus,
With a shallow response,
From oblivious stars.
Suddenly, the wind died down.
Although, those waves were not torn apart.

Chapter 7.

In a Running Water Mirror

Shadow of the Rain

In a running water mirror,
Faces and bridges flicker,
Underneath a Venetian gondola.
Similarly, the King is overthrown from His
                              throne.
As in a scene from the opera Madonna.
But, even the splendors and miseries of
                              Napoleon,
Once time threw its nets,
Paled before the monarch Moon as a gold
                              fish,
While, someone looked for a reason,
To throw hope skyward.
Therein, the transparent pulses of the stars,
Intrude into the veins of a wrist.
Whilst, wind lulled those trees,
Around a life refusing to return.

***

White sun on a white steppe.
The frosty air whirls.
That flight was canceled. Enchained,
Like a frozen bird.
Indeed, life has lost its excess of colours.
Nowadays, Saturday evening is broken,
Yet, there is no reason to be sad.
Since the fire of a salvation,
Still blesses this house!

Raushan Burkitbayeva - Nukenova

To Beethoven

Secretly, the stars eavesdropped,
But, whom do they favour?
For whom is this spotlight?
These folk are stupid. They are deaf.
So, the chief conductor intervened,
In an orbit of conversations,
Whilst stars dropped their eyes,
Amid a choir practicing voiceover skills.
In himself, Beethoven (with his shock of hair),
Played the Moonlight Sonata.
As a young Gretchen sighed,
Behind a curiously thin stonewall.
Thereafter, constellations rang like a necklace,
While comets strove for the ceiling.
Ah, sonatas key like a clean river,
Across cold ashes – the secret note of snowfall.
Yet, the light around sloping shoulders flows,
In perpetual exhaustion:
With the destiny of random meetings.

Shadow of the Rain

***

Cold winds toss a bunch of stars.
He is deaf, he does not hear.
How is he writing his music?
With his heart and blood? Please, be quiet!
He breathes immortal air.
Therefore, tears drop from the rooves of
       Dresden,
As half-starved mice in the house.
Recollect his name will last forever!

Raushan Burkitbayeva - Nukenova

Bach

Night whitens the snow,
As ice irons all folds.
Frau Bach is so strict,
But the whole family well.
A prolific father,
Writes liturgies and fugues,
While in a musical casket -
Cycle of preludes fly like a blizzard:
A polyphony of thoughts.
Their scale is amazing.
Surely, eternity flows from a sheet,
Like the sound of a pure harmony?
As for organ notes,
They children breathe music:
Choiring like a family clan -
The most powerful in the world.
Thus, with painstaking work,
And immense efforts,
(Toward the beauty of clear forms,
And worldwide recognition).
Their orchestration storms,
As a curtains of snowflakes.
Indeed, amid the lattice of windows,
At Christmas, Bach is in the living room!

Beethoven 2

Behold the depths of space and the glow of twinkling
stars.
Hearing the ether of music in otherwise oppressive
silences -
Was a plan from God Himself for someone initiated
into mysteries.
Certainly, patience and hard work are rewarded
twice.
As fascinated waves attracted by the planets.
Raise seas, which rush to hidden shorelines.
Only, night tunes reveal their depths,
Since, a deceived soul, with violent passions,
Needs a heavenly vastness. The very lyric of a moon
sonata,
Towering in its rage, like an indomitable spirit.
Thus, my heart was enveloped with an infinite
longing,
While your ear was in tune with enigmatic distances.
Obviously, these oceans of silence that shares this
universe,
Frightened the people of a lagging century.
Yet, tirelessly your perfect creations,
Allowed light to pierce their darkness. Oh, immortal
man!

Raushan Burkitbayeva - Nukenova

***

In the inky depths of the night,
Two titans hold conversation.
One is silent, the other scribbles,
Beethoven - Goethe - the spirits of the
                                    giants.
Both are so great and yet so different:
Courtly manners and a contempt for rank.
Hence, the resort town gathered legends,
While symphonies of weather are bright,
                                    then gloomy.

Moonlight sonata

When someone plays the Moon Sonata,
There is a silent dance of unearthly stars.
Each carrying the earth to heaven,
Where a cleansing light of bliss pours.
Allows the ebb and flow of moods.
And feeling, like a wave of repentance,
Amid fjords of music and cathedral buildings,
Stand proportionate to spirit and distance.
Overall, Beethoven caught with his heart
The cosmic breath of the Abyss.
As vividly as a rapid scherzo,
Memory vanished for centuries.

Elise

Drip drops sing: "Cap, Cap!"
Flying to Elise intact with their music.
As a jealous Chapel Master,
Whirls in a waltz amid spring calls.
Afterwards, children's dreams caught this gust,
For our young beautiful Eliza:
As innocent as every sweet whim.

Brahms

Hungarian Dance -
Faerie Brahms!
And dancing people.
Pushing sounds.
A curtsy of gallant violins,
Holding their embrace.
Shoulders, arms.
Boiling feelings -
Stormy delights.
And in a whirl of dance steps,
Couples spin.
Word-confessions.
A string shall deliver,
Embarrassed by revelations
On an old evening.

Raushan Burkitbayeva - Nukenova

In the past – to V. Brusov

In future
I lay in the fragrance of azaleas…
August 9, 1895 V. Brusov

Night merged with the fragrance of azaleas,
As someone's voice thrilled the silence.
He was full of anxiety, sadness,
The loneliness of a forgotten soul.

Like someone on a distant planet,
He was tormented by anticipation.
And I cried out through the thickness of centuries,
Trying to sharing the pain of pipe dreams.

Those sounds seemed familiar,
But, who reached the elective affinity?
In spite of the separation barrier,
Will we merge for a moment as a chord!

Goethe

"Oh, time, stop!"
"Faust" I.F. Goethe
How quickly time flies!
In a bottomless sky with countless stars.
Uniform kills the (free) spirit of a Minister,
Yet, passion can also tame the mind through work
and honour:
Like Faust tormented by Goethe's pain.
Your wide range of knowledge and interests is
legendary!
So, with a heart clutching at the sounds of the
universe,
The world seemed too small.
Instead, carrying his destiny through the years,
He tossed away stones to learn the truth.
He searched for himself in heavy waters.

Raushan Burkitbayeva - Nukenova

He marched without bending - like Goliath.
Fed up with gossip and nonsensical rumours,
And a spring of love in murmured verses,
He walked to immortality: furiously, triumphantly.
Rising above crowds and sins.
Meticulously summing up his fate,
Then, lamenting his fleshly hollowness,
And light of wisdom that overshadowed heritage,
You became a night wanderer of vertex songs!

Napoleon

Round, convex, light,
Breaks through the loophole.
And stares (forgetting the ban),
Through the keyhole of a museum.
On the parquet shabby floor,
With the swish of mops and shoe guards -
This Grand Commander in a velvet jacket,
Coughs enough to shake the room - chronic
                              bronchitis.
He is short, but his shadow extends over a century.
Hence, little will wash away aphorisms through the
                              prism of time:
Neither luxury, nor dusty frames -
Or the doors of Kunstkamera.
Indeed, light drowns in the cracked pits of panorama.
While red thread weaves a network of video cameras.
Inhabitants, museum exhibits.
They seem to be are married to eternity.
So, peering into the faces of visitors.
(Are you by chance my cousin or descendant),
Makes people mute? Amid modern laces and cheap
                              rings.
Over here, a familiar face is glimpsed in a crowd -
Oh, this tranche of enduring questions.

There is no music, or dancing, or reverence.
Rather, tons of stardust, boredom, and melancholy,
Force grin in his admirers.
An ill-wisher or a previous Madonna?
There are millions of vanished people -
Like snowflakes melting away in the morning.
But he was born to be Napoleon.
He gave the order: "I will not die!"

Shadow of the Rain

Marlene Dietrich

A fashion icon of sensual desires,
Like the "Blue Angel" - a frisky blonde!
And crying in the manner of a violin,
Longing for seductive nights,
The record plays Marlene's song.
With German punctuality, persistence,
She is not a woman – but a devil in the
                                    flesh!
You are now a Hollywood star, of course.
Mounted on a podium without pretense!
And outstanding men now surrounded
                                    you -
Remarque, Gabin, Ernest Hemingway!
They jumped off the deep end,
Drawing inspiration out of passion!
Through the "Arc de Triomphe" - in
                                    Morocco,
Their "Shanghai Express" carryied her
                                    away.
"This is the way the lady wants" …..
To sing before a lonely crowd at sunset.

***

Thin eyebrows in the form of a crescent,
Like a cylinder in a trouser suit,
The red lips of Marlene Dietrich,
Drip talent, temperament – and great
                                    success!

Raushan Burkitbayeva - Nukenova

To my Friend in Norway

Sometimes the stars shine gloomy,
Through a steady squelch of rains.
The Moon sticks out like a thrown butt -
From Harsh Vikings and their chiefs.
A map shows their routes.
Although, their raids are covered with clouds,
And their sails swollen with legends.
These figure are the same for centuries,
Among fearless cliffs and fjords.
Each good-natured. With a smile, warmth,
And the lingering chords of a saga:
Those songs by Norwegian weavers.
Therein, time is inflorescence and ephemeral.
Unlike the Moon keeping count and calendar,
Or planets shining in regularity.
Now, December and January play hide and seek.
Above glaciers moving flagstones.
An iceberg drifts. A friend to these poets.
Yet, their plots flow as waterfalls.
He is warmed by a southern wind from the steppe.

Shadow of the Rain

To Mandelstam

With a line of sleepless telegrams,
That poor fellow Mandelstam became disturbed.
In himself, he dreamed of marmalade,
While wandering in windy Leningrad:
Tearing chains from doors,
While his detractors pinned crimes on him.
So, he left as a shadow in the yard,
As a silver line of poetry.
Freight trains, nights, pharmacies,
And a reckless fear of humanity.
And Sonya - "golden hand" -
Holding up the bank thoroughly.
Thence, with boots as heavy as the snow,
He knew Taiga would not break any secrets.
Instead, his tortured body and the memory is eating,
Turned blue from the assaults of his enemies.
Some say a meteorite will outrun death.
Others, that the brain merely guesses at Truth.
But, Taiga honey is odorous and bitter.
Sounding more like an immortal lineation.
Ah, sleep tight in case you are murdered.
Those lines were sewn with bullets!

Raushan Burkitbayeva - Nukenova

***

The immense sea of fantasy!
Silence keeps silent patiently,
Similar to the vast expanses of Asia -
All explaining why Europe fell in love with them.
How bitter-sweet is the taste of freedom,
Over Zindan* - the light of bright planets.
Where wise, beardless, juveniles,
Pour reason into a captivity of cigarettes.
Now, heavy snows above forgotten faith,
Luxuriate like stars over slums and ruins.
The horizon of a soul may be captured in a gray cage,
While passages to the light are blocked with stones.

***

I will jump into a floating purple canoe,
With that sentimental moon.
Oh, shimmering melody,
You rewards my vigils.
And fireflies loom over the branches,
And invisible birds call into grottos.
I will sail into a harbor,
With the dawn rains.
To share a new song
With the world!

_____

*Zindan– underground prison

Shadow of the Rain

Autumn Monologue

Autumn occasionally wanders until dusk.
She cannot fall asleep in a warm bed.
With no news from her children,
She has waited for a letter for over a week.
She looked up at the stars through a
                                        window.
She missed her TV show again:
Like restless thoughts in a dream.
Yet, the willow grew sad in her courtyard -
Wedged and stretched like goose stitching -
Till a shot boomed across the lakes.
The bullet drawing a black line, they said,
As silence fell over the villagers.
Nowadays, leaves fall down in a spiral,
As threads ring through the wind,
And white haired braids in the distances,
Know anxiety will not go away.

***

Houses run down to the river,
And wave with white kerchiefs -
As fumes melt away.
Old Moon and Sun are like records,
Of these movements and messages.
From Sochi, Gagra, Essentuki.
Hiss reminders:
We are not eternal. We are Kunaks.

Raushan Burkitbayeva - Nukenova

Music

Breaking the darkness of a heavy sky,
Which overhangs with black clouds,
The music made by flows and knives:
This passage is tortured by taboos.

Not by bread alone.
From the Atlantic to the Antarctic,
Islands are like phrases on a music sheet:
Like a chord of resonant stalactites.

Do not disquiet her with a long oath.
The wine cellar is about to close.
Rye songs resound across the fields.
A young Moon glances and smiles.

Around shepherd fires until morning,
We will bask in a dairy mist.
Dombra with an inordinate tune,
Will bring reason to every Quranic parable.

And at the bottom of the sea,
Mother-of-pearl echoes in the waves.
And flies atop a vivid fountain.
And appears in a poet's dream.

It will sound to a passionate heart,
Said faithful shepherds committed to song.
As the melody sounded loud,
Across past, present and future!

Against the Background of the Night

I will reluctantly say goodbye to the night.
Dreams, like birds, soar in the sky.
I am back in my city, my body, my house.
Where have you been? Do not dare to ask me!

I will be snow, lilac and cherry,
I will sing along with chilly droplets.
I do not need an outsider witness,
Or the Moon in a greasy bed.

I will slide quietly under the roof,
I will place new nets on curtain rods.
The song of the stars and rain - I will hear,
As wings dry in a deceptive light.

Brittle sounds knock at these windows,
Like a wounded birds wing.
Stars, Moon – nothing is reliable.
But, everything need love, that's for sure!
19.01.2016

Chapter 8.

The Pulp of Enchanted Dreams

Shadow of the Rain

***

Autumn disturbs with its murmurs,
And paves the garden with foliage.
All making it is impossible to forget,
Your words.
The wind itself carries those sentiments,
Verdant and blooming,
Across the pond hearing them with unease
Of, those saddened water lilies.
Lighter than snow, softer than down,
Like a dew on the grass,
I do not weep over my losses.
Even stars can defy the blue.
So, we will leave for the wilderness,
And dress like the night in velvet cloaks.
Our crystal balls will shield us,
And give us comfort.

Raushan Burkitbayeva - Nukenova

The Great Bear

The inrush of waves was ruthless.
Seven fishermen tossed in the sea.
To prevent their boat from sinking,
They faced the storm and abyss of grief.
Seven women prayed through the night,
That the Lord should save them.
Seven lamps of hope were lit,
While their prayers and tears,
Brought seven bright stars,
Into an unnecessary darkness!

***

Prairie flowers of plain living,
Faded out like cold stars.
Although, they got back their original
                              colors,
Among low-growing grasses and bushes.
Nonetheless, an ocher colour diluted their
                              minimum.
Against Artemisia's silver shine,
While Alumina mingled with gopher:
All frightened by the sound of May
                              lightning.
There is no north, nor south here.
Sometimes, the vastness scares a rider.
Even silence fades in this county.
Where the rain and clouds are confidants.

Shadow of the Rain

***

Stop a moment,
And let streams of lightning,
Fill spaces with snapshots,
Instead of the rain…
That album was torn apart.
Its leaves turned yellow,
While smiles, tabliers,
Became as yellow as parchment.
Yet, something we will miss,
Those songs with smells and return
To the coolness of the night:
And the faces of our beloved.
That we must not forget.

Raushan Burkitbayeva - Nukenova

Music's Paradise

Silently leaving the depth of a box,
In the embrace of freedom of purple darkness,
Music wanders in the lanes,
And fills the tunnel of the void.

She sings karaoke with an echo,
And glasses tremble in the neighboring houses.
Then, the Moon dives in from the east:
Coiling into a ball amid cigarette fumes.

Hanging as hoarse icicles from the eaves,
Through the lens of a pond looking at the sky,
Now she will not be forced back into TV.
She will live as a waif.

She squeezed soundtracks into an accordion,
While on the stairs with tart wine,
Keys jingled in silence, as cautious sisters,
Spying and holding their breath in a brasserie.

And if you are lucky by chance,
To hear this delightful raving in the rain,
Of languid and ox-eyed beauty,
You will lose both quietude and strict taboos.

Sleepless roofs will then spread their wings,
As nobs wait to be inspired by attention,
To the tops of the trees and stars,
Who hear her blessing their capabilities.

Shadow of the Rain

And glass washers amid mirrored high-rises,
Remain sensitive, as a pendulum of chimes
                                   -
To her favourites with mobile coverage,
And a wind-bassoon with a super bass.

I dive into the depths of countertops,
To prostrate myself in these reflective
                                   window.
Ah, music on a curved staircase:
Striving towards the starry dew...

                    ***

Overripe, soft plums,
Shed as hail.
Our garden plunges,
            Into an avid whirlpool of sadness.
Birds sing,
                         A happy melody,
And no one will tell,
                         Who will be back...

                    ***

A Maple leave is inlaid in the window mica.
The cry of cranes in the clouds of heaven.
I hope the romantic nerve is never
                                   atrophied,
Or, fades as the voice of conscience in
                         darkened times.

Raushan Burkitbayeva - Nukenova

Bad Weather

Firs bristle,
Frozen by a blizzard.
The frost is ferocious,
All night long.
A car slips,
And recklessly,
The driver damns,
Such weather.

The roads are snowed in.
Indeed, the snow is as cinders,
Scratching the glass.
Death hides in a corner,
Sending an icy kiss.

As if in a duel,
Under precise observation,
Not all have survived.
Vehicle with a trailer,
Fell down in the ditches.

A messed darkness,
Brews with a threat.
For the sake of frost,
Winter, as a prison,
Issues a wanted list.

Blizzard grew stronger:
Puffing up its hood,

Shadow of the Rain

And wanting a victim.
So, it altering their course,
Coiling as a lasso.

And so every year -
The same harsh lessons.
Through the storms, hardships,
Life sentences.

The snow sprawls.
So do the people,
Cornered,
By shadows every day.

Under spatters of light,
We all forget -
And melt in summer,
As lean jellies.

***

Snow will fall into oblivion,
Boring like the light of a cold Moon.
Regretting broken dreams,
From a point of no return.
Even the stars were minted with tamga*.
Spruces trouble our hearts with needles,
While the moon hangs upon taiga.
Those who left will never come back.

*Tamga - a generic family mark

Autumn Etude

Sun shines as a ripe melon.
A saffron forest will gild,
The day before it gets too cool.
Who will lavish care on everyone.
Those generous tables, full barns.
The silver trills of spokes.
An oldster on a bench,
Will repairs this net in a farm warehouse.
Ah, piles of books, stacks of collections,
And the slightly parted folds of clouds,
Send maestros to the Doge of Venice.
Therein, the wind shears promising clouds,
As the oldster sets a violin
To play a farewell song.

***

I am a wood lily in a valley of dreams,
That weeps, or bursts, into happy tears.
And a frugal ant-beaver,
Will build a house as a town.

***

Great discounts in shops.
A confetti of smiles and graces.
Life goes up in prices.
Snow is tired of being tasted.

Shadow of the Rain

Moon Serpentine

Through the mist of curtains,
In a silent bedroom -
Moon serpentine wanders,
With distant signals.
The stars twinkle streams,
Of softened light.
Will your soul gently cool,
With a simple hello?
Like the abyss of space,
Bringing a shine to life!
Ah, the shiver of restless stars,
Through the prism of a glance.
It will be calm in the silence.
He will give inspiration to me -
And minutes of happiness.

***

The shadow stretched like cords,
Touching you, shyly.
A crafty light in agate eyes,
Flared happily with colours.

I send my verses to her besides.
May my sand tunnel of time,
Bring you love,
Like a phoenix, not a crow.

Raushan Burkitbayeva - Nukenova

A familiar silhouette in the branches,
Zoomed with the Moon and a lamp.
To attend life as a portrait,
Of those indifferent to you.

***

Shadows lengthen at sunset.
Leap February gives an extra day,
While silence breaks up every sound,
Contrary to superstitious notions.
Yet, bearing against spring impulses,
Ice drifts though life touched by attention.
It watches, jealously, its own parade,
Since, March does not believe in fortune
                              telling.
Yet, the frozen expanses of the steppe,
Are filled with light day by day.
As mountains send make their songs with
                              sympathy,
Above caravans of dressed grooms.
Oh, suit arrangements are made for
                              Nauryz.
And jewelry like stars made by Zergers*.
And eyebrows of moon-faced beauty,
Are chanted by bards through the barriers.

---

* *Zerger- jeweler (Kaz.)*

Shadow of the Rain

***

Before flaming lips flame are put in snow,
Before a tangle of arms is loosed,
Or a long moon keeps a cold silence -
Let this night last, and may this date not
                            end.
Forgotten worries will drown snowy
                            darkness,
And the car is cooling in abandoned streets,
But, the breath of love will still thirst,
Against snow flies on a first date!

***

Every cell, every cell,
With tenderness, I will warm.
Every news, every news,
I look forward to cherishing with hope.
Mountain river, fast river,
You will wash each and every pebble.
Every date, every date,
I look forward to, I remember.
My song is flying like a bird,
Knocking quietly against closed windows.
My sadness will dissolve in gentle rains,
May our date be repeated again.

Raushan Burkitbayeva - Nukenova

Toward the Capital!

A bucket rang loudly over the well.
The jingling chain moaned.
Do not spill the gentle sun my friend,
Which, was given by fate!
Black spruces sang in the darkness
About assignations with a blizzards.

A Christmas ball last week!
Gusar recalled in a breech bed.
Now, lunar snow like a train after carriages,
Carries in frosty sheepskins.
This winter night sparkles with secrets.
A Ural mill owner flies to the capital!

Gloom-river will lure him into thickets
The moon flies up like a shaman's drum,
While, legends of centuries vanish in taiga.
Only Moscow expects talented poets.

***

Listen to the river, to its live fright.
And how sometimes it burns in fever!
Under the wings of bridges, in the embrace
                              of winter blizzards
                    –
Trembling houses in besieged Leningrad.
Great River - mother of stanzas,
                              symphonies,

Shadow of the Rain

The forehead of the tormented Neva swells
with ice,
Like a chilled archer with white hands
Bring the sounds of sirens: of blueness.
This fog will triumphantly glide over the city.
And in the mirror of the river - a familiar silhouette,
There, the nights will brighten as chestnuts in
sconces.
And waves will gift a bouquet to the author with
respect.

Raushan Burkitbayeva - Nukenova

Toward Spring…

Slush smells like fresh linen,
Starched with winter frost.
As the sun pea – the Mimosa
Will decorate the houses on Women's Day!

Long awaited March signals -
The first snowdrop over thaw holes!
Delicate, fragile, strokes from the coast.
He, like us, is tired from sleep.

Turgid buds on the branches,
As a notebook, folded into a paper cone.
After a pause - phrases as leaves.
Their appeals multiplying in the wind!
Will Validol calm down?

It is hard to understand, though it is also easy.
Suddenly, to fall in love so carelessly!
This is the job of the spring.
And the poor, or the king, can get trapped:
Into a relapse titled as Love!

Comedy Club

News box,
Getting thinner,
While a clear picture
Is given to everyone.
A plumber's jokes,
Living near to the woods,
Gets "diamonds"
By chance from hatchlings.
We will put them on our ears:
And those of our drunken girlfriends.
Not knowing where,
This marvelous treasure is from,
Like instant coffee -
At the bottom of a mug,
We shall overseas its flavor.
Searching from advertisements to Truth.

Raushan Burkitbayeva - Nukenova

On a Raid

Ice drifts after hibernation.
It comes to life for Women's Day,
With fingers, peakless cap, and maps,
Which get used to the order and swell.
Dreams also drift from the deck to the cabin.
Amid a tight orlop of quiet nights.
The crew is subject to these routines.
In love and longing – in sealing wax.
Yet, clouds like shadows over the city,
Where brides are waiting for their grooms,
Still weave ribbons and tickle collars -
As the smell of a curl makes fine perfume!

Chernobyl

Old Moon cabochon gets muddy,
Although, renovated every month.
Each day awakening to the new idea,
Of changing plans twice every morning.
Clouds, stumble into a pile,
Now it rains, then it hails.
Our forecaster knows best.
A ghost town: Pripyat central.
Yet, a prophetic raven croaked something -
Predicting the disaster.
And ominous fogs creep,
Across already exaggerated and dark legends.
But, the white Stork is unafraid:
She, for one, still nests there.
At the hut, as a miracle of faith -
As in a paradise before it was lost.
However, residents are barred from their houses -
Pripyat is irradiated,
And only the wind wanders there...

Raushan Burkitbayeva - Nukenova

***

Like the evening twilight -
Peal sails into the mist.
Wherein starry snow-covered provinces,
Long moan like bells in a tunnel.
Yet, under these heavy layers of time,
Maybe something will remain.
At a skewed angle – of course,
While everything turns to ashes.
04.01.2015

Shadow of the Rain

St. Petersburg

With the arch of a Siamese cat,
Catching hold of a bat,
Which spreads its wings from a bridge,
Into nights turning pale under cloud cover,
To the tedious creaking of oarlocks.

As ships float, ghost- riders,
Stop a bronze horse,
As Decembrists entered the square:
With swords shining in grey smoke,
Expressing the poet is with them!

Call torments Mandelstam,
Trying to wake up your friends.
But his stamp expired.
He will be sent to Toreh* - **Tam,
To the launching area.

Ah, Cat's Eye beneath the moon, like a magnifier.
They refract time and shadows.
Indeed, it is useless to argue with ghosts.
They will change each plot as in dreams,
While the cries of gulls are heard on the casting bridge.

Night whitens. Faces turn pale.
Someone will start an affair.
And an exhausted capital -
She believing in fairy bluff.
Watches the Neva is trying to get angry.

Raushan Burkitbayeva - Nukenova

With its admiralty needles.
St. Petersburg will sign an order:
It will string an emigrant pain.
Above a cheering crowd,
Rising the echo Paris!

Of course, lead mists will vanish,
And Dostoevsky himself, barely breathing,
Will await the return from Irtysh.
And he will return to the Neva's sides,
Shut-off as a singer by this new regime.

Father-station, the claimant of truth,
Meets all his sons,
(Unbending like Karenin),
To greet enemies and gossips,
As the Gulf of Finland sends its welcomes.

Piotrovsky, the Hermitage – everyone visits the
winter palace!
With it bastion store of stories.
Including the attacks of Napoleon,
A jingle of bells, tramways,
And an auroral curl amid waves of blue.

---

* Toreh - the descendants of Genghis Khan (Kaz.)
** Tam - House (Kaz.)

Chapter 9.

Tunes of Sadness and Sorrow

Shadow of the Rain

A Frosty Star

In the tender haystack Winter snoozes,
        Indulging in reflections,
        melancholy.
Forest bend with crunch,
        Under the weight of snow.
Lazing in the sun,
        On the pearly white sand.
On the sly, she will quietly leave,
Without an escort, alone.
And someone will tenderly throw her,
        With gentleness,
A bouquet of bloomed snowdrops,
        From the thick brushwood.
Why did not you warm anyone?
        With your fierce heart,
Why did you not love anyone?
Being unapproachable and serious.
Not wanting to be frivolous,
But, tossed aside like a frosty star.
It turned out that love is still alive,
And suffers from inabilities.
Being together. Living apart...
Quick and furtive glances.
The wormwood brings this bitterness,
        As hearts shiver amid flaming poppies.
So, all stars to the fore,
        To tell you, "Relax!"
Coining a message in the sky –
        With flickering signs.

Raushan Burkitbayeva - Nukenova

Aurora

Invisible troops,
                    From northern latitudes,
Stand under a red flag,
Ghosting battlefield drifts.
The width of flashes,
Tosses the horizon.
There the crowned iceberg,
                    Is illuminated with sapphire...
Crystal palaces,
                    Of the Snow Queen.
Faceted woodblocks,
Illuminated by soffits.
Hyperborean kingdoms,
                    Immersed in darkness.
Surrounded by,
Legends and taboos.
Star watch guards,
Like rivets and buttons.
A queer hologram,
Of mountains in the sky.
Mysterious worlds of the North,
In pictures by Rockwell,
A polar glow,
Shining on canvases.
A foreboding world,
  Of joys, sorrows?
With fear and delight,
It was encountered at night.

Shadow of the Rain

Another polar glow
                              Rolls across the
                              ice.
The painting is presented,
With diamonds and crystals.
With an emerald mantle,
                              The sky floats here.
The country of Hyperborea,
                              Is steeped in
                              legends.
She was the Foremother
                              Of languages and
                              poetry.
When the immortal spirit soared,
There were no miseries.
As a lost paradise,
About which we keep dreaming.

***

"Art is just a shadow thrown by a man",
Rockwell Kent

Raushan Burkitbayeva - Nukenova

Sun – a polar companion,
Fading and getting offended.
Although, some night lasts forever -
Yet, we did not meet for a month.
We cured our influenza,
With iodine,
With pills, (Muz* –)
With the music of melted snows.
Oh, desired day,
Wherein a confession,
Of frozen rivers and enchanted poets,
Sing and admire this polar light.

*Muz - ice (Kaz.)

Shadow of the Rain

Atlanteans of Petersburg

Overburdened by the weight,
Of time,
Atlanteans seem mythic,
Washed by the rain.
Their flawless bodies,
Finely honed by the winds.
They used to have staring faces,
With oriental features.
So, Atlanteans like giants,
Are messengers of Atlantis.
Persistence – or distinct in their talents,
               They are fearless and noble.
They are adamant,
               Not deluded by false freedoms.
Snows sweep in a curtsey,
Riotous weather.
In the vertigo of styles,
               Plunged in a reverie of coaches,
While wings,
               Surround planets and singing blizzards.
They call them for a walk,
               By the clatter of hooves,
Kissing the moon,
               For as long as the bay is
               open.
Atlantis at the front!
               The darkness caresses their curls.

Raushan Burkitbayeva - Nukenova

All girls admire –
    Their perfect bodies,
So do I,
The twin brothers!
Oh, antique beauty,
You give embraces,
To the midnight sky!
A persistent blizzard,
Storms your pylon,
But the look of your Neva-wife
                        Will put a barrier
                        between us.

12.01.2015 Sary-Agash (yellow tree –kaz.)

                    ***

Neva, where is your blueness like the sky?
All these innumerable shades of gray,
From lead azure onwards - as the dragnet,
Make people ask if the Almighty is angry?
While the stars with their crystal scales,
Above this dark veil.
Still pulsate with refined and light.
Beyond that wall of the Peter and Paul,
Some called for flight: for an end to
                        Sadness!
Was it the reason why Peter the First
Built this city of fireworks?
Hitting - like a ton of bricks,
Palaces, fountains, domes,

Shadow of the Rain

Indeed, God bless the Tsar!
Yet, rain drizzles half the year,
And souls often sing the blues,
Amid locations for cordial people,
(An ancient lineage of intellectuals).
Where a special spirit reigns:
Spilled along with a cocktail of tenderness.
Oh, aesthete, like a thin sandwich -
Your city-chic stands amidst the swamps!

***

Blue heavens are splashing,
In the azure waves of Kronstadt.
As curls of the blossoming ashberry,
Became crisp through bumblebees!
Oh this wonderful time of flowering!
Yet, a nagging feeling in the chest,
Makes this cadet in a hurry for release:
Culling Lilacs along the way.
Thus, a cruiser whitens above the harbour,
And "Aurora" lulls at the night.
Listen, your crew returned from a passage,
While the first mate did not postpone his
date!

***

Silences in an autumn garden.
Wandering alone,
As birdsong dies down.

Raushan Burkitbayeva - Nukenova

Oh, let gimlets of rain point,
Towards webs like small seines,
Falling over a human face.
That mowed wheat,
Grew sad for some reason,
As a pompous goose amid moon lakes.
It grew fat over the summer,
While agile flocks headed to the house of a
poet!

***

Late January - and blizzards have started
again,
Hence, in the desert, windows delayed our
words.
Each running a race with the snow,
Until the nearest forest, and nearest river,
Witnesses snowdrifts whiten into pyramids.
However, I still wander along the avenue in
circles,
Hoping to catch the wing,
Of some soaring bird. Thereby, revealing
my craft,
And proving it wrong to judge me harshly.
That river paves the way for someone,
Through rocks, waterfall thunders, and the
ages,
While rain often sounds out of place,
Amid timid grasslands playing their games.

Shadow of the Rain

Look, shaggy couples wake up in the
morning,
With Poetry – the pulp of enchanted
dreams:
And critics appraising my strange
catchment.

28.01.2014

***

Summer flies by quickly.
Again, the city falls,
Into dreams about any vacation.
So, a man asks for leave:
To sauna near a river,
Whereby twigs,
And pies (from a hot stove),
Induce our mother's happy laughter.
On the wagon - a pile of hay
Of solar straw.
Now tired of this noisy city,
He returns to his village home!

Raushan Burkitbayeva - Nukenova

Trans Onega, Trans Ovrazhye

Through chatoyment of organza,
                              In a faded window,
A paths of light and tears,
                              Allows a quiet alley to be
                              visible.
Pearl flashes in the darkness,
                              A crucified bell trembles.
A deacon reads the last rites of the day,
Thunderstorms fly across a floor.
And cringed spruce freezes -
                              In a glass with blackened
                              silhouettes.
To walk, we refuse,
Instead, a poet will break in the house.
That mill flies up on wings,
                              As barns, cottages,
                              everything, creaks.
A pale Chamomile tells our fortunes,
                              As Porcini mushrooms do
                              their magic.
And grasses knit macramé,
                              Into thick mint brews.
Carmen, born by Merimee,
                              Ah, the west surrenders - old
                              pander.
And in the morning - bright and fresh,
                              Turnips wash their heads.

Shadow of the Rain

Shine clusters of Kizhi,

>Facing ferocious howls
>without fear!

03.12.2014

Raushan Burkitbayeva - Nukenova

A Quay of Dreams

On steamy windows in a tram,
The fall clung and quietly fell asleep.
So, like the frames of old movies,
We sailed into frosty houses.
- To whom is our rent to be paid?
- And where is the owner? – is he crazy?
Yet, these houses were chosen,
Because princesses flew from the nest.
Tenement houses – rented as shared apartment,
As courtiers keeping the manners and etiquette,
Of gentle cousins.
Long time ago did this Russia disappear.
Its splendour being that of a lost era.
Ah, the greatness of Russia, the royal house.
With laced scarves, fans, ornamental sighing.
With a Parisian air - with sadness from the past.
Its exiles still wandering under a cruel fate:
Their roots remaining among the birches.
Were they the messengers of a Silver Age?
Do they seriously hope for their dreams to return?
Nowadays, taxis drive them from birthday parties,
Into a maze of Continental streets.
- Madame, here is your change - merci, merci!
- I will drop you closer to the entrance.
- In Russia - the house with the helpful servant.
He is waiting for me, but snow starches the night:
Veiling both roads and backstreets,
From a time more comfortable and free!

Shadow of the Rain

Palaces keep (Sheremetev, Yusupov,
                                    Fontanka), their
                                    shores,
While a Paris winter is like a Russian
                                    summer -
Dull rains, boring summer gardens.
Yet, in memories, one has no obligations.
Instead, every evening looks backwards.
Turgenev – the captive of Pauline Viardot's
                                    charm.
Do not stir up "A Nest of Gentlefolk".
The Duncan Road snakes like a scarf.
A faithful sphinx waits on the doorstep!
An ageing Tatar sweeps the yard.
                    —You are late today, sir!
05.01.2015

***

Raushan Burkitbayeva - Nukenova

Pierre Martin Offant

Again, like a bloated dispatch,
A broken cloud floats.
And after canceling his hiking trip,
The artist works in his workshop.
Yet, untaken pathways scream in reproach,
Making his coat glower in its closet.
Look, that piano is exhausted by lessons,
And this goose has been fattened for fois gras-
Although, each farmer has tempered his attacks.
Ah, every gourmand gathers birds on a scaffold,
In a jaded world tired of Paris,
Looking at sick horizons.
So, the tear-stained windows of a balcony,
In a royal park dropping without sunshine,
Allows Nature to faint,
Whilst twins grimace in a puddle.
Oh, my honorable friend, my dos *
I am offering you Calvados.
But, you miss the steppe so much,
Since in Biscay waves you hear the Caspian Sea.

Dos*-friend (Kaz.)

Shadow of the Rain

To Bella Akhmadulina

Like a feather from God's hat,
You are airy and weightless.
Going along an invisible way.
So, graceful ... and the snow,
Which wrapped each window and door,
Will dance around that staircase.
Oh, your admirers do not believe -
Your hand slipped out of the ring.
And this terrible news,
Pierced the soul like an arrow.
You were a muse and honoured:
A descent of heaven; an elf.
Your unique voice,
Sounded as a farewell sonata,
Over saddened Moscow,
Embracing each verse like a poem.
But, the snow became salty,
And tears dried your cheeks,
Greatly endowed,
Like once proud black silks,
Since, they only caught the contour
Of your divine hands.
Hence, embarrassed by revelation,
The landscapes of a pounded river
(Squeezed into marble armour),
Allow no place for wild herbs.
Beforehand, hunted Mandelstam, Dovlatov
And Pasternak: keept sweet sonnets,
In ears washed by milk:

Raushan Burkitbayeva - Nukenova

Whereby a fervour was given to them,
Resounding in its own rhythm.
As for her paintings, she sailed on.
Although, it seems that her presence,
Will be long among us,
Albeit reflected in fragments,
Of the radiance in perfect phrases.
All meaning, halls freeze, echoing,
Her breath and lines.
Yet, death crept up enhancing grief,
In her silver temples.
And our souls emptied out.
As frigid bells ring.
So, after the blizzard, she left,
For a place where fragrances ripen.
Where, paralysed in a frame of watercolors,
Chilled flowers still grow crimson -
Neither regretting their date,
Nor stiffening in a sorrowful curtsy.
Indeed, each a man refusing to hide tears.
Nowadays holds a trembling candle, as if in a trance,
And lingers in a corner – near tthc piano.
And December blows its first snow...
Similar to swan feathers,
And taking her to royal chambers,
The reborn one,
Is pleased by eye and ear.
She seems fragile, but with the power of spirit,
She sews strings on prophetic lyres.
Incredible chords,
And enchanted hordes,

Shadow of the Rain

Getting drunk and shaking the air,
While silenced decibels,
Ring before every word,
As a Bella sigh!
07.12.2010

***

She lived in the spacious workshop,
Devoting her whole life to Art.
Yet, unable to cope with sadness, or
longing,
She drowned grief in the wine of poetry.
But, a blizzard struggled through cracks in
the ceiling.
So, dropping her voice, she listened to a song.
Remembering Bella's divine style,
Wandering homeless around Presnya.
She recalled he had lived next to her:
Her worshiper, her husband – a painter.
Nowadays, dissolving night colours into
dance,
While outlines to silence the ear...
He served her without fading light into
shadow -
Facts encompassed by care and a vigilant
void.
And keeping these image for the coming
century,
Saw an artist and poet, matched in the
family!

Raushan Burkitbayeva - Nukenova

To Akhmadullina, to Mayakovsky!

Occasionally, words conceal truth,
As tracks are lost in the dust of centuries.
Oh, arrogant grass,
Which germinated between interjections.
And daring to guess in flashes,
Like the blade of a dagger.
Of course, only Love is always right,
Even when separated, or strained.
Thus, desperate verses have been born
From this abyss of doubts,
Tearing between these two:
Wherein genius is driven from a house -
Rinsing letters like linen,
And mercilessly stirring up archives.
Poet, your piece of art!
Is doomed by a ruthless axe…

Vysotsky – a Flight to Paris

You fly, leaving the weight of grudges and silence.
Yet, the she silver of wet wings on outspread roofs
Again lights a road into the night.
Once, I believed you sailed in the sky like a satellite:
A guardian of love dozed off – in a Parisian airport.
Somewhat tipsy and swaggering a bit.
Indeed, my best friend is always ready for hardships,
While booking us a hotel in the city of starry dreams -
With views from the windows into infinity.
Ah, Madame Love will register each lodger,
As the moon raises Her eyebrow in amazement
At seeing two people destined to cross paths!
Oh, Paris! Forgive our whims again.
And tolerate every poets' fantasies.
After all, their memory got lost in alleys
Mazing your magnificence - you will keep your
                                    mysteries.
Like a bartender in the rain shaking a cocktail,
With the spicy aroma of pastries.
On bare nerve broken lines by the wind.
Hey, my phone pulsates under the pressure of song,
Like a bubbling voice in spring through the frost.
Perhaps this globe and scale for Vysotsky was too
                                    tight?

Raushan Burkitbayeva - Nukenova

***

Rains, snow blizzards.
Do not part with your sky house for centuries.
They release herds of heavy clouds.
As a river rushing to meet its fate:
As the cycle of water and love in nature.
Your melodies glide along rainbows.
Birds, cherries, blizzards and lilac waves.
And clusters of thunderstorms like roses,
All fill this world with allure!

Shadow of the Rain

"In vino veritas"

To Z. and M. Kakimzhanov

All notes of sadness and grief,
And the sweetness of a gentle dawn,
Looked over the shades of day,
Into a zenith melted by summer.
And clusters - all the nuances of rain,
Moods etc, carry bursts of bad weather,
Like a tuneless sing song.
Yet, wine keeps those years within,
A ruthlessly, recklessly,
And rabidly burning vineyard.
It is easier to pull down than to build.
Your flush is noble: brave.
Old barrow - keeper of the centuries secrets,
You knew those depths as a cupbearer.
Hence, drink thickened quietly,
While soaking in pitchers and purple red.
Indeed, the Sun, himself, drinks depthless air,
Through a straw – slowly getting tipsy.
Here the vineyard is renewed again,
As green vine tears,
With tight little fists, breasts,
All filled with juice,
And teasing starlings who will cool them down,
By giving a high flight to verses.
Ah, the Rubaiyat of Omar Khayyam,
Flames with a ruby fire.
Luxuriating in clouds of fog,

Raushan Burkitbayeva - Nukenova

Our poet was captured by a tavern,
Oh, eternity – astute cooper,
Adept at sloping shoulders and bodily joints!
The beam refracted on a ringing edge,
              Still shivers as a passionate night -
                            moaning.
              Herein, a Divine nectar sparks,
              And spreads through the veins.
              A sip of wine – and we will repeat,
              His love in the sunset of a bygone time!

In vino veritas – There is truth in wine (Lat.)

***

To Rollan Seinsenbaev

In the darkness of days through the fog of
                                    bitterness -
Your novel seeds a ray of light and
                                    goodness.
And grains of wisdom and sprouts of truth,
Will upspring in rich harvests.
We are proud of you We love you and
                                    respect you.
You are the voice of conscience, worthy
                                    Kakharman*.

_____

* *Kakharman - a hero, warrior*

Chapter 10.

Anticipation of Spring

Shadow of the Rain

***

The canopy melted away from bliss...
Now rain, then hail, then snow.
Yet, mad flirting by a star made things
                                    long,
While, revealing her passionate look.
Oh, how tempting are expanses,
Along with delightful dreams!
Your eyes beckon with aquamarine,
Your features are so attractive.
And the star falls tiredly
Into your open palm.
Like a Universe in a small snowflake,
Everything rings and sings at your touch.
In a necessary metamorphosis of day and
                                    night,
Do not look for brutal truths.
Instead, flourish as a fallen star -
In curves and melting peaks.

Raushan Burkitbayeva - Nukenova

***

From spring to spring,
As if in a long sleep,
Through fog and snow,
You run to see me.
And the still of the night,
Hides again.
You fly to see me,
My song, my love!
Scattering stellar music,
With an enlivened piano.
And the motif floats,
Through a veil of rain.
Ligatures of simple words,
Will then tie thoughts in a line.
You are the hero from my dreams.

Anticipation of Spring

Like a culled leaf -
In a dry day, passing into separation.
The whistle of the crosswind,
Brought night into the embrace of boredom.
Against dreams,
You see a shrill sunrise,
While towards spring,
Outstretched avenues,
And an orphaned breeze,
Will sing lonely songs outside our windows.
He calls his friend,
From apartment 20.
Maybe they will fly together,
Over a silent capital?
Hey, do not worry,
About news from a newspaper!

Raushan Burkitbayeva - Nukenova

***

The long-awaited snow of February!
Stirred up like a beehive...
In an underground cafe on a table,
Inverted chairs.
Glasses rattle melodiously,
At the counter.
It makes no difference now:
Deceptions, lies.
Snow flying into the night,
And the whole city lights up in the
                                    morning.
Through the sadness - forgiving laughter,
Giving us hope for better times.

Shadow of the Rain

Love - Paranoia

As a March madness,
Love is comparable with paranoia.
And hopelessly winds howl,
Although they should not be blamed.
This is how old Moon plays with a wave:
One day ebbing, another flooding.
But, blossoms grows and quietly melt.
Oh, how sweet are their torments,
And how deadly are separations.
The further they are distanced from us by fate,
The fiercer they get in their passion.
Yet, outrunning snowfall,
They will sweep away all barriers:
Trembling and dissolving like flames,
While strings tear with a melody.

Raushan Burkitbayeva - Nukenova

***

Come in broken dreams.
It is night time in this city.
So, the colours of a spring rainbow,
Will echo, filling mountains.
Cheering the autumn landscape,
With a favourite song from a movie.
Be a hero from a film scene,
A planet sailing by a window,
Through the call and cry of alarming verses.
Please feel the joy of meeting,
As weightless as the evening frost,
And as tender as light.

The 8ᵗʰ of March

Gambling stakes are high,
When gliding kisses on the run.
A bouquet of flowers in a "hyped" March.
Some say Ladies fondly cherish these
messages,
Like heady aromas in spicy air -
Like sparkling winter and creative springs.
So, a crowd of men standing at the ATM,
Overshadowed the love of your dreams!
Yet, credibility is prolonged for a year,
While cards shine with a triumphant ace.
Another February fell asleep behind my
door.
Again, the bustle of the 8th of March
endures!

***

Red, yellow, and blue -
Stars are alive. Any questions?
One asks, they give an answer.
They love you, and they see everything.
Only old Moon waits outside the window.
She grew up with you,
Like a glacier filled with light,
That ripens as a summer apple.
Thereafter, sunrises stretch to the planets,
While stars dance with the Milky Way.

Raushan Burkitbayeva - Nukenova

Ah, a spilled glass of milk,
Mirrors stardust in clouds!

***

Spilled black ink...
The sun snoozes behind a hill.
Those rumours blackened you for nothing,
But, now you sing with other ladies.
Look….. that bridge hangs as a dragonfly,
While words thunders in empty buckets,
Who disturbed these thoughts?
Certainly, you left with a sprightly step.
Afterwards, the river flowed calmly,
And stars burnt in silence,
As a favourite waltz played in the park.
Some children play there too.
But Moon only gained weight and went away.
Summer departed into autumn.
A blizzard howled with anguish.
Yet, we have enough patience until spring.
Look ….. that bridge again: hanging like
                                    an earring.
A star breaks into the abyss,
And there will be real feelings.
For a man as solid as a wall!

Shadow of the Rain

***

In the desert night,
Only the wish of a candle trembles.
And incorporeal creation,
Flickers in flashes above a stove.
But, the wind that knocks at a window,
As an unwelcome guest in the darkness,
Is in a jealous anger,
Is never leaves me alone,
While cold rain tirelessly poured,
Into a culling of fragile flowers.
But, I will not forget that I am loved:
Or that you were loved by me!

Raushan Burkitbayeva - Nukenova

In a Café

Tired of iron embrace by the frost,
Irritated snowstorms tear at the frozen asphalt.
They run from constant worries - dull prose,
As brakes screech akin to an alto.
Ah, trees-skeletons stand along the road,
As rivers stumble across concrete boulders.
Come in the café. Throw away the bans.
Warm up your soul. Forget all your sorrows.
Through a snow wall, in a whirl,
Where voices are not heard, my head swims.
Trust your heart. Believe the song,
With its lively smiles and simple words.
The violin moans, or cries, ruefully.
Ice floats in an amber glass.
These pains will go in the morning. Everything will
                        change,
And relief will re-polish the glasses.

Astana, 26.12.2007

***

Let the fall
Colour the festive grizzle,
With a thick paste of henna.
Let her ask sleepy pines
Their secrets.

Shadow of the Rain

Where do dreams fly away?
Birds take them away
Into a heavenly azure.
And they melt without a trace.
"Stay" - they beg.
But silently, without question,
Years are running away...

***

It snows. It rains.
Long nights. Short days.
And troubling memory,
With beckoning lights.
Between running verses and days,
In a land of tangled roads,
Where is a song of joyful meetings?
You are cold without my love.
You awaken cold spaces.
My prayers and gentle looks,
Will wake up the warming vastness,
While chantant jingles drip,
On Jazz patterns.
You have been given to us by fate,
Like a flying music motive,
Taking us to another world,
And making our dreams come true.

Raushan Burkitbayeva - Nukenova

***

My endless grief,
Flies on a snowy field.
I still wait for you.
Come back to me, my dear!
A poet wanders Like the rain.
My soul suffers with him,
And takes off all my masks.
Now, clouds and thunderstorms will pass
                    by.
And faces will glow with happiness,
Once lovers will meet again.
Oh, this old globe keeps revolving.
As a leaf drops across years of time.

***

Awakened by the spring a long time ago,
My wings are still hidden behind my back,
Although, your voice is slightly hoarse,
In the night. I hear it behind the wall.
Now, the wind whispered all his secrets,
Through a window.
Indeed, he brawled until dawn,
Scaring everyone in the sleeping quarter.

***

The Sun grows cold on my window frame,
As it obliquely sides,

Shadow of the Rain

Into evenings within quiet courtyards:
Therein imprinting leaves in the sand.
A glancing tree snoozed,
And insidiously, a bell kept silent.
Strangely, autumn embraced its parting.
So, wrapping a scarf around her,
Winter - like a jealous mistress,
Gave a cold look towards the threshold.
And from heaven, a tangled flock
Of doomed, whirling, snow flies,
Thickened across a twilight river.
Be patient until the spring.
Your sadness will melt as a candle,
Warbling like rings bursting into a dream!

07.12.2008

Raushan Burkitbayeva - Nukenova

Phone Call of a Friend

To Y. Koshkin

Life is playing hide and seek with me.
Maybe I am doing something wrong?
Days, however, run away without looking back,
And my enthusiasm is scattered like ashes.
Ah, flashing ideas will whirl,
Over those block houses,
And then fade away, turning cold:
Through the rejection of the gorged minds.
Albeit living in different dimensions
Under the same roof.
Sometimes, two (occasionally three) generations,
Incapable of hearing each other.
Surviving like ripe, juicy, cherries,
I once picked in a garden.
But, now I am like a gate-crasher,
And tired of moving in shadows.
Yet, lilacs will be torn into bouquets -
While evenings are indifferent to the elderly.
Listen, newspapers rustle as leaves,
Until only the stubs of a tree remain.
In which case, tell the air to breathe today.
Is my city poisoned by smog?
No - I will sing an octave higher
To the morning and rush on my journey.

Shadow of the Rain

***

Cupid's arrows dulled.
We have not stood up for love.
Nor throw darts at targets.
So. there are no secrets full of erotica -
Only accessible beauties.
These days emptiness gapes in the heart.
These are tired day awaiting the shadow.
And on the winding path,
Advertising will poison picture shows.
The circle is closed. There is no cure from boredom.
Now, vicious cities seized us,
While noises break the silence.
But our mountains are impartial,
And the rifts of a quiet river,
Live amid azure eyes made pure.
Ah, the sunset is clear.
And tireless prayers
In mosques, churches, and the blood,
Reveal Life to be a battlefield,
In the name of truth and love!

Hong Kong

To S. George
Glass-concrete jungles -
And artificial bamboo forests,
With garlands of flame like night coals,
Allow thin arms to rise skyward.
Oh, Hong Kong blooms! And the mountains,
Eclipsed by the towers of skyscrapers,
Gathers admiring glances from tourists.
Yet, once knocked over by these heights,
Great Buddha in copper womb
Still keeps his magic crystals.
God almighty, he is everywhere.
Please send us good and happiness.
But, fog hides the statue,
Refusing to let the fire of his soul shine,
Or warm and inspire us.
Instead, the rings of an stretched string,
Bridge the past and present.
What will happen? We do not know yet.
Some are in yachts, indulging in dreams,
Some are in junks, slicing through the water.
Yet, future days prepare surprises,
When flying like a seagull...

Shadow of the Rain

China – in Passing

In a rickety boat,
Two lairy lady anglers,
Put out a rod:
Stretch a fishing line.
Then, two young fellows,
Floating nearby,
In skintight T-shirts,
With athletic bodies,
Paddle smoothly.
What will they catch today?
Ardent comrades?..

Multideck tourist motor ships, white luxury yachts,
motor boats, sailboats, cargo barges and crafty junks,
ply between the islands on which concrete and glass
skyscrapers are formed like bamboo thickets in a
fantastic city. Underground and underwater tunnels,
intricate roads, monograms; the life of this Asian
metropolis is constantly in full swing! Only a 34
meter copper Buddha (frozen in endless meditation)
blesses these swarming people.
A few hawks hovering above the hustle and bustle
of the world ... for some reason there is not a single
gull in sight. The thick greenery of spreading trees
and shrubs covers the slopes of mountains and hills:
splashing them with the bright colours from flowers
emitting the fragrance of flavors. However, I do not
see bees, or bumblebees, which is strange. In these

parts, nature exhibits diverse flora and fauna. Maybe it is because there were less people once?

A group of young cadets in white naval uniforms came to breakfast. Military uniforms have always been attractive to ladies of tender ages. Medals for valour and honour jingled alluringly on puffed out chests like necklaces. One cadet's face went scarlet like a ripe apple on a plate. For their part, waiters were keeping an eye on the fiery fire-fight of long slanted eyes...

02.05.2014

Copper Dime

My grandson found in a closet,
A shabby penny.
He dangles it,
He plays with it.

I will ask my grandfather,
What can I do with it?
What can I buy
At the kiosk?

Weighing in his hands
This trifle penny,
Although, hitherto dozing,
The old man cheered up.

- Oh, buddy this is,
Priceless stuff!
He was surprised
At his stupefied grandson.

I remember my first
Shiny penny.
It was like a medal
Of boyish fights.

I got this penny,
For something,
When I gave a lesson
To a bully.

Raushan Burkitbayeva - Nukenova

I recalled man-to-man talk
With my father.
And I still keep this penny

For honour – there were no harm,
From a purple bruise.
I put this cold penny
On ice.

What can you buy?
Yes, a mere trifle.
But, my grandson did not
Unclench his fist...

Chapter 11

The Music of Lines

Shadow of the Rain

***

Sky - a cloth made of satin,
Sparkles as New Year's bling.
Shadows of the past – on the carpet,
Snow, promised to us in November.
And porcelain plate whitens -
Om a lunar virgin's torturous face.
A frosty arrow freezes-
Lonely, jaded twin.
The table is set for one person.
Although, an untouched dinner cools.
I will rush like the ringing of bells -
With a snow-dance on a cold January!

No Haps...

Half serious, half playful,
Rain washes away traces of the wheels.
While petals as white of roses,
Flew into my window.

Half serious, half playful,
A direct question was posed:
"Will you go with me?" The answer was
                              simple,
But, the roses turned yellow.

And the wind whispered something,
And the twilight deepened.
None of you understood,
That you said farewell to fate...

***

The capital is braced for a blizzard!
It will make its way with a howl of
                              troubles,
While, those with whom you share shelter
                              and bed,
Acquires chinchilla furs.

Celestial as a ray of sunshine!
Is an imprint of parting on the heart.
A thorny kiss on the cheek,
Proves a spluttering of feelings.

Shadow of the Rain

Stilling my insatiable eyes,
You disappear with interrupted sleep,
Yet, flowers watered with the moisture of
                                    night,
Are as heavy snow – or your voice through
                                    the window!

Just do not put love on a conveyor,
Which makes fire by a random spark!
Gill-flirt looks for a fan in a purse.
Macho will make a super star out of her!

***

I wish I could return to those parts,
Where houses are smothered in lilacs:
Twined with hops, sleepy sloth.
Where frogs' a cappella,
Amid the warbles of nightingales.
Over there, the blues are spread beyond,
Snails with hide horns,

While hard worker-ants puff aloud.
This gate will open wide for the spring.
Surma is ready with new eyebrows.
"Shtander - ball" will take off to the sky!
There apple ripen with dreams,
As you and I - right after them.
Therein, a donut with a golden crust,
Appears so tender, tasty and hot,
It is as if mum remains at home.
Ah, I will go to kindergarten,
Where a glance becomes slanting -
And my dad with my brother braid hair...

Shadow of the Rain

Dos –Muka- San

*In the memory of Sharip Omarov,
Bakhytzhan Zhumadilov*

Sweet with windy chants
A tulip galaxy flies!
Through the pain and blood
Of Anrahaya swords,
All imprinting moans,
In dull granite.
Korday Pass -
The rift of centuries.
A shaky bridge
On a rattling sky.
And someone is doomed,
In miner's cage:
Vanished round the corner of eternity...

Raushan Burkitbayeva - Nukenova

The steppe is impartial.
The mountains are silent,
Menacingly, drawing near,
A fox malakhai.
Dombra sings.
Taking away,
Sad floods,
With an eagle's wings -
Gilded strands
Hanging down,
With a flow of tunes.
The youngster on a stage, on a screen,
"Kydasha" desperately calls you!

13.01.2012

Shadow of the Rain

Zhansugurov – Merke

To Erzhan, Ida
Bronze roses of manure,
Fertilize the way home.
Flying from childhood through the storm,

The motif of a mountain river on the slope.
My smiling old grandfather,
Will glimpse as a ray on the face.
There your shadow - jig,

Grows with each passing day at the porch.
And the evenings with a whip,
Fly to meet the flock.
Our hosts are waiting at the fence,

Laughter as bells ring.
And a statuesque old man,
Protects our house from misery.
Our sisters and brothers,

Are happy around this long table.
And here at our homes threshold,
Your warrior shadow,
Freezes ablush, strictly,

Casting eyes upon the abandoned day.
And strangers arranged their life
In our house a long time ago.
Yet, your voice will not wake them.

Raushan Burkitbayeva - Nukenova

The boy forgot Alshee* in arbor.
Puppyish delights will startle,
The dormant yard with excitement.
You are just a passenger for them:
A depleted fence singing the blues.

And this house has got much lower,
While the trees fused with the sky.
Neighbours – are closer and much loved,
As our prayers ascended to our grandfathers.

Above your home on a plane,
You soar high like a bird -
Like a snowflake on the decline,
Like wormwood, lily of the valley, flesh...
(All smells to be framed by a song,
Will sparkle as the mountain Marinka)
And they will be easy and light!

02.11.2011

_____

* *Alshee asyk - dice (Kaz.)*

Shadow of the Rain

***

The needle stumbled,
On the vinyl disc.
This inevitable arrow,
Changed the world.
Made moaning a rebellious runaway:
Whistling a merciless whip.
The rush of persistent tenderness -
Will dance among dying candles...

***

A hospital courtyard,
Like a well.
A heavy wind,
Pierces leaves.
In the House - in colour,
The ward's windowsill
Is full of flowers.
Tired branches,
Clung to the window.
There, trees are like guards!
Nightmares,
A last breath.
The first day crying...
They are used to it,
Sharing sorrows,
And happily waiting,
They recognize me.
08.10.2014

Raushan Burkitbayeva - Nukenova

***

Stars shiver in the morning cold.
The Sun weathered on cheeks in the cold.
Looks squint in a mirror of puddles:
Putting ointment of velvet roses.
Rain turned to snow overnight.
Dancers whirl in a spiral-fuete,
In an irresistible volatile happiness.
Do not fly away - after your reception in
                              vaudeville!

2012

***

My city, my lair,
Tired from the daily bustle.
These roads are in patches and sores,
Since, the ghost of ills and poverty haunts,
Shuttered windows in a box.
Oh, family fights and troubles,
Keep wise and kind people,
From stubbornly dragging their woes
Across black windows, like an abyss,
Of vanished light amid one-handed souls.
That moonbeam was drunk -
As it scoured your wallet,
And poisoned with bitter truth,
My inveterate eccentric.
So, directed at high peaks,
Like the scarlet coin of the sun,

Shadow of the Rain

Swallows now twitter in the sky,
And live by a campfire of squirrels:
Whistling on a railroad,
As whispers catch up with the violin - breeze!

***

I wait for this moment,
Every year,
Eagerly.
On dark-skinned branches,
Full of mysterious inceptions.
After a growing,
And maturing moon -
Allows flowers to bloom,
In wave after wave.
Of inflorescences,
Bursting across the eyelashes of stamens...
Like a bee,
Before is too late,
Enjoy the sweet fragrances,
Of hot languor,
Of blooming gardens,
Of shy thunder.
Then, in a whirlwind of pollen,
Of fulsome croaking,
In fruitful writings -
Allow this promised paradise,
To curl before willows,
With honeyed earrings.
Ah, these grasses,
Are smothered in flowers.

Raushan Burkitbayeva - Nukenova

Here comes the Spring again…

Gardens veiled with colours often spread,
The nightingales at dusk before dawn,
While scatter roulades like cherry petals,
Allow Birch shadows to pattern the air.
Ah, fragrant mists lure people into darkness.
So, beware shrubs and grasses that sway in delusion.
They embraced with anguish and sing the lilacs blues.
Filled with magic, these warm April days,
Beguile. Only yesterday, the bark on a peach tree,
Depressed sights among ranks of gallant saplings.
Similarly, magazines, as on fashion plates,
Use sticky leaves when clapping their hands.
Here, every day – a premiere of wedding dresses.
For honeymooners hoodwink my fellow men!
Like butterflies and bees. Like decorations.
On flavoured meadows amid rivers of refreshments.
Yet, to be sad in such days, my friend, is
                              unacceptable.
Target your love. Is it really unreachable?
And what do I hear, nothing but groans,
With branches of chestnut under your crown!

Shadow of the Rain

***

A stubborn column was stunned,
As he looked down upon everybody.
Their homely garden had been transfigured:
Covered with tender flowers.
So, he admitted his guilt,
And fell in love with the beautiful spring!

Raushan Burkitbayeva - Nukenova

April

Purple foamy rolls of lilacs,
Embraced by boiling rain,
While, the mystery of new inceptions,
Was hidden by a trembling April day,
As tears from the flesh of greenery -
Of solid trunks and branches,
Of passionate birch bleeding juices,
Allowed a nightingale to whistle.
Then thunder marked their first joys,
As a dawn of dandelions,
Glowed like blossoming apples,
After leaving fresh footprints in the grass.
Oh, I turned a blind eye to laughter:
To roads mired down in gossip.
Yet, laughing, since emphasis is never
                          noticed,
Forgot about sleep and sorrows,
Arranged in dates by violet willows.

***

Waves of chestnut streaks,
Were veiled by a frosty rime.
As light reflected in the eyes,
Of a frozen crystal vase.
Only, the lilac branched out rampantly,
As a gentle teasing cloud,
With shadows growing on a wall,
Where zephyr hastened the day.

Shadow of the Rain

Thence, candles lighted in mirror -
Became two flexible stitches of passion.
Yet, a new song from the sheet,
Is needed to heal old wounds.

***

Pink and white May will break in,
With thunder in a purple sky.
And from the shelter will rise
A raving mad forest.
From then onwards an impenetrable
                                    thicket,
Will smoke the moonlight with clouds,
Of sweethearts waiting for their first dance,
After receiving the advice of a bird cherry.
They do not care about bans and threats!
Or, the eternal call of the invincible.
Rather, noisy showers and thunderstorms,
And the hoots of deaf owls,
Must mushroom around their skirts -
Breathing pure ozone.
Yet, a crown with yellow umbrellas,
At the top of dandelions,
Promises air filled with mint.
So, swift piercing clouds,
And bees, like tipsy in-laws,
Allow an intoxicated twists of tthe winds.
Oh, quails will run across your path,
As the song heard from the village,
Prevents couples diving into the grass.

Raushan Burkitbayeva - Nukenova

***

The whole garden is spangled with petals of
                               cherry.
Wind puffs away at gentle pollen.
The shadow of a witness wanders - like
                               third wheel,
And creeps towards the porch as a cat.
Now, branches jade, recalling the heat of
                               embrace,
While the lips of petals turn pale in the
                               moonlight.
So, cool rains alone will capture the whole
                               garden.
As a guitar bypass.
Thus, old winds lull birds on the branches
                               of willow:
On wet leaves – like tears from a mournful
                               moon.
And spring grieves. Sad at her motives,
Until everyone meets again. Until the sobs
                               of a wet string
                               sound.

***

Embracing steppes and mountains,
I am flying on the wings of a song!
Doubts, quarrels, cease.
I envy the sun, the streams.
Over there, grapes are filled with warmth,

Shadow of the Rain

And vast fields of solid spike droops -
Wreathed with hops and roses.
As was childhood island on a loving
                              continent,
Where my home became the land of my
                              ancestors!
All keeping the legacy of our fathers:
And intoxicating branches of the lilac,
Which obscures our porch from the Sun.
Oh, the enlightened faces of brothers and
                              sisters,
Oh, the joy of meeting and the bitterness
                              of losses.
Our hearts understand. It needs no saying.
And the soul is wide open like a door.

                    ***

As in a silent desert,
Saxaul droops,
Burned by the hot sun,
Not knowing the taste of moisture,
Or a cloudless sky.
But, single and proud,
Each swan falls in sorrow,
To the ground as stone.
The same way I am choking,
In Vanity Fair,
Among people – lonely.
Indeed, it is cruel,
Like gray skies,

Raushan Burkitbayeva - Nukenova

Once broken with thunder.
Or, raindrops beginning to knock
On the roof of a house.
1971

***

A stuffy July night,
And a refreshing balm.
You come to me quietly,
But, only dreams - not in person.
Oh, those sweet intoxicating lips,
They touched me.
I wish all of this were real.
As it is now, it is a wonderful fancy,
Waiting for a physical embrace,
While words, I will not voice them all...
Beg for your love:
Shall we make a miracle in reality?

***

Tell me, what does "marriage" mean?
An end to sweetness and light?
The answer is simple – courage.
But, this crown is heavy.
Other worries will come,
And morning mists will disappear.
However, knee deep in work...
Love becomes a lie.

Shadow of the Rain

***

Why is it called the Black Sea?
It is in fact akin to heaven.
Only, the grief of orphaned relatives,
Can be called black.

***

A vast sea of bitterness,
Sprawled on the ground.
So far, it is indifferent -
Your destiny to mine.
It does not know yet,
As it steadily absorbs salt,
That somewhere in a distant country
I was born - Assol.
Indeed, on a magical morning,
From out of the blue valleys,
The young handsome man will come to
                                    me -
Green heralded.
And the sky will turn scarlet, like those
                                    sails,
While my prince will come,
With dreams on the edge of truth.
1971

Raushan Burkitbayeva - Nukenova

Assol

Having experienced bitterness and joy,
And having tasted the honey of May,
In my heart, I remain the same Assol,
I still live -yet underloved.

And my heart is tormented by hope.
So, I look into the horizon.
- Oh, where are you, my brigantine?
Come into sight – I beg you.

In such ways, travelers in deserts long for coolness.
Wishing, as they do, to drink ice-cold water;
While wanders lonely and looking for delight.
He is ready to break the ice.

My soul, like a seagull, over the expanse of water,
Is tired. It will rest in an experiential wake.
And, soaring high, with joyful eyes,
This precious ship will arrive!

Shadow of the Rain

In the Park

Heavy clusters of tender lilacs -
Like lovers hiding in coolness and shade,
Spread the fragrance of jasmine and
                            warning:
Saying beware of him, sweetie. He will we
                            will betray you.
So, in the flowery bliss and foam of boule
                    de neige -
My honey, will you comfort my heart?
And bring candles alight near the chestnut.
Oh, I am so tired and sit by that fountain.
Now, the smell of wine fills the air,
While, only narcissus proudly shines.

***

A small little Sun,
Shines with a smile and bright eyes,
Thank God for such a miracle,
Developing delight in us all.

***

And time is the best healer.
And the world is huge and single.
Yet, every inhabitant is a seeker,
Of its hopes and their other half!

Raushan Burkitbayeva - Nukenova

Lieutenant

Spring, April, lilac and a ball...
As butterfly, hovering!
Oh, slender young lieutenant,
You burn with passion.
You sparkled like a crystal,
Revealing ups, downs,
Dreams, hopes, and promises.
And the nights were so long,
So delightful, so gentle.
As if in lava, everything boils -
But, my lieutenant is not sleeping.
Oh how fast time passes by!

Captain

Oh, scorching besotted summer,
Friends, girlfriends, a thin waist,
As insatiable as skillful:
As tempting as insidious.
Oh, this charming captain!
An unsinkable daring, but air-minded.
In love, in friendship, and in business.
Strong, handsome, stubborn and cheerful,
Powerful, as almighty as Allah.
Like a bright light, or a magnet,
He beckons night butterflies.
Indeed, his life is in full swing.
Oh, how fast time flies!

Raushan Burkitbayeva - Nukenova

Colonel

How short was that Indian summer!
With its warmth, tender, and mature view.
And its taste of fruit. A reward for effort.
Certainly, all can be solved. Everything is so easy.
However, hearts can beat timidly.
Oh, how young she is and proud.
But, our Colonel cheerful - playful,
Put on weight and got lazy:
Proving Larks can be so fastidious.
And, young ladies can be venomous.
So, days suddenly shortened,
And nights became times for boredom,
Dethroning our iron Felix.
Now, this useless man sleeps all the time.
Sooner or later, everything ends.
Not everyone is destined to be happy!

General

He is a brave general, is he not?
He drained the cup of life to its dregs,
Totally tasting it to the bottom.
But, there was one cherished dream,
Which came to him on dark nights:
Weaving both rest and sleep,
Into a seductive and sinful day -
Although, hopeless and absurd.
This dream (invisible like a fairytale),
And as fragile as a melting snowflake,
First awoke him as a lieutenant.
The Rake. Don Juan. A Dandy.
Yet, Spring, April, lilac and balls,
Produced a young general!
So, he scanned ladies with straight glances-
While his wife was somewhere around.
And fire flashed in his eyes,
And his heart ached from sweet pain.
Yet, his wife told everyone - in a fit of anger,
That his son was a womanizer, just like his father.
But, women in springtime charm men:
Who are then besotted by beauty.
As sons rush to meet their girlfriends.
Oh, how fast time goes by!

Raushan Burkitbayeva - Nukenova

***

Oh, this young Lieutenant!
He is such a rascal, such a mischief-maker.
Herein his waltz surrounds the General's
                                        wife,
As he whispers in her ear, what is the next?
But, this poor fellow blushed, he is so
                                        young,
Nevertheless, from timid hands grow steel
                                        claws.
So, he put his arms around her waist.
He carried her into a furious dream.
Holding her helm,
Like a ship's captain, or a lion.
Now, the Colonel is very careful,
Brown-nosing the General's wife.
He, is like a crystal statue.
He whirls her in a gentle dance.
Oh, Spring, April, lilac and balls.
How keenly everyone watches.
Oh, one's head goes round -
As a balm are the words of love.

***

Our enormous world scares me,
With its billions of roads.
Although, our way is not long, or dull.
Indeed, we will only cross doorsteps,
Since, I am not afraid of each zenith.

Shadow of the Rain

Ah, dozens of unfinished business deals,
Call us with honking car horns,
As a flight of arrows from tower cranes,
Allows one thing to worry me:
Will our paths cross?
Or is it maybe?
Perhaps you will not be able to find me?
1971

***

A drop of dew on a petal...
The drop of a tear on a soft cheek...
Raindrops drip and snowflakes swirl,
Leaves whisper something to someone.
Somewhere under this heart and in warm
soil,
A sprout will announce himself with a
wince.
"Hello, spring clears the sky"!
Yet, I drove to you on a thirsty afternoon.
Truly, everything is a miracle - the magic of
a miracle!
Do not guess or clarify why?
All these miracles are given to us .....
Not by magic, but by heavenly love.

***

I could think once.
That'll get us far.

Raushan Burkitbayeva - Nukenova

As far as Havana in Cuba - for the festival.
There, we will become part of my life.
All suddenly making our world huge:
On the faces of envoys from different
                                    countries.
On smiles and songs,
While a fountain of reckless youths,
Named this "Friendship" …..
In Cuban-AMISTAD.
So, we will be a symbol of unity,
For anyone who is going to the parade.
We are diverse, have different views,
But have a single wish.
So, our world is always beautiful,
When people are free and united.
1978

***

You were not in Cuba,
And even if you were,
I did not see you at the carnival.
Now you can only dream about it:
Those rhythms, the mad rushing,
The rave of colours,
Dazzling patterns,
All woven by the night.
Yet, it seems there are no graceful women,
In our world.
Only those who dance rumba and
                                    pachanga,

291

Shadow of the Rain

Each dancing and singing their vulgarity.
Like fireworks in a sea of flame.
So, have as much fun as you can, my
                                friend.
Have some "refresko" and "sorbetto" -
Cool down your temper with a drink.
What a holiday. What a miracle.
Personally, I forgot about my worries,
Amid the fake palaces that float along the
                                Maleco,
Ah, carnival creators,
They are still singing and dancing.

Chapter 12.

Arabesques of Love

Shadow of the Rain

Egyptian Women and Slaves

Muddy waters of the ancient Nile,
The fervour of the African heat.
But this is not the reason of my swim,
Even if a breeze under the veil.

A light shadow glides like a ghost,
While the lotus opened its petals.
You are so far ... although I am near,
Your feet are so light.

Envies the shadow caitiff thy slave.
The one that bears the fan.
A poor man exhausted from excitement:
You hover like a butterfly.

At night, a shadow will merge with the beloved.
I am in inconsolable grief.
So, my song quietly flows like a teardrop:
As a lotus in your hand.

Darkness descended on Egypt again -
A sign is given from above.
Maybe you descend to me -
You found me as a solar eclipse.

Muddy waters of the ancient Nile,
These boats quietly glide,
As Cyprians lure me.
Surely, Isis shall bless us!
1996

Raushan Burkitbayeva - Nukenova

Nectar of Love

An amber drink for God,
As Nefertiti prepares herself.
In the midday heat, on the road,
Would you like to have some beer?

Vivific is this nectar,
Its secret is kept in the temple,
Where young and old drink it.
Do not mind this fresh Ambrosia.

The Pharaoh eyes will light up.
The hop will hit each temple.
How passionate are the words of Akhenaten,
Yet, they will close again.

The energy of the sun is in this beer.
It plays well in the blood,
Today the Queen is happy.
So, he confesses his love to her.

Drain the love potion,
And behold the sacrament of the heart.
Let this night be joyful,
Die in my arms.

Forget those reptile girls,
Do not be a prey for them.
The lotus is tender and thin:
Its fragrance allures you.

Shadow of the Rain

In the Temple of the Sun, the Queen,
Prepares this nectar for her spouse.
Oh, Divine spear hand,
You will be baptized by a brewer.

Sultan Baybars

Sultan Baybars,
My great ancestor!
Where did fate bring you?
Steppe guest,
You come here rarely.
Only a flock of birds will get here.

Wind driven tumbleweed,
Which lost its roots in native soil,
In a distant desert.
Now, raving from misfortune,
You proudly stand for a cherished dream.

The ruler of Egypt,
Tough as a headsman,
Powerful and cruel.
In your heart -
An orphan cries:
A sprout torn from the soil.

Your servants,
Bend low out of fear,
Fiercely hating you.
You were not happy
In those distant lands,
Without seeing the steppes.

Voice of Dombra,
And songs from the steppes,

Shadow of the Rain

Played in your heart.
Ah, gray feather grass,
Like the grief of mothers,
Illuminating sadness.
To drop off by drinking,
This intoxicating drink.
To fall asleep in the arms of a steppe girl.
You cannot relax -
From a royal torture.
How harsh is your path in life!

Sphinx's Mystery

Treasury of ancient knowledge:
Old Sphinx faithfully sits in silence.
As guardian of those giant creatures -
The Grand Pyramids.

Argument in the Tavern

I would like to be a eunuch,
Said the poet to a sculptor.
To praise all women,
To spite the townsfolk.

But, the sage objected to that view.
Contemplation is vain.
It seems you are a fool,
Living in endless anticipation.

Why does the Creator give us,
All the splendours of the senses,
So that we can created own palaces,
And toss aside servility.

As a taster drinks nectar,
From those ripe, edible, figs,
We have been given this grace -
And can touch innocent virgins.

Weeping Willow

Why did you bend,
By the pond?
Why are you sad?
The water trembles,
A tear rolls down.
Falling into the water,
Like a pearl,
Vanished in the abyss.

And heavenly singing
Not regaling the ear,
Still allows cheerful eyes -
Wan from sadness.
The veil fell down -
Revealing the face,
Of a sad moon.
Then the ring rolled off.

The flower in a harem,
Fades without caresses.
This handkerchief got wet:
The colours blur -
While the heart in a chest,
Can pinch out of pain.
This paradise is unbearable:
What is worse than slavery?

Bracelets and rings,
Are as shackles.

Shadow of the Rain

Also, Chinese silk,
Does not allure the soul.
I wish I were a butterfly,
To fly away on the summer steppe.
To jump and to sing
As a barefoot little girl.

There is a vivid carpet,
Of scarlet poppies.
And the air of freedom,
In vast expanses.
Can run around,
Like a thrifty colt:
Drinking clean water
In a pond.

Water surfaces,
Breaks into ripples.
I wish I could turn into a white swan:
To expand my wings,
And fly to those parts,
Where in distant yurts,
House a whole family.

The Fountain of Bakhchisarai

Frozen like,
Lovely maidens.
With sinuous waists -
The willow stands,
Sad and sorrowful:
As flutes melody
The look of a dove
In a Falcons Tower.

A boundless vastness,
Is seen from there.
This freedom,
Beckons and besots.
Yet, sleep is serene,
As in a pink childhood:
Alexandrite,
Changes its colour.

The dove parted,
Being freed forever.
And pearls of tears,

Shadow of the Rain

Fill the fountain.
Do not dry,
The sorrows of the river.
And bend in anguish,
The willow's figure.

The Fountain of Bakhchisarai -
Filled with the tears of slaves.
The figures of immured doves,
Seems bent from grief.

Rendezvous at the Palace

The night is veiled,
Like a starry mantle.
The cricket sings a song,
Amid gardens,
Where pathways lead,
To quietly sounding shoes.

Timid Moon
Illuminating this path,
How lovely is love!
I wish I could, somehow,
Get to Seraglio,
To meet my sweetheart again.

And silhouette will flash,
Between the bushes,
As a vague shadow,
Of the beloved.
I do not have the strength,
To wait for a date all day.

Thank God,

Shadow of the Rain

There is a burqa.
The type that will veil your face.
So, the eunuch is bribed -
And sleeping like a prude,
Our date gets closer.

Night cover us,
With your veil.
In a dark gloom,
We will be together,
This summer night,
Till the dawn.

Sister-moon,
Veil your face.
Let nightingales sing louder.
My beloved,
To leave you is torture,
I will fall asleep in your arms.

Idyll

Cool breezes will blow from the sea.
A couple is quietly wandering along the shore.
Timidly, tenderly, they join hands,
Quivering from an engines howling.

A lighthouse keeper shouts something from afar,
While waves drown out the noise.
Away from our eye's those two left.
They are comfortable with their great age.

Only the past is behind us.
They are alone by the sea.
And the sound of the sea is magnificent:
Like the fires of a distant hope.

The Moon is silvered by gray hair:
The pearly light of their heads.
Like they were in the old days,
On Olympus, at the meeting of gods.

In Backwaters

Emptied and faded,
Is this house without you.
Silence and sadness,
Now reigns in this house.
The ring of spare keys,
As forgot badge -
Will not sound again:
In my cozy backwater.

After healing all wounds,
And patching all the holes,
The Knight, my brave soldier,
Revived his spirit.
If the enemy, again,
Breaks your wings,
I will accept reproach.
I was lucky.

Raushan Burkitbayeva - Nukenova

I will kiss you,
And heal you once more.
And with the fear of parting,
Give you away.
Such is the fate of all women -
To wait for their beloved ones.
To endure without reproach,
To cheer and praise.

Oh, the brave hero,
Of my novel,
I will not forgive you,
For your cheating and lies.
Do not go overseas,
To a cheap hangout.
In our bay you will find,
You are in a familiar backwater.

Shadow of the Rain

Enlik-Kebek

Love - God's gift,
As a revelation.
The fire of passion,
Flight, inspiration.

Not every soul,
Will be touched with it.
Only to honour, dignity,
Is this gift given.

Courage and strength,
The baldness of Batyr,
Wit, justice,
Serve this world.

As a sappy,
Spring sprout,
Young Kebek
Desires feats.

Sadness and sorrow,
Painfully squeeze,
The heart, like a Falcon,
Languishing in captivity.

As in a trap,
This raging beast,

Raushan Burkitbayeva - Nukenova

Is deceptively quiet:
Beating against the firmament.
Soul burned,
As a boiling cauldron...
Of sad fate -
Nysan revealed to her:
A fatal love,
While a sad demise,
Lies ahead,
Like a crown of thorns.

Fair few bold feats,
Young Batyr performed,
To earn his honour.

Like wings,
Are good luck, honour.
But, the heart languishes -
Dragging somewhere.

To kill the blues,
Kebek went hunting,
In a distant land.

He let go his,
Berkut-friend.
He is like a shadow -
Above the steppe.

The hills and valleys,
Ahead - Mount Khan.

Shadow of the Rain

Once Genghis Khan
Sat on in.
Stopped dead for a moment,
Winged help,
Began to circle,
With strong wafts.

He rushed down,
On a fox, as a stone,
Put out,
Like water, the flame of life.

Finishing off the vixen,
And taking off her fur,
He went on,
A seeker pleasures.

Wandering afar,
The sunset turned pink.
He rode on a hill,
And looked at the steppe.

Smoke sweeps,
There, far off – people live.
In the gorge – a village.
There will be a place to sleep.

He rushed there.
And suddenly by a rock,
He froze – as a vision,
Like a flower in a dream.

Raushan Burkitbayeva - Nukenova

Tall,
Slim, like a gazelle.
An opened forehead,
And a voice as a flute.

Tight braids,
Lie as silk.
Eyes like a whirlpool,
Drag to the abyss.

This girl,
Is of strange beauty.
Bottomless eyes...
Baksy foresaw this.

Like a ray of sunshine -
Is the look of this girls' eyes.
Love is like a fire,
Ignited from a spark.

After jumping,
Into the deep end,
You have broken,
The honour of family.

Like the wind in the desert,
- Invincible,
So blinds passion,
When you are in love.

Father betrothed,

Shadow of the Rain

His beauty to another man.

A bride price is paid,
And they went to the abyss.

A daughters' dates,
Were sealed by the family.
You - unconsenting -
The laws of the steppes.

She ran away with her beloved,
At night in a cave,
Enlik hid her heavenly face.

Relatives and groom,
Have been looking for them for so long.
Preparing a cruel vengeance,
For them.

Love and happiness,
Their age is short,
As a spring flower.
But man is cruel

They will trample the flowers,
And mix with the soil.
They are powerless,
Against the greedy crowd.

Crying and screaming,
Didn't reached their ears
- Spare the baby! -

Begged Enlik.

Killing all three of them,
The crowd cheered.
Growling and howling,
They were torn to pieces.

Their grave is on a hill:
Enlik and Kebek.
Their fame kept their memory,
Through the passage of time.

And the traveler is in a hurry,
To bow to relics.
To spread this sad story,
Through railway halts.

Belly Dance

Our Turkish boat
Rolls in carpets.
The expanse gives us,
A river coolness.

At the water surface,
Shakes your belly.
Dance Bayadere:
Sparkling are your eyes.

Ring of a drum,
As a call to battle.
And like a tuning fork,
Swaying your waist!

Transparent, light,
Garments as gauze.
Movements are vivid,
Dance, Gulistan.

Night Guest

Why are you tiredly looking,
Out of the elm window?
You do not sleep at nights:
Perhaps the rain's cry awakens you.

Drumroll,
Will you wake us in the night?
Maybe, I will knock for a loop,
- My God, where are the keys!

A night guest chilled to the marrow:
Anxious, keeping silent.
He drinks his cup of tea,
With no rush.

A ray of hope extinguished.
Where are you from, my friend?
You are as a kerosene stove,
Which once burned.

A scar left on the heart,
Does not always hurt.
But, you are yourself.
- Be quite, my daughter is sleeping there!

- You told me that father,
Perished in Afghanistan.
Why did you not call? -
Pride is in our blood.

Shadow of the Rain

- Yes, looking just like him,
And as stubborn as you are,
Apologies are vain.
And flowers are belated.

It rains again,
Blackening the elm.
I would fall into sleep.
If my heart had not cried.

Raushan Burkitbayeva - Nukenova

Rainbow

A rainbow in the sky!
Like a symbol of happiness:
A bridge of hope,
A glimmer of light in the storm,
Splashes of colours,
Seven pure rays.
As if armfuls
Of spring flowers.
A heavenly mosaic -
Bracing freshness.
Oh, a sigh of relief,
Grateful tenderness.
The thrill and delight,
Of a celestial fire.
As if the Almighty,
Had put out his palm.

Shadow of the Rain

Old Songs

Only yesterday,
These songs sounded.
From windows,
They flew as birds.

The boys,
Took me out.
Where did these wrinkles,
Come from?

Harshly singing,
Polad knew the same songs,
And my heart,
Ached with longing.

And those dresses,
Were tight long before.
Movements, alas,
Are not smooth.

We all wanted,
To look like -
Edita Piekha.
And sing like her.

And we easily,
Achieved success.
And life seemed,
Infinitely long.

And your grave confession,
On the desk,
And in my heart,
Left its mark.

School thresholds -
Platforms for a start.
We are scattered by life.

Other tunes,
My son sings,
But the old songs,
Are as sweet as honey.

Chapter 13.

Guiding Star

Shadow of the Rain

In the worlds of love - amiss comets -
The road to trusted orbits is closed for us!
The earth will not break the reality of our dreams -
The lights beckon the midnight sun.
Who dreams and remembers the names -
Are given love not joy,
For gloomy raptures of parting!
M. Voloshin

As a guiding star,
Love ... Through heat and cold...
Will guide you through the desert.
Oh, I hope that she will not leave us!
We will push mountain ranges,
And will keep everyone from the abyss...
Through snow and fog – you still shine:
As the Star of love, the star of hope!

Raushan Burkitbayeva - Nukenova

Man

It is in a man's nature -
Risk and passion,
Chase and rank,
Wine and billiards,
Amorous victories,
Hunting and fishing.
Notes on duty.
Hardening fights,
Football and bullfights,
A drifting brig,
A wife – Caryatids:
Helm, field, rings,
Dragoons and hussars,
An ataman, a grenadier.
A gloomy corsair,
A fighter, matador.
A favourite or rebel,

Knight and seeker.
A player and goalkeeper,
A hopeless dreamer.
A Caliph and the Tramp,
(He is his own master).
Dresser and dandy,
A Sheikh, Beduin.
Seaman - Admiral.
Navigator - pilot.
Soldier - General.
Smart polyglot.
He can take liberties.
Overall, he is
Just a little boy.

Raushan Burkitbayeva - Nukenova

Autumn

Flexible reeds,
Bend on the wind.
Droplets, raindrops,
Fall in the forest.

Pines - like sisters,
Dance in a circle.
And a mottled handkerchief,
Floats with the wind.

Birch leaves,
Shinning as foil,
And resin like tears -
Cranes fly around.

Shadow of the Rain

The delicate webs,
Of openwork lacework.
Painted diligently,
As scarlet foliage.

Last days,
Warmed by heat.
All the leaves tremble,
As cyclones blow them away.

Clouds are round the corner,
And the cold is coming.
Gloomy, boring, evenings,
Will be brought by the winds.

Raushan Burkitbayeva - Nukenova

Return

Twenty years later,
I am back.
Those old men, whom I knew,
Passed away.

The kids have grown up,
They have their own children.
Their pathways overgrew,
While your footprints faded.

And no one here,
Will call me out,
Won't open a door for me,
Or offer a welcoming smile.

The dove flew off.
Where do you live now?
You will not sing me a song,
On the phone.

And the neighbouring girls,
I will not recognize,
Their voices ring as before...
But, only mother waits for me.

Flowers and Children

Double flowering asters,
Proud roses,
Silently bowing,
In a mournful pose.
The mistress is gone,
The one that caressed them,
As if they were small children,
She watered them.
Daisies and phlox,
And prudes,
Delight the eye,
After a long road.
And chrysanthemums,
Until early snow,
Wait patiently,
For baby steps.
Children and grandchildren,
Wander around the world,
Maybe they will ride over,
To mother.
An aged mother,
Waits in the courtyard.
To give her warmth,
To children.

Mother's Dresses

Hung in a closet of suits and dresses:
From cashmere and crepe de chine,
Ragged brethren wait in solitude,
For madapollam and gabardine,

Bright colours pleasing to the eye,
Out of capricious fashion, we are ageless.
We are always welcome for our mistress,
But, somehow she had forgotten about us.

We are natural as snow and water,
While the mistress knows the worth of crimplen.
She does not like that cold prison.
In the heat and cold, always together are we.

Granddaughters and daughters put dresses on.
- How hopelessly out of fashion they seem.
But, they keep the warmth of our mistress:
These warm memories give light.

Some time ago, slick was trendy,
And it was also good for cool weather.
So, we run through the puddles in mother's shoes:
Wrapped in shawls in the January cold.

We knew the value of things:
Books and tons were precious to our hearts.
Now, things are getting old, and masters pass away...
On the bookshelf - Tolstoy, Veresaev.

Mother's Hands

Mother's hands never got tired...
Serving up porridge in the morning.
She cooked, darned, hand-knitted,
Or planted and weeded in garden.

Mother's hands caressed, compassioned,
Healed all of us when we were sick.
Put ointment on our wounds:
We timidly hug on mother's apron strings.

Mother's hands never had a dull moment,
Carefully picking berries and fruits,
Making preserved food for the winter,
So that kids would eat with pleasure.

Mother's hands covered us,
Plaited tight braids,
Gently picked thorns out of our fingers,
And prepared us for a long journey.

Mother's hands blessed us,
Fed grandchildren, bathed in herbs.
No matter how much we glorify them,
We are forever indebted, in an enlightened sadness.

Raushan Burkitbayeva - Nukenova

***

Before we used,
To write letters to each other.
Confided our sacred secrets to a pen.
Postcards, messages,
And parcels,
Full of wishes,
As toast in a feast.

I do not believe,
In phone calls.
They have less soul -
Only a cacophony.
But we have little time,
To strike a couple of lines.
On a white sheet of lies,
With marks of omission.

Shadow of the Rain

***

As you walk uphill -
You bear your load easily.
Life stretches so languidly.
More walking,
Problems – with laughter.
And enough time for everything.

As you walked down,
Problems were slowly solved.
Now, years fly as an arrow.
No time at all,
You have got to give an answer.
Here they call you to a lectern.

Forgive Me

I cannot have a peaceful sleep,
At night.
Tears choke me, clasping the throat.

I do not want to accept,
This loss.
Pain and conscience, smashing drills.
I cannot sleep easily at night,
I am far away in summer lands.

I could not bid you a final farewell.
Forgive me, mother, for that.

***

Do not break my heart, do not...
Since, through the shouts of crowded
                              streets,
I will rip through the bars of a fence,
And close my eyes from the glare.
And melodies, pure sounds,
Will resound in this hour - as if from a
                              screen,
While a flood of separations like a wave,
Dries my throat from its fountain.

Ai-Suluu

Expanse of heaven,
As a star tent.
The moon is wrapped,
   In an airy veil.
I will kindle,
A ritual fire.
Water is poured,
In a bronze jar.
Stars, like sisters,
              Flash in the darkness.
Flames dance,
              And so do I.
- Spirits of shamans,
              Help me.
Chase away sadness,
And any night dolor!
Healing herbs,
Miraculous roots,
I will put in a boiling pot,
Which is like my mind.
I am preparing these potions,
For healing.
My dear,
              You will wake up at once.
I will light,
A strong fire.
I will wash our wounds,
With this balsam.
A women waits,

By your faithful horse.
The road beckons,
In southlands.
The seeds of faltering hope,
Will upspring,
A blurring of vision,
Will fade away.
       My dear,Here you are awakened from
                  sleep.
Familiar ringing,
          Of bracelets and rings,
In the silence of the night,
           Caught your ear,
So in distant lands,
           You came to me.
And your sleeping sprit,
Lifted me again.
This magic fire,
Burns down.
And the sun's rays,
          Pushed back the gloom,
The beloved,
Outstretched am embrace,
And your Ay-Suluu,
Falls asleep in these arms.

Shadow of the Rain

Autumn. Rain. Grief and sadness.
I know their song by heart.
There is no boundary for this love.
No riot of colours. No Indian Summer.
But, stars will throw off cold snow,
Since, hungry people crave affection.
And clouds will hide mountains,
While disputes die off at night.
Autumn. Wind. Rain. Parting.
The hearts does not accept boredom.
The stars might melting at sunrise,
Yet, a melody is born.

Raushan Burkitbayeva - Nukenova

To Munira Maevna

How radiant are domes!
And merging with a turquoise sky,
Their glide reflects in the lake,
When seen from a distant village.
Again I pray,
I do not dare to forget you.
You shine like a minaret,
While without love, there is no joy...
Again, I will sluice myself with icy water -
Keeping sadness in quiet lakes,
Since, I remain faithful and in love:
Albeit jingling with broken strings...

***

Shadow of the Rain

To Aitkul Baigazy

How pure were the rivers!
With playful rainbow bottoms.
And elder broad-shouldered brothers,
Playing dominoes with us.
They fed us with tasty Marinka,
As we caught butterflies with a net,
And ran down a wet footpath,
To secretly meet girls.
Ah, we wrote our first messages,
As guitar strings tore apart,
And our fierce excruciations,
Were witnessed by a strict Moon.
But, childhood rivers got muddy.
Oh, cities, why are you so cruel?
Veiling severe snowstorms,
In my albescent temple.
Now, with a ruthless hand,
I fell trees along the road,
While an unrelenting smog,
Coveres the city with a sultry veil:
Obscuring everything.

M. Gulnar

The spring came,
As sole mistress to everything.
Do not stand up to her,
Do not.
After all, those crossroads,
Saw girls flying like a flock
While in a hubbub,
Eliciting love.
Then, the city surrendered
To glittering charms,
As windows witnessed the light -
Being washed by rain.
As if on cue,
Split into pairs,
Under a red umbrella,
We would walk hand by hand.
And give way
To jeeps.
Oh, blossoming boulevard,
You besot everybody.
Melting as if a dream,
Into a wheezing winter,
Before an angry march
Sweeps away snowdrifts.

Nostalgia

Nostalgia, nostalgia...
For places that are gone:
Tight black braids,
The marvelous light of slanting eyes,
Pushing my way through lanes,
Through old houses.
But only echoes in my ears,
Remain – along with the creak of trucks wheels.
Oh, these lovely faces,
Will not see them anymore.
Now we are quite different,
So who will welcome us?
Maybe around the corner
Mum's voice will call us,
As we run home from work,
While (for a moment) her face will flash.
She will cook whole plates,
Of pastries and patties:
Offering jam to taste,
And will chase away our sadness.
Ah, from dawn to dusk,
Loving faces will abound.
How painful are our losses.
Nostalgia, nostalgia...

Raushan Burkitbayeva - Nukenova

Nowruz

A cold March is drawing to the close,
And sweeps the last snow away.
Now, clouds crowded at the pass,
Will anxiously flying in the air,
Until they swell inside a loose bud
With bursting pain in their chests.
Ah, they have reached an extreme point,
Wherein feelings try to crash out,
And every day brings nearer,
A suspenseful happy ending.
Indeed, the sky reflects frightful,
Grimaces - amid puddles and swampy muds.
While, without waiting for permission,
A fringe hangs from tree branches.
Its Spring – and the bride broke into,
That boring house without scruple:
Scattered lawns,
With the petals of delicate flowers,
Suddenly, birds chirp from a height.
And, throwing off their fur coats and sheepskins,
Silhouettes get more graceful,
As the touches of a thin contour,
Define artists, poets, and their pieces.
1.04.2002

Hotel

Still full of suspenseful anticipation,
Songs carousel our faltering hopes.
They keep the warmth of past meetings,
Between hotel snoozes and meditations.
Hence, our footprints on those walkways
                                    are not disturbed,
While a creak of wheels resounds in the
                                    chilly gloom.
Now, the night robe thrown over a chair.
Like a candle can burst on a celebratory table.
As the new century, our new guest,
Walking in darkness with a slight fright:
And dabbed by a frozen finger blindly,
With a sleepy Fate – something almost
                                    Vestal ...
But, the sounds of a new musical score,
Allows shadows to wander at a ghostly
                                    distance.
Ah, these calendar days groan like
                                    instruments,
Blown by eternal ranges in the landscape ...

                    ***

A night excited with ringing cicadas,
And the fascinating dance of shadows,
Awakes our garden to the moonlight.
Listen - a nightingale sings with passion.
So, I revel in the tenderness of hands,

Raushan Burkitbayeva - Nukenova

Fascinated by the curves of each hip:
A, the iridescent beat of two hearts,
Does not cease all night until morning,
Since, the smell of the night and the mint
                              herb,
Merely stupefy your beauty -
As all earthy poets prove right,
And the stars talk to one another.

***

Lonely night,
Not warmed with caress.
The humid light from a window,
Under an indifferent moon.
Rain rustles softly,
When reading fairytales,
And stars of steadfast hope,
Are not yet visible -
Like withered leaves,
Or pages turned yellow.
Now, time rewinds again.
Let them live in silence:
These thirsty lips,
Craving for a belated love ...

***

Oh, how reluctant you are to leave bed,
Like the bumblebee, immersed in the
                              nectar of a flower!

Shadow of the Rain

If only the hand of a clock could be
stopped...

***

Forgotten worries,
Of bygone days.

Broken hearts,
Of seduced ladies.
Old roads are,
In snows of sorrow.
An equipoise of doubt,

Disturbing
endlessly.

Sweet tears,
    Of reminiscences.
A series of shadows,
In forgiven offences,
And a pile of letters,

Strewn across a
hill.

With rose petals,

Of awakened
passions.

Raushan Burkitbayeva - Nukenova

***

I remember those songs by heart.
I will throw a sad, crumpled, basket, after
                              them.
Along with scraps of caustic - chilling
                              phrases.
Then, I will sweep away the fragments of
                              that broken vase.
And refuse to cherish ill-will –
                              acknowledged
                              garbage.
Instead, I will keep my loving life.
I will bring a bouquet of chrysanthemums,
And make up the plot for a new scenario.

***

The autumn plaited,
Golden braids.
Grasses soaked,

                              With Sun and
                              warmth.
The wind threw seeds,
In a river as mementos.
An old windbreak,

                              Getting stuck in a
                              web.
Lush armfuls,

                              Of colored leaves.

Shadow of the Rain

Rain cuts like a blade,

                    Scattering wounds.

Like a pile of letters

                    Old and
                    unanswered.

As fires over the river,

                    Close the circle.

***

Shadows are blurred on the sidewalk,
And lights were on all night long.
And the silk of a coloured sari is cool,
Like the mysterious outfit of a river.
Of course, over time they will be too small,
To crush an ice-block.
As blizzards howl instead of songs,
And anticipation behind that wall,
Develops ice shackles, which will not melt,
Or be broken into pieces.
You are working on the tune of a new song:
Something in tune with the rivers cycle.

A Piece of Poetry

Branches swell with sticky buds,
And the smell of spring is in the air.
Each leaf is laced with a ligatured script,
Although, brushed aside by greedy hands.
Look, veins also swell at the back of a head
-
As convulsive lips breathe deeply.
Yet, I pierce like a fork,
Through the space of spheres and invisible
cubes,
While the limp thought of lagging
Behind that hypnotic bridge,
Suddenly turns into a new song -
Only then, will it becomes a hit.
So, like a glassblower I play with fire.
I can expand and get burned.
But, even when losing a cherished though,
I cannot mindlessly smolder.

***

Clinking needles weave a web,
As evening sunsets refresh themselves.
Restless birds fly in the sky,
While stacks are laid down in the
boundary.
Oh, shivering branches interlocked in
sorrow,
Said night suddenly become longer.

Shadow of the Rain

Autumn plays Nocturne on the piano –
Spreading the light of shadows.

***

Wind tears at the leaves of September,
As at the pages of a calendar.
Autumn, as mistress, sets the table,
Yet, the trunk of a shy birch is graceful.
Now, waves polish amber stones:
As a quiet September evening flickers out.
Look, memories will grind the edges of
                              bright days,
While your footsteps will disappear on the
                              sand.

Chapter 14

Contours of Memory

Prose

Bloomy Dwelling

I love spring. As a starving beast throws itself on food, I also inhale frosty winter air. Indeed, I avidly breathe the heady scent of jasmine and tender lilac, while lazing in the warm rays of May. Assuredly, showy bunches of lilacs, graceful tulips as wax candles, chestnuts greeting passersby, the dense greenery of shrubs sheltering a pair of lovebirds hiding from prying eyes - each animates me. As such, air gets heavy from this flowery infusion of scents: from these blossoming trees and flowers. All intoxicated through white and pink petals mixed with the floral aromas emitted from the uniform buzzing of tireless bees. Each hanging in the air like a cloud - resembling huge vanilla marshmallows from a distance. This is like a honeymoon in nature. It is a season of love, ovaries, the beginning of a new, fruitful, life. Every living thing in nature being absorbed in the bliss and delight of trying to leave offspring as the fruits and seeds continue their generation. Oh, I remember, when I was a child, we would immerse ourselves in this atmosphere of a flourishing kingdoms and observe the awakening of mysterious worlds. Of ants, fire-bugs, bees and ladybirds ….. all being our fellows.

Hence, a child removes any boundary between himself and wildlife. In a sense, children organically melt into this swarming world. Therefore, this is an amazing time for the discovery of surrounding existences. Capturing, as it does, the entire imagination. Like a small tadpole, one moves in this whirlpool: it is one's element. One wants to try everything. Even eating sweet acacia and clover leaves - or green apricots.

In nature, everything is harmonious. Permeated by an unwritten, but established, law and order. There is nothing unnecessary, superfluous. Even ants fight because the crumbs of a cookie fell from one's mouth. It is hilarious! Remorselessly, beavers stubbornly drag grasshoppers to their dwellings, which we, ourselves, accidently squelched yesterday. Everyone is in business. No one takes time off, gives orders, or makes a fuss like machines. And the same thing happens every day. In this wonderful world, each morning is on schedule.

But I had not found my place in it yet. So, I observed and examined my childhood. Only the shouts of my elders distracted me from younger felloes. "Well, I am not hungry, I already ate, leave me alone. And I do not want to sleep either. There, at night fireflies are waiting for me, cheerily winking like flashlights from willow branches ..."

I could only tag along behind my elders for night fishing. There, they would catch enormous crayfishes and marinkas and, maybe, they would even allow me to shine a flashlight on them. After all, tomorrow, I would be as avid angler, eating marinka with pomposity: so yummy!

If only I could sneak off from my parents. However, I was afraid of frogs, toads and cats screaming like crying babies. They scared the hell out of me. Okay, I was continually drowsy after a heavy dinner. I could hardly keep my eyes open. It was exhausting and I was enjoying a balmy daydream – as bloodsucking mosquitoes were alone able to awake me.

In the evenings, to get rid of us, the adults would tell us horror stories about the dead and cemeteries. "Leave my hand!" My heart was sinking out of fear, while my temples were throbbing and legs turned numb. So, we sat petrified with horror. Afraid to make a move. Then, we were taken home as if hypnotized by the adults who faded into the night. We, on the other hand, were cuddling our mothers out of fear - "leave my hand!"

Nowadays, our children live in the age of television. After watching horror movies and TV shows - and sitting for hours at a computer - they have lost all interest in books and outdoor games.

But, in those days, our elder brothers and sisters developed their own performances in the courtyard on the subject of "cemetery passions" ….. along with an interest in the novels of Alexandre Dumas. They choose their own actors for the role of D'Artagnan and Milady: for the Queen and Cardinal who fascinated young audiences.

If younger children were like angels, friendly and open-minded, then our elders lived by other laws. Sometimes, by harsh realities. I remember how they hung a cat from next door on a tree when she strangled the cock of Bogachkovsky. Certainly, our elders had their own cruel and harsh rules, but we did not really want this adult life.

About ten families lived together in our neighborhood – families of different nationalities, a real "Internationale". We lived in "barracks" comprising of two, or three, rooms connected to each other like wagons under one roof. We did not really have any amenities. We burned coals in a stove. We shared a toilet and shower at the bottom of a courtyard. To my recollection, a water pipe was behind a fence – we carried drinking water in buckets. Yet, every family had a small piece of land for a garden and barn. Old-timers had hencoops. In general, everyone had a small household meeting their general needs.

In the spring, our street was smothered in greenery - with blooming trees and flowers. Cherries, apples, peaches, apricots - all fruit trees standing like shy brides under a pinkish-white veil of inflorescences, Bowing their crowns, but assailed by bothersome groom-bees. In the gardens, flatbeds were planted with tomatoes, cucumbers, eggplants, peppers, dill, parsley and potatoes. From an early age, adults had always taught us to take care of these "vitamins". Our only honourable duty was to water these vegetable gardens and flower beds on a daily basis.

Buckets were made of tin cans from tomato paste and condensed milk. At that time, they were sold in three and five-litre cylindrical containers. After the lid was opened, the can was emptied. Then a handle, or a rope, was attached to a wire and it was turned into a bucket. Along the main street, there was a small irrigation ditch, while at the bottom of the yard we had a main ditch. We water-carriers took water from there and watered everything that was planted. However, our neighbour, Maksimovna, remained vigilantly against us every night. What a pain in the neck she was. Looking the part, her nose was as red and fleshy as a strawberry and she had a whip in her hand. She could be described as overweight. A condition possibly contributing to her ceaseless complaints. We children were afraid of her. She sat on a stool as if it was a throne to maintained local order. Indeed, the entrance to the yard was strictly regulated to unknown people, particularly to admirers of the blonde beauty, Natasha Tambovtseva.

Every morning our street arose to cock--crowing. From early morning, the roar of truck motors from Tambovtsev sounded, as well as the sneezing and snorting of Bogachkov's motorcycle. Women were busy in the kitchens, firing up their oil stoves.

We, the kids, enjoyed the gurgling and aromas wafting from Tambovtseva's door, along with the gentle and melodious voice of Aunt Shura. She was the one making magic at her oil stove: like Aladdin, Clearly, she always offered us delicious pancakes. She had two daughters. The raven-haired meanie Galka, and a blonde sweetheart, Natalia.

Bogachkovs lived right across from us. Their son, the handsome Volodya, was a friend of my older brother Mukhtar. They had a big and friendly family. Their children were already grown-ups.

Argimbaevs lived across from my nanny. They only had daughters, my friends Alma, Janna, Gulya. Their parents, Uncle Medel and Aunt Anna, had been friends with my parents.

Maksimova lived next to them, albeit on the other side of the wall. Our family nurse, Galka, eventually became a doctor.

Thus, my memories of early childhood are related to our street and warmed by the serene image of my nanny, Mama Poly. She was a broad-browed Russian woman. An exceedingly modest person with a very kind soul. Affectionate, hardworking, inaudible and strikingly kind. As such, she always had a gentle smile on her face. She worked every morning, cleaning the service apartments of First Secretary of the Regional Committee. She also did grocery shopping in the Obkomov buffet - that is why she always had plenty of yumminess on her table.

My nanny's husband, Uncle Yasha, was fluent in Kazakh. He used to like talking with my grandfather.

Our family lived in two rooms. The big room was for my parents with three children, while the other small one was for my grandparents from my father's side.

I remember myself as a roly-poly, rosy-cheeked, little girl, always creeping away from my home to nanny's.

Once, the whole street took fright because of my howling and shouting. It happened due to the fact our cock attacked me and started to peck my head. Uncle Yasha then knifed the cock, since he was constantly hurting kids.

Every morning, when my parents went to work, I would crawl to my nanny and sleep in her bed. However, my own grandmother did not love the girls apparently, so I compensated for this lack of tenderness in my mother Poly.

She loved to stuff yummy things into my mouth. This is the reason I was a squab kid. Moreover, I followed my nanny everywhere. Whether in the garden or kitchen. She was constantly busy with housework. Unsurprisingly, I went bathing only with her. But, other women continually kidded me about our nanny: "How come your daughter is Kazakh"? She would say uncle Yasha knows the Kazakh language and that is why I was so black-haired.

Mama Polly and Uncle Yasha lived with their daughter Anna, her husband Nikolai and two grandchildren - Kolya and Sasha. The elder grandson, Kolya, was very quiet and obedient. He was like a girlfriend to me. I conducted my first medical practical experience on him. Whenever he cut himself, I would put a plantain leaf on his wound. I picked thorns and painted them with green antiseptic. He had bad teeth some saying they were black "wormy" molars - not to mention having red hair and being generally freaky. As for me, I made this poor fellow eat bulbs of garlic.

Sasha, his younger brother was smart and unaffected. Therefore, Kolenka uncomplainingly endured my healing for the two of them. Once, Kolya and I tagged along behind the elder and went to a chemical laboratory, which was across the street from our yard. The chief was scary, hairy, with a gray beard: like a sorcerer. He was busy doing something: pouring liquid into glass jars. Yet, after being sucked into his experiments and got off the elder's tail. We started to cry at the top of our lungs thinking he would turn us into toads. The nurse came running to our rescue.

We additionally liked it when Mama Polly and Uncle Yasha took us to the river to swim. The water in the river was clear with a visible bottom. Our older brothers caught crayfish and marinka there. I remember how I was afraid to pass over the bridge. I walked with such fear that my stomach started to ache. I walked in the middle of the bridge, even though it was about two metres wide. When I was feeling dizzy from the noise of the water, Mama Polly laughed: - "Our Raichka is such a crybaby!" Unarguably, when she went to neighbouring yards, I would hold the edge of her dress: everybody was afraid of the neighbourhood boys.

At that time I wore glasses, I remember mother sat me down at the table, gave me a litre jar of peas with mixed beans and made me separate them into two jars. One jar for peas, the other for beans. What an irksome task. Meanwhile, Kolya was waiting for me. Afterwards, we'd run to the bottom of the yard. There Mama Polly was busy with her animals. Some silly chickens fell into a basin of water. We pulled them out and they dried. But ducklings are clever. So, we protected the poultry house from hungry cats who attempted to catch careless chickens. Geese and turkeys are pompous: they pinched us. We did not like them and chased them with a spray. However, in winter, Mama Polly would cook a delicious goose with apples for New Year.

Nanny was a noble cook. What delicious Easter cakes and pies she cooked. But most of all we liked her coloured eggs. We tried to break these eggs one against the other is such way that ours would stay unbroken. Truly, we were more of a hindrance than a help in colouring eggs with different dyes.

"Christ has risen!" - We shouted to the guests. "Hush" – nanny calmed us down. On such holiday's we not only celebrated openly, but maintained traditions. Beyond doubt, Mama Polly prayed to icons in secrecy.

It was not allowed, of course, since she worked for the Secretary. However, she always venerated God in her heart. That said, we lived under those old, but fair and honest laws. "Thou shalt not kill, steal, condemn." Apparently, these were the reason why Mama Polly was illuminated by a special light of peace, purity, and kindness. She would always greet people with a smile, offer food, listen to their sorrows, and warm them with her love. She had horny hands and gray locks under her kerchief. What is more, her eyes were continually ready to start crying, She had a very vulnerable soul.

Dear nanny, forgive us, your heart was not strong enough to endure all our pains. I could not cure you as I promised when I went to medical school. My nanny had a heart of gold.

I also brought my future husband to our street (for viewing) as the groom. Nanny gave us her blessing.

Indeed, our old street was like an x-ray machine. It displayed people's light and dark: their good and bad sides. People lived in a narrow circle of mutual understanding and respect, selflessly helping each other. Yet, we children lived in an environment of total care and protection. Our neighbours looked after other children when their parents were busy. Furthermore, strangers were stopped by sharp-nosed Maksimovna. She guarded the peace of our corner of paradise better than any watch.

But we, the kids, felt free and easy, every cubbyhole of our street had so much to offer and the large irrigation ditch at the end of the street seemed like a whole river to us. Everywhere we could find a wonderland of new discoveries. Following heavy rain in the garden, we collected worms for fishing. A favourite amusement was catching butterflies with nets (aquatic, black, elegant, big-eyed dragonflies), which we liberated after careful examination, because they are useful and ate mosquitoes. As for butterflies, we dried them for our collections in the herbarium.

Today, in our cities, there are no longer cherry, or apple, alleys with clouds of elegant beautiful butterflies, Neither is there a need to call these heavenly streets "compote" in mockery. Nowadays, monotonous standardized blocks of micro-districts tower above streets with planted poplars alongside.

Only in the song does it sound nice: "spring will spread poplar fluff". However, in real life, it causes a lot of unpleasant troubles, including allergic reactions Once, I became convinced in the wisdom of the Japanese, deifying a branch of "Sakura" - blooming cherry. They can find harmony in one simple flower, I thought. In these soulful contemplations of the world, they find the sources of their creations: they clarify themselves and rise spiritually.

As an aside, our capital - Alma-Ata was once known for the world-famous Oporto. After all, it didn't bear the name "father of apples" for nothing. This is not the case nowadays. I remember the unique fragrance and taste of these huge rosy and juicy apples, which amazed us by their size and texture.

Why is everything going West (like mammoths) in our time. What will we leave to our grandchildren? Our memories? This whole generation witnessed the disappearance of the Aral Sea.

Rivers and shallow lakes, the climate getting worse. Saigas, muskrats and many other inhabitants of our steppes will soon survive only in pictures and diagrams within an encyclopedia.

We had the great Union of Soviet Socialist Republics. We had the Soviet ruble, which was more expensive than a dollar: now everything fades away. This is a time of great change. While in other countries "capitalists" are trying to preserve and increase national wealth, we have the exact opposite. We live for the moment, yet how will we explain to our grandchildren that everything was lost. Everything is moving abroad. We rob ourselves. Our actions cannot be described as reasonable.

Sadly, this is the end of the world. In pursuit of the ruble, we have lost eternal values - hard work, honesty, decency. What type of generation will grow in this thoughtless world, wherein each feathers its own nest? Every mind eclipsed, a time will arrive when people feast amid a plague. When will we come to our senses, but when will a kingdom of kindness and faith reign? After all, life is cyclical, and I believe this new loop should lead us to the light of a prudent life.

We, adults, shall not deprive our innocent children from the happiness of childhood.

It is hard to believe that our tradition of unlocked doors for our homes will vanish. Now, each person barricades himself behind metal fences, or an armoured door. Former good neighbors – with shared customs and borders - require a new currency, passports etc. But all this is a formality. At heart we are all the same

– a single whole. Humanity, overall, has the same life values, open to each other, without any nationality.

During one of my visits home, I did not find our old courtyard. At the site of the old barracks, a new two-storey house (owned by a "money-bags") had been built. All previous lodgings were knocked down as if by a hurricane – the Paradise Island of our childhood was gone. It is bitter and it hurts. I understand that life changes, of course, but our neighbours had moved into apartments in a new micro-district – a civic "improvement" in their living conditions. Nevertheless, as a tree may get sick after transplanting, in the same way people cannot immediately get used to these new homes: they are homesick.

Contrarily, on the outskirts of villages in the Kazakh steppes, amid mountain settlements at the foot of the Caucasian peaks, in the tea houses of Uzbek Mahallah and on Birch mounds in the Russian countryside, old proud gray golden eagles (old men), gather in the evenings – Aqsaqals holding their deliberative conversations about life. Local philosophers arguing about the wisdom of rural living.

They recall the last time snow was heavy, also they predict what the harvest will be this year.

In Ukrainian villages and Kyrgyz kishlaks (all summer long), Malvinas glow in a scarlet shade as traffic lights and fleur-de-lies sway with yellow balls and blue eyes - garden pansies and wood lilies shyly hiding in their shadow. Red lilies loom cheekily and "four-o'clocks" timidly open in the evenings. When touched, their seeds scatter in different directions, like sparks.

Back then, in all villages, girls would tell fortunes through observing field daisies and asking them "does he love me or not"? What is more, house-proud female villagers after being done with housework would sit under the windows of their homes, husking sunflower seeds and chewing the fat with passers-by. After getting tired of gossip, the most vociferous of them would break into song about unrequited love. Indeed, melodies about these common human feelings flew like birds from the Donetsk steppes to the Kazakh. Additionally, feather grasses swayed in the breeze, like plumes, echoing these sad, soulful, tunes.

People are the same everywhere. They have the same values, same illnesses, same sorrows.

As multi-coloured pieces of glass roll as in a kaleidoscope, all making up a new mosaic, these fragments of the brightest impressions - moving to new places - created my colourful mural of fresh perceptions.

My father, as a young promising party member, had been constantly transferred from one place to another. For our part, we followed him as "tumbleweeds". This was a painful process for my mother, but for us children, by contrast, it meant new adventures and new discoveries.

Clearly, in these new places, Mum got engaged in the cultivation of her favourite flowers and tended a vegetable garden. Dad helped her in the evenings. He even tried the Michurinsk experiment of crossing different varieties of cherries, apples, and cropped shoots between various vines. However, we had fun by watering the seedlings from small watering cans, while realizing the importance of the ameliorative measures.

Raushan Burkitbayeva - Nukenova

The first strawberries, the first radishes (grown in Akkol village), remain in my memory as the pioneers of our horticulture. Once dad (he was then the head of the Local Education Authority) brought us turtles and hedgehogs from a business trip. We mucked about with them, but still the Big-Eared one managed to escape. I cried so much because I got attached to this funny creature. As for the turtle, my brother and I pestered it with our care, and then we released this tortured beast into the wild.

After a short time, our father was transferred to work in the city again to gain promotion. Once more, we parted ways with the countryside.

We lived on Kachalov Street in the same house as the godmother of our younger brother Berik - Zhatboloy Shakhanova. She was in charge of the regional library. Clearly, she had graduated from the Higher Party School. She had two children. Her daughter's name was Gaziza: a tender, light-skinned, exquisite needlewoman. Furthermore, she has a son Saken – a swarthy, silent young man who was the same age as my older brother Mukhtar. So, Mama Jenya (this was what we called her) was an educated woman. She read all the latest books. Most of all, she loved the genre of political essays, memoirs, publicist writings. She and dad voraciously read the memoirs of Winston Churchill and members of the Kennedy clan. In the evenings, they held their endless political discussions. Thus, we renamed her "Iron Lady", taking into account how similar Mama Jenya was to Margaret Thatcher - with her backbone and adherence to principles. I got this love for serious books from her. Yet, considering I spent a whole year working under her guidance, it seemed odd that I failed to pass the competition in the first year for admission to medical school.

For her part, our mother worked in a kindergarten as a manageress. Both I and brother Serik went there.

As for dad, he had been reconstructing the former People's Court building for housing; he planted fruit trees - taking seedlings from the orchard of the kindergarten.

Then we moved into our own house, which was located on the same patch of land as the house of Zhatboly Shahanovna. We felt easy knowing the district store, kindergarten, and dormitory of the cultural and educational school, were nearby.

Kachalov Street in the town of Jambul forms three circles. The school named after Abai is located between them.

On the school sports field, we kids from Kachalov Street scattered coloured peas across the streets and arranged our children's battles. One side of the street competed with the other.

Temirov Esen, the eldest son of the Director of the Cultural and Educational School, was the ringleader of one side. We went to the same music school He was one year older than me: well-read and thoughtful. Their family was very friendly. His little brother, Nurlan, was the same age as Serik. He became a sculptor. As for Esetik, he was a notorious bully. He became a police officer. Juniors were quiet: Dulatik and his sister Karlygash. The mother of the family, Aunt Munira was a fashionable woman. She was a piano teacher. The grandmother of this talented family was sublime and sedate in manner, always covering her head with a large white silk kerchief. She even carried water from the next water pipe and seemed to have a royal bearing.

Uncle Zhora was the head of the family, a cheerful and simple man. He was good in playing dombra and sang well.

The Meyer family lived under one roof with Temirovs. Their son Pasha was my best friend. We used to invent all sorts of competitions, one day it was cross-race, the other "war games". Especially we loved night hide and seek. We would dress up in black and hide in ditches, behind bushes. Then we would go and scare our neighbours from across Ninka Babkina. We hung a potato to the window on a thread, thereafter hiding in an irrigation ditch while knocking this portal by a thread. He was scared. His parents looked after him following school during the nights. When the boys came to see him (they were sitting on a bench), they would flash with their flashlights and mess up dates. Also, we stretched a string across the road so that when a car drove with its headlights on, this gleaming string looked like a thick rope. The driver got out, looks around and saw it is a thin string, then the driver would swear in the darkness. Of course, we choked with laughter in the bushes.

Until the third grade, I spent all my time playing football and hockey with the boys. Then, I was moved to the other side of the street: to the girls. There, a red-haired merrymaker Valery Konovalov was in the saddle. Curiously, all the girls were in love with the blue-eyed Vitalik Steselev. His parents were teachers in the high school named after Abay. His father, Aleksei Semenovich, was our physics teacher in the sixth grade, while his mother, Nina Grigorievna, was assistant principal. She walked with a dignified sweep - like a peafowl. Valery's mothers aunt, Valya, was her older sister.

Valery was an inventor; he knew a lot of games and jokes. Very often, we would be carried away playing until it was dark and our parents started to look for us. Once, I tied my younger brother Berik's leg to a gazebo with a rope. At that time, he was still crawling. However, he was terribly heavy, so this was far from easy. Afterwards, I ran off to play. Yet, when I came to senses he was gone. He had untied himself and crawled away. It even turned out he had fellen into a ditch. Thank God, there was only a little water there, although the mud was sticky and viscous. Nonetheless, his overweight head had nearly choked him. Luckily, I managed to pull him out. I washed him and never left him unattended again. Thereafter, Berik was always bumbling behind me like a tail, even though I ran and jumped more mindfully. Indeed, I was a tomboy with my skinned knees. I hated wearing dresses. My elder brother nicknamed me - "lanky girl"

An additional insult was "Modesty adorns a Lady" – Obviously, he would have preferred me to weave paper curlers in braids. He was always chasing away boyfriends. He was severe with us, but always protected us from others.

Raushan Burkitbayeva - Nukenova

At the time when our younger brother Berik was born, he was sixteen years old. I remember him being ashamed of our pregnant mother. But then, he cared so much for his younger brother. Once I came home to find him sprawled on a couch as white as snow and doubled up from pain. I immediately run to mother's office - fortunately it was across the street. We took him to a hospital.. He had a perforated appendicitis. While he was alive, he took care of me and my sister. He passed away at the age of thirty-four. During those last years, he was seriously ill with chilled kidneys from a business trip. He told me that I certainly have to have one more baby. "Children - are the flowers of our lives, and the more of them, the more beautiful the world is"

Mukhtar was a great athlete; he had a senior degree in table tennis. He took our younger brothers to the sports school and played football with them. He was strict, but a fair judge in children's disputes. I remember he was proud of me when I went to the Havana International Festival of Youth and Students.

Back then, he worked as a foreman. Indeed, after graduating from the Hydrological Institute, he traveled around the Muyunkum deserts building irrigation canals and wells. He worked and lived in trailers on the steppe. In the evening, he and his brothers would go to local farms to drink milk, or koumiss. He would always carry a magazine with him "Kazakhstan әyelderi" - "Women of Kazakhstan" - with my photo on the cover. The heading said I was a delegate at the XI World Festival in Cuba. Hence, he proudly announced to the hostesses that I was his little sister. Following this, they would brighten up and prepare a lamb in honour of their guest.

When I came home on vacation from Karaganda, he proudly told me that thanks to my picture in a popular magazine, he has eaten a whole flock of sheep. Well, good for you, you are welcome!

When my elder passed away, I felt as if a defensive shelter had been taken away from me. Yet, I feel his support during the most difficult moments of my life. As we say "Arhuak" - his spirit protects me. Sometimes I see my brother in my dreams - it usually happens before turning points in my life.

Obviously, we all come into this world crying and leave it with a last gasp. But when young people leave, this loss is irreparable and hurts the hearts of their loved ones. Such wound never heals.

Back in those days, towns were full of sparrows. Entire flocks of merry, mischievous, little birds bathed in puddles after the rain. At night, eating mosquitoes and midges, they would fly like hang-gliders, or bats. Adults scared us by saying they drank blood and admired the colour white. So, in the evenings, we took off our hair bows, which were snow white. Relatedly, sitting on benches and listening to scary stories about the jacket-strangler, we did not notice how naughty boys tied ribbons in a strong knot. A prank meaning us girls could not scatter in different directions.

In spring, girls twined flowers into their braids and wore wreathes of dandelions and blue-eyed bell-flowers like a crown. As for the boys, they constantly played battles in alchiks, holding "Lyanga" competitions.

"One couple, two lures" We had no idea what it meant. They have their own games. Yet, the most common games were hide-and-seek, ball games, cops and robbers, "shtander-stop" etc. We played volleyball without nets; we all stood in a circle. The one who missed the ball, sat in the middle and got hit by the ball going forwards. If anyone caught the ball, or returned it, then this player was allowed to get out of the "hole". None of us could wait for winter to come. We preparing sleds and skates. Certainly, wearing fluffy knitted gloves made by the caring hands of grandmothers, along with sported socks for skates, were worn with pride. Overall, we spent hours skating on the highways, at the same time as the boys were showing off with their tarpaulin boots - sliding down from the hills.

We built entire winter cities and ice palaces, filled rollers, played snowball battles.

Catholic Christmas, of course, was before the New Year. Therein, scents of vanilla and spicy muffins wafted around streets from the houses of German families. Aunt Martha would always invite us to visit, warm us up with hot tea, or coffee, and offer us cake. Then, each of us would take a little sack of foreign candy, or biscuits in the form of wonderful animals. I kept the candy wrapper in a box with other wrappers. Beforehand, we used to collect them, as well as cards and pictures of our favourite movie actors in order to exchange them. Vyacheslav Tikhonov, Vasily Lanovoy, and Oleg Strizhenov, were our idols. All the girls wanted to look like Jeanne Bolotova, Ariadna Shengelaja, Isolda Izvitskaya, Elina Bystritskaya. We cut out dolls of cardboard and made coloured removable dresses, or suits for them.

The boys collected stamps, models of airplanes. We even went to hobby groups for styling and design, making miniature ships in the Palace of Pioneers.

Then, all at once, everybody started to buy East European Shepherds. Our dog's name was Dinga. All black, only a white spot on the chest like a butterfly. When she was a puppy, we wormed and vaccinated her. We treated her like a child. My brother Serik with his friends Otto, Eric, Sergey took her to the VSAAFN, where dogs were trained as if in school. They participated in exhibitions, showing acquired skills. Our Dinga got a medal.

Four-legged friends were inseparable from us and went on picnics with us in the mountains. In winter, we tied them to the sled, and they rolled us over the snowy roads. We rolled all day long, so those in their evening out clothes were soaked to the skin and after they froze in the cold, rattled like chains. Fingers turned blue. At home, parents rubbed pungent turpentine into our skin: they gave us hot milk with honey.

New Year was our favourite and most memorable holiday. Fluffy fragrant trees shone in every house. Mum pulled out a box with Christmas decorations. The whole family decorated it with winter beauty. Dad strengthened it in the crosspiece. Mum gently released coloured glass toys hung from cotton wool. No one could wait to hang these sparkling toys on green prickly branches. Beads, silver rain, and a garland of coloured light bulbs completed this New Year's outfit. My elder brother Mukhtar set up a five-pointed star on top of the tree. We put Santa Claus and the Snow Maiden at the foot of the tree. Here we go. The tree is ready. Everybody was stunned by its sparkling beauty. Each tree toy was made and painted by hand. Beads entwined the silver ball with intricate monograms; here were the strobiles - that is a hut, icicle, snowman, and a ball like a spotlight. Every decoration was a work of fine art. The magical outfit of New Year's beauty sparkling with a myriad of stars and the flash of light bulbs. They looked like fireworks. This beauty was breathtaking. Now decorations are all the same and unimpressive.

All houses got prepared for the New Year: baking pies and cooking various viands. Indeed, a New Year table should be generous, so that the next harvest will be rich.

The shots of champagne corks, cheers, the firing of rockets and merry chanting spread through the wintry streets. Everyone making a cherished wish at the New Year. "They say whatever you wish on New Year will always come true."

Then Orthodox Christmas came. Girls read fortunes, sitting all night in front of a mirror and trying to see the face of "Mr. Right". Children went caroling from house to house. Valery Konovalov (wearing a coat inside out), danced to a drum roll. As for the kids, we gathered up yumminess, which would be eaten later on.

Each season has its own way. Except late autumn and early spring with their cold rains and sharp wind gusts, making the heart sick, and creating conditions whereby it was impossible to run around the streets. We had to sit at home and play with the cat Kuzya, although it spent all day snoozing near a furnace. Previously, this furnace was stoked with coal. Then, when we had natural gas, a blue flame flashed inside, heating adjacent rooms.

One summer, when the windows and doors remained open, a pigeon flew in the window. Kuzya started to run after it, then caught it and bit its wing. Wounded, the pigeon huddled behind the buffet, where the cat could not get it and fell silent. When I came home I was so tired from the games, I lay down on the sofa and fell asleep. In my sleep, I hear rustle and bustle. I got scared, calling out: "Who is there?" to the silence. I was scared to death. Maybe thieves had broken in through the open window and shuffled into the closet. I was paralyzed with fear. Now they will come in and kill me. Oh, suspicious noises again, even though I could not hear any steps. I took courage in both hands to get up from the couch, I looked around, but there was no one. Yet, something rustled behind the buffet. A man would not fit there. Probably it is a mouse. So, I took a look and saw the pigeon. My brother and I barely pulled out the poor guy. He is wounded and couldn't fly away. We bandaged the wing, giving it water and feeding it with breadcrumbs. A few days later, it flew off, away from the mean Kuzya.

In some of the summer holidays I, my brother Serik and sister Rose, took to the mountains – to the summer pastures at Uncle Mahan's, mother's cousin. High in these mountains in a valley, shepherd yurts spread their hemispheres. Flocks of sheep and goats grazed on those green slopes, resembling white clouds. Moreover, noise from constantly chewing cows walking pompously near the mountain river - and a herd of horses descending down to the clean waters - deafened everyone. Uncle Mahan was in charge of all these animals.

We stayed in one of the yurts with the milkmaids. Early in the morning, when a thick fog hung over the gorge and a mountain coolness poured heavy dew on the grass, the milkmaids got up for morning milking. However, we slept soundly under camel blankets. In the evenings, we tried to milk the cows, but were afraid of them. We helped to drain their milk, nevertheless, which poured from buckets into jars like a white river. In the morning, it was taken to the city in milk tankers. In the milk plant, it was processed, turned into fermented baked milk and made into clotted milk and cottage cheese - a favourite delicacy for kids. Nowadays, these Milk Rivers are shallow, since most dairy products are made from powder.

Obviously, shepherd houses made from felt were amazing. As in a fairy tale, a magic tablecloth allowed wining and dining. In the same manner these yurts could be assembled in a matter of minutes. First, a skeleton is set out, then tightened by a lasso and insulated by felting. In such housing, it is warm in winter and cool in summer. Furthermore, no insects got inside. Also, yurts were decorated with hunting trophies - wolves, foxes etc. At night, we would open a "smoke hole" at the top and admire the starry night lying in bed. A universal yurt once served Kazakhs as a sauna. The heat was administered by boulders rolled down from the mountains in the valley close to the river. Thence, a fire was kindled around the stones making them red-hot. Afterwards, a yurt was set around this space in such way that the stones were inside. The felt cloth preserving the temperature and the heat of the stones - as the laying of a thermos.

Bunches of herbs were hung there, including tickseed, mint, oregano. Additionally, people took off their clothing, entered the sauna and took their seats around the hot stones: smearing their bodies with honey. Sweat flooded from them. Then they went to the next yurt, where they washed with water and an infusion of herbs. They had a massage – by hands as experienced as any on a chiropractor. Each massage reviving both joints and bones. Those who were younger ran to plunge themselves into icy mountain streams, following which they went back to the "steam room". After such procedures, one looks 10 years younger.

In the evenings, lying around dastarkhan sipping fragrant tea from mountain water boiled in a samovar and twanging the dombra, everybody anticipated beshbarmak. Sorpa bubbles in a large cauldron. This meat was already cooked. However, thin pieces of dough were added to the broth: along with thin slices of onions infused with spices – "Tuz-Dyk". The pieces of dough were then taken out and put on a platter with meat – following which Tuz-Dyk is poured. First the sheep's head was served on a first platter and "Jan-bas". Then a large platter with meat and dough was served. The head being offered to an honoured guest, who sat in the red corner - Torda. He butchered it and then gave it to all those present. Children got crispy ears. Others get "keen eye", daughters in law - "a singing sky".

This was a whole ritual. The meat was cut into pieces. Everyone got a piece. Brother-in-law got brisket, daughters-in-law got ribs, men - buttocks and thigh-bones, women - vertebrae. Everyone was involved. Afterwards, mi-palau was prepared, by opening the sheep's brain-case. The beshbarmak was eaten by hand. Hence the name of the dish - "five fingers". It was much tastier like this, rather than eating it with a fork. The old men would then wipe their oily hands on their moccasins – on leather boots as soft as a husky. "Et etke, sorpa betke" - "Meat to meat, broth to face". Sorpa – broth was served with katyk - sour-milk cottage cheese. It made the eaters sweat and their faces shine. They were so full that the condition of a "noble burp" ensued. This means that guests enjoyed the food. Then they drink tea again; to keep things hot: the saksaul was stuck in the pipe of a samovar. It gave a special flavour to the drink and kept its warmth.

Meals were accompanied by long instructive conversations. Kazakhs love striking words and appreciate the wisdom of ancient sayings - as much as they love eating meat. They can spent hours listening to oral chronicles and legends. Indeed, steppe tellers named Kuishi were surrounded by special honours. Simple in design, dombra allowed cultural memories to pass on from one generation to another. They preserved the treasures of the Kazakh steppe in folk songs and kui. Talented sons and daughters adding their precious contributions to this treasury.

They had their own strict laws, a special steppe philosophy. Wise Beys resolved disputes fairly. They held fair trials. Kazakhs valued their age-old traditions and good name. Their personal word identified with honour and dignity. Oratory honed as a Damascus blade. In the competitions called Aitys participants won due to ironic and worthy narrator-improvisation. Even today, they draw large audiences of fans through their felicitous words and implied meanings.

This nomadic way of life forced people to fit their households accordingly, All starting from demountable dwelling to baby cots called "Besik" - a great invention by steppe peoples. Within it, a child was deposited as in a baby cot after being dried and isolated under a blanket. Moreover, a kind of drainpipe for urine had been made from sheep tibia bones drilled with a hole - "shumek". The child was then placed in this baby cot and shumek was inserted between its legs. Apparently, it was especially comfortable for boys. Curiously, the body was secured with strips of fabric - and afterwards reinforced with ropes on a crossbar. Children's "surprises" flowed through a tube into a clay pot - inserted into the bottom of the cot. It was like a personal toilet. The child was always dry. Certainly, there was no need for any baby linen, or diapers. The sole necessity being to put the cot onto a cart and go ahead to another location.

I also used Besik when I had my first son Yerzhan. At that time, we lived in an employee dormitory, so my child grew into a healthy and calm boy. Although my father-in-law upbraided me for using this relic of the past, the wisdom of our people seemed limitless to me. Later, when my second daughter-in-law hung baby linen all over the house, we remembered the merits of besik.

Of course, the second indisputable treasure of Kazakhs are horses. On Lugovsky stud farm located in Zhambyl region, stallions of the Akhal-Teke breed are raised. Their famous ancestor is Absinthe (1952-1975), a pureblood stallion, on which in 1960, Sergei Filatov became the first Soviet Olympic champion in equestrian sports. In his homeland, a monument was set up to him.

At six years old, a steppe boy is given his first yearling. From that age onwards, this yearling is his faithful companion. Indeed, boys care deeply about their four-legged companions and prepare them for races.

In the spring, when the steppe wears its most beautiful coat of red poppies and bluebell flowers (scattered around on the green velvet of emerald fields), the villagers go to the Toy, which is a feast for all the people from the surrounding villages. If for Christians and Catholics the biggest holidays are Christmas and Easter, for Muslims it is such holidays as Nauryz. The arrival of the New Year with the first spring sunshine of March. Clearly, at the moment of awakening and rebirth of nature, Nauryz is a holiday of renewal and a celebration of life.

Yurts are scattered all across the land as felt skullcaps, wherein a generous dastarkhan is laid. The preparation of seven cereals in a ritual Nauryz-koje drink is also offered to guests.

At this time, horsemen get ready for Baiga horseraces. Their horses becoming exited in the process. Indeed, they line up in a chain and scoot upon command. People cheer for their favourites with whistles and whoops. Supporters bet on animals that will come first to the finish.

These poor beasts are like a national currency. If farmers do not have money, they pay with their herd, or cattle. The horseman who wins the race, is like a national hero. A winning horse is then used for mating to improve livestock.

People always keep in their memory when this race was won. Additionally, full-bodied men test their strength against each other in a horse battle called "kokpar", wherein each tries to take away a goat from the other. Young horsemen cheerfully wink for the start. They are aware that a hot kiss from a local beauty awaits the winner. Hence, this pursuit of beauty is called "Kyz Kuu" - catch the maiden.

In any case, all villagers keenly follow the competitions and react very emotionally. Woe betides those who embarrass themselves. The looser being barracked by painful metaphorical lashes to his male ego.

In the evening, excited youngsters have fun, swinging on "altybakan" as the wind carries soulful melodies throughout the steppes. Folk tunes are echoed at every turn. Furthermore, dombra in the hands of skillful performers can convey the feelings of these boy without words. Therefore, a girl's face is often seen to blush like a tulip. Albeit, trying to hide her black eyes from any embarrassment. Only her ring-laden thin fingers, fidgeting with tight braids, show her excitement.

Yet, vigilant young women "Jengey" - the wives of older brothers - see everything. Oh, these notable matchmakers! They know the secrets of love and they help prepare the way towards a girl's heart.

Spring arrives. The world awakens from hibernation. Wrinkles smooth under the warm rays of sunshine. People's hearts have not grown old; they are open to love, like a guitar for a song. Just gently touch the string and this instrument will sing as a nightingale.

Happily drinking a brew from the milk of a mare - Kumys, courage strikes the head with new thoughts and spreads warmth throughout the blood. Brothers-in-law flirt with young women and the little sisters of their wives - "baldyz". Cheeky jokes fly from young women to dzhigits as the shuttlecocks of badmintons. The dombra echoes them. Peals of laughter waft over the evening mist. Couples in love, and restless children, play on swings.

A warm night covers the gorge with a starry blanket. The noises of grasshoppers and crickets abound. "Who's hooting there?" It is an owl. His feathers adorn the "Borik" – headdress of girls. Mysterious nightlife sets in. It is time to sleep. We go into our yurts and drown in the soft Korpeshe. The first rays of the sun - as plashes of sunlight - go through the "Shanyrak" and holes (eaten away by moths in the felt), allow our faces to peep through. We hide under the blankets. The elders get up, they have some work to do, as for us we sleep, since we are on summer holidays.

Shadow of the Rain

After waking, we run down to a mountain river to wash. The water is ice cold there; sleepiness vanishes as if by magic. We return to the yurt in a cherry mood, where breakfast is already served. Fresh milk, baursaks, kurt and sour cream. In the morning, dzhaylyau is filled with an intoxicating fragrance infused with herbs and a variety of colours, sprinkled with fresh morning mists. In the mountains, there are plenty of healing herbs; it is a complete green pharmacy. Just do not be lazy, go pick some herbs; this is natural medicine from all ills and ailments.

Childhood years in a person's life – they are like a moment of dawn in nature. Children are like angels - pure and innocent. Children's worlds are a paradise on earth - wherein reigns happiness, kindness, and an openness to the light. The world wakes up in that dawn. There is nothing sweeter than the faces of sleeping children. What will the world of the future be like? Well, it depends on these little cuties. May good thoughts come into their heads, while their hands do good deeds!

Our national poet, Muzaffar Alimbaev, loves these early hours of dawn. Sometimes, he wakes his companions in the village before dawn, saying: "Get up quickly, while everyone is sleeping – we will get plenty of pristine fresh air!" There is a philosophical wisdom for such a situation. "Dew point" - the awakening of the world. It is as mesmerizing as the hours of the evening crimson sunset.

During the daylight, a child watching the world around recognizes incomparably more than during years in school and universities. Since he is part and parcel of this world: the main cog in this complex mechanism of life. A child comes to know this world without help, or pointers, from teachers. Apparently, this is the most useful lesson. Indeed, childhood lessons will be the starting point of one's life chronometer: the foundation of knowledge. Thus, the further we move away from childhood, the more we need to go back to those years.

Understanding the world comes as an insight, no matter how difficult and confusing it was. To understand it, the vectors of good and evil, lies and honesty, strength and weakness, demands a clear set of guidelines in these fragile minds and hearts. Everyone chooses his own way. But, a child's notions are originally pure and innocent. Their direction in life the ship that will make depends on us adults. Among the confusion and chaos - a happy childhood (like a lighthouse), will indicate the right way to goodness, honour and justice. Thence, will come the kingdom of reason and prosperity!

1996

Shadow of the Rain

Station of my Childhood

The road is calling me again. Without hesitation, I take a ticket for the express train. Honestly, I do not like airplanes with their angularity and aloofness. I feel much more comfortable and relaxed on a train. The carriage meets me as a good old friend, opening hospitably at every door in a compartment. Suitcases and bags make themselves snug - hiding under the lower couchettes. All goodbyes are said. And now, the railway station with its eternal bustle slowly starts to glide as a movie frame. A semaphore signal stands stretched out as a strict check-man, giving us the green light.

Soon, the smell of sausages and boiled chicken wafts around the carriage. The stove cheerfully buzzes. So, we will drink hot tea. The train has always acquired this lively atmosphere, new acquaintances are made, and everyone feels cozy as at home. Whistle stops and villages flash outside the window - as our dear land amazes passengers with its vast expanses.

The shades of evening fall creepingly. After satisfying any aforementioned curiosity, my companion, a blue-eyed baby enjoys a balmy sleep. So do I: falling asleep to the sedate clack of the wheels.

Our memory has some interesting features. Every time I pass by this station, it touches me with its invisible hand...

From an unexpected shake of the compartment, I wake up and anxiously squint into darkness behind the windows. Did I miss my station? Not yet. I calm down and fall asleep again, but at every train stop, I jump: "Is it my station?"

Every time I anticipate this encounter with trepidation. And here it is finally, Meadow Station.

As if a huge wave overwhelmed me, I find it hard to breathe. Images of a distant childhood run over one another, as the kilometers of this road.

- Home sweet home, lovely places! Hello, my bright world of childhood!

Through tears, I can see the face of my grandfather with his sly smile. He looks like the famous Aldar-Kose with that arched look in his eyes and rosy disposition. Grandpa was tall and broad-shouldered. His regular features accentuated by a mustache and beard, whereas wrinkles scattered from the corners of his eyes. Years had slightly hunched his figure. Yet, grandfather's face was suntanned, soaked with salt and the warmth of the sun: the generosity of the places where he lived his life. His name was Tleubay, his brother's - Tleukul. They also had nine sisters. Tleu means begged.

Grandma's name was Tyndym, which means a lull. She was white-skinned, of corpulent habit, but also soft and warm.

For his dark skin, grandfather was nicknamed Karashalom, which means black old man. When he reached out his calloused hands, people saw his strength and gentleness. My brother and I hung on them like a swing in our early years.

- Hello, dear grandpa! Here I am back again.

All the best memories of my childhood are connected with my grandfather. I did not like kindergarten, though my mother worked there. I could barely eat cream of wheat, or take a nap. Every day, I ran away from the kindergarten. At that time, we lived across the street. Shortly after arriving home, my folks would dutifully bring me back, while I cried from the top of my lungs. Tangentially, I always looked forward to summer when my brother and I would be taken to grandfather. Nothing could hold us in the city. There was nothing special in the place where the parents of our mother lived, except for a salt marsh, where there was freedom and fresh air.

My grandparents lived on the meadows. Indeed, vast green meadows stretching around the village - this is where the name of our village comes from.

My little brother and I followed our older sister Rosa everywhere. She always lived with our grandparents. We went to the meadow to gather dung, and then piled it near the barn in a huge pyramid. Grandma burned dung in an outdoor stove and baked flat bread. We also ran to get some water; it was a few streets away. Our sister walked ahead of us, balancing with a shoulder yoke as a ropewalker in a circus. With pride, she announced to local bullies that we were her relatives from the city, so they did not bother us.

Each morning grandpa drove cattle to pasture, while every day we intended to help him out, but always overslept. Nonetheless, we had to get up early before the sunrise, although grandma did not let anyone wake us up: "Let the kids sleep before kindergarten". Our sister sniffed, "What sissies, cry me a river" However, the day was already getting hot. So, my brother Serik and I guiltily went out of the house. As usual, grandmother was busy near the stove in the courtyard. Everywhere wafted this distinct scent of freshly baked bread. Never again, did I have a chance to eat such delicious bread –the type my grandmother used to cook.

My brother helped her to kindle the samovar. My sister and I set out the dastarkhan: sugar, sweets, homemade butter, sour cream, milk. Here everything is ready. Indeed, the freshly baked bread was cooling and exuded a delicious smell. Our samovar was on the boil. Yet, grandfather was late for morning tea. Thus, my brother ran outside to find him. Curiously, he was riding his donkey with a large box in one hand and holding its reins in the other. "This is for the kids" - he said, handing the box to grandmother. We found candies inside.

- "Oybay"! – Grandmother shouts – "you want them to lose their teeth"!

- "What are you talking about, they will not eat them all at once", - interrupted grandfather.

Then, we all sat down to dastarkhan. Grandma poured tea. Grandfather sat in the front corner. He was pleased with himself: he made us kids happy. We had breakfast at a leisurely pace, until grandpa told us what he had seen at the station - who he had met.

After breakfast, grandma and my brother worked in the yard. Thereafter, grandpa gave us donkey rides. Yet, my sister and I were still busy with cleaning the house and helping my grandmother cook lunch. Grandfather's house was a clay adobe; even the floor is made of clay.

Shadow of the Rain

On the occasion, of our arrival, grandpa would always kill a sheep. He artistically butchered the carcass, generously adding salt. Grandmother then cleansed the insides of the sheep and proceeded to cook Kuurdak. Thereafter, the meat was kept in a barn, hung from the ceiling where it was ventilated, and finally stored in a dry area. After all, elders did not recognize refrigerators in those days. Unrelatedly, my brother and I were afraid to walk alone in the barn; we thought some strange creature lived there, even though my mother was born in this little low old house – which was now the barn. Slowly, evening set in. We all run into the meadow to greet the flock. Grandfather sedately walked behind us. Certainly, we gamboled like baby goats, while grandpa playing with us. Then, worn out, he went to join other elderly folk who waited for the herd. Albeit comfortably sitting on the grass. Here, they met every day to exchange news. "The children have grown. Your grandson is almost a dzhigit! How is your son-in-law doing, how is your daughter?" The elderly discuss all of life's occurrences deliberately and with keen interest.

The last names of my contemporary Kazakhs are derived from the names of their fathers and grandfathers. One can tell many things from this: who was one's ancestor - a hunter, a shepherd, or how many midwives delivered babies, or where did one's daughter-in-law originate from. So Koyshibek, Koylibay - the owner of sheep, Zhilkibay - the owner of horses, Baymolda – a wealthy mullah, Ushkempirov - three old women, Koibagar – a shepherd Tungushbay – the firstborn, Kenzhetaev - the reckling etc. Unarguably, these poor people (in gratitude to God) named their children Kudaibergen,

Rahmanberdy which meant given by God. Yet, their children often died from diseases, or starvation. In such cases, parents begged the Almighty to preserve them by calling them Tokhtar, Turar, Toktasyn – let him live, or Omirzak - long life. Moreover, to ward off the evil eye, they sometimes gave offensive names such as Itbay – the owner of the dog, Zhamankul – a bad person.

If only girls were born, the last would be named Ulbolsyn, Ulmeken - let it be a son - in hope for the birth of an heir.

Also, children were sometimes named Amangeldy Zhaksylyk, Amanzhol, which means godspeed, as if blessing them.

Only Bai children were given euphonious, sometimes menacing, religious names - Abdulhairov Ablai, Ualikhan, Amirkhan ... Often parents would give consonant names to children, thinking that one child will keep the other. Interestingly, this tradition was preserved until recently. For example, children were named Askar, Aset, Asel, Asem or Aizhan, Nurzhan, Yerzhan, Marjane. But this rather reflects the proclivity of Kazakhs to versification. After all, back in those days anyone could take part in Aitys – a competition between singers-improvisers.

These chronicles of Kazakh names are the living history of the people: human lives and times.

With the arrival of our new lives, moreover, new names appeared such as Soviet, October, Mels, Tractor, Vilen, Stal, Kim, Marlen...

Assuredly, the names of my peers are as follows: Kuanysh - joy, Nurlan - radiant, Arman – dream, Bakhyt - happiness – each one sounding lyrical and concise.

My mother's name was Zharylkasyn. In itself, Zharylkau means God bless. This is a masculine name. Explaining his reasoning in this matter, grandfather stated he had fathered ten children, but disease and famine took away nine of them. Only my mother survived. So, grandfather did not have an heir. A fact forcing him to raise his daughter as a boy. Hence, she grew up as a lively girl. Certainly, no matter how hard her parents tried to talk to her, she still decided leave the village - eventually entering university and then getting married. Moves preventing any return to the countryside.

Yet, the elderly man started to grow sad, so my mother decided to give them her first daughter, while she continued her education. "Merciful Allah, he did not take the last child away and gave us grandchildren" - thought my grandfather, looking at us.

Suddenly back, shouts resounded, "They are coming, they are coming!" - mouthed the vociferous village boys. All in all, we found ourselves running after them to meet the flock. Now exhausted and satiated, the beasts were approaching the village like a huge cloud. Cows were walking ahead steadily, swinging sideways with bulging sides, whilst goats and sheep minced behind them. Young owners greeted them with cheers and drove them into their yards with cheerful whooping.

Raushan Burkitbayeva - Nukenova

Our cow welcomed its hostess by shaking its head. Unsurprisingly, we fussed around grandma impatiently; everyone wanting to milk the cow. Yet, nothing worked out and we were compelled to be satisfied by helping to drain fresh milk. Thereafter, drinking it with relish. Grandma looked at us tenderly: "Drink, drink, my foals, there is no such milk in the city". Then, butter was made out of this milk, as well as sour cream, ayran, kurt. In such a way, we have seen with our own eyes where milk comes from.

Endlessly, grandma still bustled around the house and, after having dinner, we climbed on to the roof of the barn. There, our sister prepared a bed for us. We peered into the starry sky and chatted about something, before falling asleep.

Naivety is such an amazing trait in a child's soul. When my mother was pregnant with our little brother Berik, I wondered why her belly kept growing. "You drink too much tea" –I told her with anger and took her cup away. Grandma laughed: "You cannot do this; soon your mother will buy you a brother, or sister". Honestly, I did not really want to have a little sister, because I was afraid that Dad would love me less. Yet, father made renovations to the house and soon after mum gave birth to my little brother. I remember how many guests there were in the house, mothers parents also came. They looked at the baby with tears in their eyes and thanked God for this grandson.

All night long, my brother and I jumped from the screams of the baby, watching mother feeding and swaddling him with interest.

The most interesting moment was when my mother and grandmother bathed the baby. "When he grows up, he will play with us?" - We asked. "Soon, soon", - replied grandma.

When it was time to start dry nursing, we took him to grandfather. The kid was a fun, roly-poly, tiny grabbling. When mother showed up, he began to cry, as if he was angry at her for a long absence. After which, he started to beat her chest with his tiny fists, but no longer cursed.

He turned one year. Grandpa killed a sheep. We prepared the rite. Grandmother's girlfriends came. Everybody sang songs. One of them, the most agile, tied his legs with multicolored string then cut it in the middle, while brother took his first steps. He walked with clumsy footfalls and stretched his arms as we were threw candies and coins, jumping joyfully. For his part, the kid was cheerfully smiling: feeling everyone's attention.

Now he is a grown up and serves in the army.

Personally, I will never forget that day when grandfather knocked us out. It happened during morning tea. My sister bought us candies - white cushions. Grandpa thought it was sugar, and took a piece of candy. Then Grandma stopped him. Grandpa got furious and grabbed the edge of the tablecloth before shaking it in grandmother's face. Bowls flew to the wall, all the dishes piled up. Grandmother calmly stood up and took us into another room. After grandpa had calmed down, she re-set the dastarkhan and came to get us: "I got so old, I see nothing. Forgive the old man". We laughed at his gaffe and went back to drink tea.

Raushan Burkitbayeva - Nukenova

My brother and I loved to listen to grandpa's stories about his tough youth. However, he did not like recalling the time when he hacked for Bai in childhood. But, when my grandfather was talking about Turkish rural electrification, his eyes glowed with youth and joy. "It was hard, earthworks were unusual. Yet, it was an unforgettable experience - meeting the first working crew"- he recounted. "Indeed, signs of new life lit up in each family as bright light bulbs" Overall, it was surprising for these illiterate labourers that such advances allowed their children to write their names on a sheet of paper. Nonetheless, it remained a great pleasure to sign on behalf of our grandfather when it was time to get his pension benefit. Being illiterate himself, he rewarded us with a coin for this work.

Until the end of his days, my grandfather turned on the radio with particular trepidation and listened to the voice of the broadcaster. It was strange to him how this box could speak and sing in different languages - as if it was alive. And we, in turn, were surprised at how grandpa could tell the exact time without looking at his watch. Grandpa smiled: "Life whispers to me". Maybe this is why grandfather prayed every day - given that we were told in school that God does not exist and that it is a fairytale for poor people.

Yes, a lot of new things have appeared on our Kazakh steppes in recent years. Could grandpa ever dream that his children and grandchildren would be doctors, teachers, and engineers: that rockets would be launched into space from our land?

All of this amazed and delighted my grandfather. But he did not trust technology. His old donkey seemed safer to him. Moreover, he sometimes disappeared, or rather was stolen, by naughty teenagers. Without hesitation, therefore, we went looking for him. Every time we found him in a different place. Then he returned home happy with his faithful companions.

Indeed, my grandfather was a merry chap. In this vein, he once came up with an interesting history about our little brother.

A long time ago, a brave warrior Batyr lived in these parts. He defended the poor. He was fair and generous. He had a damask sword ornamented with precious stones. Before his death, Batyr buried it in the desert, so his sons would not fight for it.

"When you grow up" - grandfather told his grandson, - "we will find this sword. It will be a good bride". After all, back in those days, the poor often remained without a wife - if one had nothing to pay for her. Dear grandfather worried about the fate of his grandson as if forgetting that we have moved on from those times. Now, no one buys a bride or fights for a sword.

When grandpa came to see us in the city, he would always buy ice cream. He did not eat it; he would just look at it with a smile saying: "snow in the summer". It was the same during his last visit. He was so old, he got lost right next to our house. His ice cream almost melted.

Last summer, grandpa's donkey was stolen again. However, he found it tied to the usual place. That said, he did not trust doctors. So, he left quietly and without any complaint.

Raushan Burkitbayeva - Nukenova

All people from the surrounding villages who knew our grandfather gathered to bid him a final farewell. Everyone loved him for his rosy disposition. We children did not understand where our grandfather has gone. But all our childhood memories are connected with him.

In the evenings, when she had done her housework, grandmother spun yarn, quietly singing old songs. We watched the spinning wheel lying on korpeshke, cupping chins in hands. It spun like a top, winding wool into elastic thread. Then grandmother knitted warm fuzzy socks out of this wool for us. Our grandmother was a needlewoman. She knew how to make homespun rugs - tekemets, alasha, kiiz. The elderly would always bring presents and knit warm socks whenever they came to see us.

Time flashed passed. At the end of the summer, our parents and elder brother came to take us home. They stayed a few days, helping the elderly with household chores. We hated to leave, but I had to get ready for school. I wish I could run far away to the place where the flock pastures on a meadow and turn into a frisky horse. Grandpa would tell us: "Go back, children, you have to study, you will be great people, and I will come to visit you".

Grandma would give us a pot with sour cream and butter, fresh bread and kurt for the journey.

Grandpa talked with father, asking about the health of his parents - who lived with us in the city. He was keenly interested in news of the city, in places where our parents went for leisure. We were more interested in what they had brought us from the south. "You will see when we get home" – mother said.

One day she gave us smooth, round, stones, taken from the beach, and taught us to play with them. We ran away to learn this new game.

My sister, however, was better in these matters than I. She deftly tosses up a stone meanwhile picking up another lying on the floor and catching the first one. Our parents brought goodies from the south, fruits from our garden, vegetables. Mum admired our tan and how we had grown over the summer.

A few days later, we were taken to the city. After the death of grandfather, our parents decided to take grandmother and sister to the city. Once, my grandfather gave an alarm clock to our grandmother. She had never parted with it, lovingly winding it up and listening to it tick. "So, this is how the heart of my Tleubay beated", - she said. When the alarm clock broke, my grandmother cried. She calmed down only when it was repaired. Until the end of her days, she remained faithful to our grandfather and loved him. She passed away right after him.

The ragged beep of the train interrupted my thoughts. Here it is, the dear railroad station of my childhood, even though new buildings tower nearby. A few passengers are fussing.

Again, memories rushed back upon me. My sister and I, and women from neighbouring houses, were running down to the railroad station in the evenings to see the passenger trains. They offered the sleepy passengers hats knitted from dyed lamb's wool. My sister also knew how to knit them. So, we ran around the platform cheerfully, looked with interest in the windows of carriages. Yet, the train slowly took off, carrying passengers away to an unknown world.

Nowadays, I am here in the carriage again and the painfully familiar railroad station is behind the window.

Sadly, there are no longer vociferous neighbours, nor those caps. All that is connected with this station now seems distant and as bright as the stars. Here, my childhood was left behind me. Goodbye, old railroad station! Goodbye, Grandpa! The train slowly moves away from the station of my childhood. It is gathering pace. There are a lot of milestones ahead, a whole life.

1985

Firecrackers

Winter turned out to be snowy and frosty. The village dozed when it was covered with snowdrifts - as if with a thick fur coat. Rare freight and passenger trains swept past with a roar like a flying arrow over numbed steppe space. Indeed, if you look at Algabas from a railway embankment, it seems like Batyr stretched out on a white rug at the foot of the Alatau mountains. Albeit covered with a felt blanket, and tranquilly smoking an endless roll-up cigarette - puffing thin wisps of smoke into the bottomless sky.

At night, in every yard, staunch dogs barked harshly, menacingly rattling chains that protected households from frequent uninvited guests. Packs of wolves circled around dwellings. The steppe was getting short of food, and they had started to pay visits to villages more often - making predatory raids. The villagers tired from bloody devilments, began to keep a night watch - riding around their snow-covered streets.

"Hey, Zhumahan, it's your turn tonight" - a neighbour called Murat: a man wrapped in a long frosty sheepskin coat with a shabby fox fur cap.

"Here is the shotgun, but do not give it to the kids, tomorrow you will pass it on to your neighbour".

The road lost traction throughout the day like a mirror smooth under the sunrays.

Round about lunchtime, whispering and constantly laughing, rosy-cheeked young village girls in bright colourful shawls walked this road: creaking in their boots. Rarely, some cars drove toward the city. Here, the whole gang of restless village kids came back home from school. For them, winter was a time for endless fun and skating, often on makeshift sleds, or simply on bags and cartons.

In winter, the length of light is short. Here, already the dusk lays with a thick veil over the village.

"It is time for my watch, put on some warm clothes Atanchik", Zhumahan called to his son. "Is mother home?" She is working until late again; probably she is at some kind of meeting. Koke, let's go, we will ride on the cart, maybe we will meet mum on the way", - the son said.

There were about five kilometers between the village and the central manor. This was the usual (forced) daily jogging distance for many villagers. The situation with transport and gasoline was bad, especially in wintertime, and many villagers worked in the "centre". So, they were forced to go back home on foot, unless someone gave a ride.

The teachers' council dragged on until late. Rose Asanovna, a mathematics teacher, anxiously peered into the mist outside the windows, "How will I get home?" Well, finally, the debates ended. Afterwards, she went to Algabas with her coworker.

It snowed with wet and sticky snowflakes, making it difficult to walk. "A teacher's eternal burden - these notebooks. All they can do is pull shoulders by their heavy weight, Its only acceptable if there are good grades". Oddly, they were lucky every day, Someone would pick them up and give a ride, but now, as luck would have it, there was little apart from dead silence.

No lights, no sound. Women tried to get ahead of nightfall, putting on pace. They are halfway there. Ahead they could see the silhouettes of mazars.

Toward the evening, it suddenly gets colder. Snow became hard and prickly: painfully pinching faces. "O Allah, save us, shall the spirits protect us from misfortunes!".

Fitful winds blew over the tardy travelers. Hearts started beating faster from a quick walk, producing a booming noise in the ears. Suddenly, a prolonged plaintive howl wafted out of the darkness. The women were petrified with horror. Wolves!

A neighbour, with a stifled cry slowly fell to the ground. "Saule, get up, wake up!" – Rosa shouted, rubbing her temples with snow.

Nevertheless, subdued nasal howls merged with icy gusts of wind and swept throughout the stark steppe. It was coming. It moved away. Then it seemed to surround them like an invisible noose. Looking around, the women tried to catch a galloping gray shadow in the whitish mist.

Leaving her coworker alone, Rosa began convulsively fumbling in her bag: somewhere there must be lighter - one she had taken away from her students for smoking during recreations. Scattering notebooks around, she tore pieces of paper and enkindled them. Suddenly, the steppe was illuminated with bright torches, like flashing lights. We have to make more noise to scare away the gray robber. Shaking out the bag, she stumbled upon the firecrackers with which the students terrorized the whole school during recreation.

She began to set fire to the fuses of these firecrackers and throw them in front of her. Noisily exploding, they enveloped space with smoke and the smell of gunpowder. She stuck the remaining long firecrackers in the snow and kindled them. Like missiles, they flew into the sky and exploded with a crash and a deafening row. Having arranged these fireworks, she anxiously looked at her fellow traveler – who was starting to recover. "Saule get up, cry, and make some noise".
Hey hey hey!
Grey, hungry villain,
Get out of here, get lost,
In the cold winter night.
What are you looking for this time?
Get back to your crummy hole.
Hey Hey Hey!
I am a mother of three children.
And they are waiting for me at home.
Their love is hotter than fire.
Why are you trying to scare people?
Sly steppe villain?
Wolf, frightened by the dustup made by these women, started circling at a distance. However, the teachers kept the fire around themselves ablaze, with notebook sheets flashing brightly: blowing in their faces both warmth and the hope of salvation.
From the village, the sound of gunshots and the screams of approaching rescuers was heard.
It was Rosa's husband and son Roses, who were coming to the rescue. They noticed from afar the twinkling

lights on the steppe. "Faster, there is Mum. We have to save her from the wolves!"

Whipping the horse and deafening the vicinity with whistles and gunshots, they rushed to the signal lights. Wolf, sensing a serious danger, reluctantly trotted onto the steppe; his empty stomach convulsively gripped by hungry contractions. Thus, ranging his ferocious grey eyes round from his might-have-been take, he slowly moved away from the road.

After this incident, all those who lingered until late in the "centre", would always carry a lighter, matches and firecrackers - Chinese magic wands, the miracle of fireworks, as they kept in mind the experience of these brave teachers. Moreover, men took not only weapons, but also firecrackers on the night watch.

Hey Hey Hey!
Who are you, night villain?
Are you hardened gray wolf,
Or a bold ravenous thief?
Join us in the conversation.
I know a thing or two.
Hey Hey Hey!
Get out from the village soon,
You cowardly and greedy thief.
The ferocious watch is coming,
We protect our land,
And every house in the village.

Raushan Burkitbayeva - Nukenova

Kerchief

"Oramal ton bolmasa da, jol bolady". "A kerchief is not a fur coat, but it opens the floodgates". Hundreds of times I have heard this saying, and voiced it many times when presenting this modest gift to guests.

"It is the thought that counts".

This age-old custom of our people, offering a gift, means blessing our parting guest. Yet, there are funny instances, when your gift – a caftan, a piece of fabric, a costume, etcetera, comes back as a challenge after being through several hands and houses.

Yet, our tradition - not to go, or let the guest go, with "empty hands" – is courteous. So, when someone pops over and one is not ready to take them in, curious incidents occur. This is especially true in rural areas. Stated so, most of these gifts are chosen specifically for each guest personally, as a keepsake.

"Oramal ton bolmasa da, jol bolady".

I recently felt first-hand the meaning of this saying and the wisdom enclosed in these simple words.

Yes, it was a true sign of faith. Particularly when meeting my elder sisters after forty long years. I knew, of course, that Maya and Raya Ayazbekova had studied in Moscow – straight A students and beauties both. Nonetheless, their parents and little brothers Skandarbek and Ermek lived in Dzhambul, not far from us. I went to primary school there.

During one of the holidays, they brought me a gift from India: a silk kerchief.

Genteel with pink ornaments, it passed freely through a wedding ring, streamed along my shoulders like a ray of sunshine and warmed the hearth of ancestral homes, as well as distant, mysterious, countries.

Thus, my handkerchief accompanied me to Moscow, Cuba, Karaganda and Almaty, before quietly waiting for me in a closet in Astana. "Қyzdyn zholy zhenishke" – a girl's path is thin.

My sisters had become professors. Truly, over these long years, we were separated by cities and time and had not seen each other. Now, this unexpected meeting at an exhibition in the new capital was synchronous.

Raya apke came over to see me. It seemed as if my silk kerchief united us again, An occasion reminiscent of the tender May poppy fields of childhood: of times when the enlivening faces of those nearest and dearest had left us.

In Almaty - Maya apke treated me with her culinary delights. Conversely, Raya apke showed us a scarf and sweater made from black coloured Indian Lurex - which my mother had given her on her wedding day... My mothers and sisters' parents were no longer with us, but we cherished their memory and treasured their gifts, because they were a part of their loving hearts.

Ah, belongings, photos, outlive their owners. Flea markets, antique shops, museums, utility rooms, attics and basements are all piled high with the evidence of someone's life.

And maybe someday my granddaughter will try this kerchief on as an heirloom, while reminiscing of us...

The Door

"Uh, oh" – an old door was harshly hooting, choking with bouts of a dry cough. Its tightly closing creaky leafs, with chipped paint, made it look scaled.

She could not remember herself young, or rather new - or recall when the lightwood greedily absorbed an indigo coloured oil paint that proudly gleamed across a tin sign indicating the apartments # 16-30. As for her childhood amid a circle of whispering, risible, green curled girlfriends in her home forests, she simply despaired. Yet, prior to those terrible moments when cutting pain had knocked the blue sky away and a heaviness and vertiginous fear shot through every cell ... things were bearable. Then, as notches of memory added rigorous touches, the recollection of oiled gloves and axes returned. Some of those girlfriends have already burned in the insatiable roar of the fire-breathing furnace. Perhaps she was lucky, because the front entrance was made for her.

Moreover, for more than 10 years she had kept her watch. In summer, this would be underpinned by attempts to get rid of creaking. All meaning, life was much easier during a snowy winter, since she was fully appreciated. After all, people carefully closed the door on their way out, allowing her to snooze among powdered and fluffy snow blankets; her girlish dreams of flying in the frosty air following careless chats with her slim girlfriends on the forest skirt notwithstanding. In the next entrance hall, the old door had been replaced by an iron armoured door. So, she, the poor thing, will be taken back to the village and recycled as firewood. That just proves the ingratitude of humans. They appreciate you as long as they need you. But, being afraid of causing outrage between residents on the first floor, she felt a bit down - swaying in tune with a blowing wind. Uh, oh ... the cat and dog are so annoying. They scratch swollen leafs with their claws, while boys with their balls and heavy sneakers, want to kick her as hard as possible.

And, of course, rainfall – bothersome spring, or autumn cold showers. These times were always chilly, wet and uncomfortable. Especially on lonely, long, rheumatic night, when moisture soaked through, and each cell ached. As for the eternal draught and gloom on the stairwell, no comment could suffice, Albeit, there was no one to talk to. Sadly, apartment doors, upholstered in faux leather and cold-poof, or these freezing metallic beauties from a different world proved impossible...

Only this lonely short-sighted old woman from the first floor, tightly closing the door on her way out, suited her as a soul mate – she was the only one the chilled door waited for...

Raushan Burkitbayeva - Nukenova

The Key

A mantel clock stand. Two ceramic angels drearily looking at each other, while perched on the side. It seems they are about to take to wing and fly away to a melodious jingle wherein the pendulum imagines a time beyond mind: a place where my memories live. After all, my loved ones have gone from this hectic life. Along with friends and compatriots ….. my contemporaries.

Eric Kurmangaliyev has died. He had a unique voice; such talents are born once in a hundred years. At home, he was treated with irony and a lack of understanding, although by Westerners - with admiration. His shrill thin voice now sounds as if generated from an old music box - the echo of bygone days. Faima Kozhabekova and I were at his concert. We saw the enthusiastic faces of the audience and conservatoire teachers. Yet, the closed-off face of Eric (framed with curly black hair) was tense.

It was in Alma-Ata. A slender young man stood on the stage, embarrassed by the warm welcome of his metropolitan audience. Afterwards, his performance was followed by a barrage of cold, random, critics and ordinary people. So, he decided to leave for Russia. In order to be recognized at home, you have to go through rejection in your homeland: to pull up roots, to break through the asphalt of the Arbat. In a sense, as grass impresses the sophisticated connoisseurs of Europe, following which one can return to the steppe with one's head held high!

Shadow of the Rain

On a stage in Astana Congress Hall, Eric-Meruert sang – once he had reached manhood. He had the same facial expression always. Looking like a winner, he wiped beads of sweat from his face and did not look at his audience. Instead, he looked inside himself. Compatriots exulted. Bravo, encore! The Steppe Lark fell silent forever.

A mantel clock stand. The key was lost when moving. I will take tweezers for plucking eyebrows and wind up this old device. Are the angels slyly smiling at me? They say something, gesticulate, but I do not hear them, even though window glass shelters me from street noise. Maybe the angels have flown away...

I cannot talk because of pain in my post-operative throat. I am in the hospital of the Ministry of Internal Affairs, I had my tonsils taken out. They were choking me every morning. Angina "licks the joints and bites the heart" - we were taught in medical school, but life teaches us otherwise. The pain from insults, the loss of close friends, and our fear for children hurt our hearts even more harshly and deeply.

A hospital room illuminated by the shining face of my friend Gulya Dzhekbatyrova. She had a charming plangent voice. The whole bedside table was stuffed with overseas jars of compotes from the Sovminovsky buffet: her trademark potatoes - baursaks and cervelat sausage, "Oh, I cannot eat it!" - "Do not worry, you can give them to Marat. He is starving in the dormitory without you".

Ah, Gulka, Gulechka. All our fellow students of Koba, inhabitants of Almaty, were welcome guests in the apartment on the street of Shevchenko - Baiseitova.

Raushan Burkitbayeva - Nukenova

Every evening, tired hungry field officers, investigators, local officers and graduates from the Karaganda police academy gathered at your parents' house. You served them culinary delights, delicacies. They sang songs and recalled cadet pranks, while your Koba rushed here from Frunze to see you. Looking back, Beatles songs and "Bir Bala" played until the morning. Then we all shifted to Theater Park, enjoying the sounds of fountains and the rustle of the oaks. Altai Mukhamedzhanov - Khosha - son of the well-heeled writer Kalta Mukhamedzhanov (with his burring, insinuating, voice), telling entertaining stories from the lives of famous people - about meetings with Chingiz Aitmatov - a co-author with his father.

"Bir Bala" was a prophetic song for you, Gulechka. Koba once took you away to the capital of Kyrgyzstan, just like that, in a gown and your father's slippers. He took you away forever. Now, your son Nazarik and Koba have been orphaned after your visit to the dentist. Your gentle, caring, voice felt silent. Your smile faded. As an angel, you flew off into the sky. Theater Park emptied. Our fellow students scattered like autumn leaves. The generals and colonels (all already passed the fifty mark), no longer shone amid guitar strings, or glistened with silver on their temples. These days, with pain and bitterness sounding like a hymn for departed youth, sounds "Bir bala". A single monument in the parks of Almaty, where our children dated each other, abides. Places where, our grandchildren fussed around. "From spring to spring, like in a long dream, you came to me". Yes, clog up fountains, springs and rivers. Let them jingle and nourish both soil and gardens with life-giving moisture. Thank you, Imangali Tasmagambetov. The current mayor supports this revival of rivers and fountains. May he hold not only a shovel in his hands, but also a guitar. Certainly, this bell will not fade at your porch". The key of our beloved city is in safe and strong hands. Again, these new and old songs play in the parks until morning. Almaty – Alma-Ata is my first and last love!"

Raushan Burkitbayeva - Nukenova

"Flights in Dreams and in Waking Life"

My spectacular flight over those tiled roofs and peaked spires (characteristic of European cities), is suddenly broken off by the shrill sound of an alarm. Fragrant parks and fascinating landscapes remain, however, in waking consciousness. A trivial reality streams through heavy eyelids like a blinding light. Where am I? Oh yeah, in Astana.

Oh, those fearful and quizzical glances by the young beauty Aisha-Bibi – looking out from the picture by Duzelhanov after returning from a night journey.

For three and a half years, I have been waking up in a foreign city, in a different environment. Here again, I am amid familiar surroundings, among familiar things in my metropolitan apartment. Curiously, the people and events of those years in Aktobe flashed as if in a film series. All meaning another bright page of our biography (brought to us through Maratkali's new friends), provides unforgettable stories and good memories.

This Nauryz broke into our slow-paced lives bringing changes. So, returning to the capital, my creative projects focused on cooperation with the magazine "Youth". A move obtaining membership of the International PEN Club from the hands of Abdizhamil Nurpeisov. Indeed, he filled in the form himself and joked: "your double last name is too long, shall we leave just one, your husband's"? – "But then my father will be offended. Is it hard to bear this double burden of responsibility as such a fragile woman?"

Shadow of the Rain

Of course, Nauryz merely awakens nature. Something accompanied by the sounds of numerous new buildings in Astana. Overall, the capital changes with each passing day. It feels like another city. Only the appearance of the old square convinces me of the reality of what is happening. After all, this new city is located on the left bank of the Ishim river. Its modern buildings similar to frozen glass icebergs, or giant towering crystals, Each one of which transforms the ancient steppe. Commentators have even said they are like the gifts of winter to lush spring - everyone of them heating the imagination. Thus, the new capital mirrors the next generation in its new millennium!

My parents, however, will remain eternal romantics and sentimental dreamers. Similar, in a sense, to snails carrying their unchanging way of life, while cautiously looking around at their painfully partings with familiar foundations. Unlike our children who belong to a different time: with different values and priorities. Indeed, there is a wind of change and renovation blowing.

Each time has its own legends and myths, its idols and ideals, its love stories.

Love is the overarching aim and the unit of true measure in a human life. The mirror of its value and significance.

Love – is a school of hard knocks, with its lessons and mistakes: its discoveries and losses. It is an eternal generator of ideas, as well as the criterion of achievements to each individual person. Hence, listening to the stories of our contemporaries, especially the older generation, I am more and more convinced of its foreordination. In the non-randomness of a chosen path, since everyone on this earth has their own mission, their own cross. On the stellar map of the skies, the route of a human destiny is traced. If one wanders in a wayward fashion, one will come to a dead end – as if in a trap. Clearly, one's intuition (that voice of the heart), is the azimuth in this journey. And love usually comes out as a guiding star.

I was amazed, therefore, by the story of Abek about the war. By his admiration for the poetic hymn of love by K.M. Simon - "Wait for me, and I will return."

For him, love and infinite faith have helped millions of our soldiers to survive in this terrible war. Staggeringly, he felt that through the prayers of friends and relatives, the lives of those who came back from this bloody Hell have been saved.

Akin, therefore, had gone through these terrible years (although he did not kill a single enemy soldier), by conquering the readers of many countries with his words and books. Indeed, the name Abdizhamil Nurpeisov now drew awe and admiration from connoisseurs of the high style. So, by the end of 2006, audiences in both Moscow, as well as five cities in Germany, listened eagerly to the words of our patriarch through his new novel "The last duty".

The fate of the disappearing Aral Sea had excited everyone who had been involved in the magic of this book's presentation: a project on which Abeke engaged himself for many years. Undoubtedly, despite the age of the author, one was struck by his youthful enthusiasm. His look was bright and his thoughts sharp. Moreover, his images were fresh and lush: irresistibly plunging his hearers into the whirl of activities and interweaving destinies of the novel's characters.

Interestingly, the writer was unexceptionally self-rigorous. Contrasting, possibly, with his love for his grandson and his caring attitude towards his wife and daughters - never forgetting, of course, the charm he exuded when communicating with friends. Also, the stories of his meetings with famous people of the Soviet era were fantastic! What names! Only the greatest talents and unique persons.

I thank God for this curious encounter with Abeke, even though each of our meetings was a gift: an engagement with something grace-filled and great. God bless him.

In one of his visits to Aktobe, I got a call from Maratkali wherein he said with excitement: "Senin shalyn keldi! - Your grandfather has arrived". In fact, our Abeke was younger than many of our friends with his young soul! Additionally, the fate of another elder cut me to the heart. Yet, I will not disclose the names of the heroes in this other story of love. Instead, I will outline the silhouette with some telling strokes. Imagining, therein, how those girls felt, who were acquainted with such handsome men back in the days when they were young. To this day, they find it easy to turn the head of any woman, although 80-plus years. All I can say is that this character was a blue-eyed, slender Kazakh, a winner, a sophisticated aesthete ….. the head of a friendly and respected family.

His eldest son bore a remarkable resemblance to his father, but by a twist of fate, they had been separated for many years. However, among certain students, he found his missing half-brother and met with his father once again. Even more surprisingly, their children, grandchildren of one his grandfathers, met in Moscow - where they were students of the same university. Undoubtedly, there is no escaping fate. Explaining why first love came back to this man's life with his grandchildren.

To conclude, an interesting thing happened with my fellow student. His girlfriend was given in marriage to another young man. Years later, the little sister of my fellow student (who studied in Moscow), married the brother of that young man. By some quirk of destiny, their families had intermarried. Here is how fate turns out: their roads had crossed.

But, what is most incredible is the feeling of characters who have been saved over the years by their commitment to theirs ideals.

Shadow of the Rain

Stories of the Herdsman Rakhat

This year winter turned out to be harsh, long, and snowy. So, each soul yearned for warmth and greenery. Indeed, waterlogged muddy yards, broken city roads - splotched with clusters of mud – and surrounding worn out cars were utterly depressing. Yet, with the first warm gusts of wind wafting scent from steppe grasses, so every weekend we felt inspired to leave the city. It was like breaking away from the cloying cages of our apartments to hidden homes on the expanses. The spirit of previous nomads relentlessly calling us on a journey to new horizons.

Our tireless friend, Tazhgali, greeted us on these occasions. Accompanied, as he was, by an exuberant jingling spring world stretching around us like an emerald silk carpet - dotted with tulips and cornflowers. Clearly, these were special moments filled with jubilant sounds permeated by heady fragrances.

Our friends, the herdsmen were happy to see us. Cauldrons steamed, cooks performed religious rites (like in witchcraft), while our Sasha Zhukov led them as a chef. Indeed, he seasoned these foods through his nipping jokes in fluent Kazakh. He also wielded a knife and ladle as skillfully as a traffic wand in weekdays. What is more, as befits a true cook, he was of majestic proportions like a fiery titan.

Overall, the herdsmen were fussing: preparing for a ceremonial review of forthcoming events. Thus, following the arrival of General Maratkali, Erzhan, his eldest son, and I (his wife), they started to address me as a poet.

Firstly, we were taken to a "creche" - Kashar, where young camels were kept. Usually, they are hidden from prying eyes. One of them, however, was a fluffy and frightened beast that was to be given to our son. Obviously, the lad wanted to get a notch on its ear. After all, it was a gift to him from Tazhgali. Said so, its huge eyes, with long, trembling, eyelashes, seemed the same as the big eyes of Yerzhan himself. Hence, they gazed at each other with amazement and delight. He cuddled this warm, downy, lump in his arms. He did not dare to cause it pain, as the herdsmen usually did. Curiously, curly goats fearlessly approached us and licked our fingers, demanding to be held aloft. Meanwhile, their anxious mothers shrank away from overwhelming guests. Following these adventures with surrounding wildlife - and capturing it in a photograph - we went into the yurt, wherein the festival of dastarkhan had been prepared. Drowning in a pile of blankets, eating steaming Surpa and all the delicacies of steppe cuisine, we then listened to jokes and stories from our friends. As guests on the steppe, we were seen as messengers of God. Therefore, we were wined and dined with the best the house could offer - whilst entertained on a noble scale.

Now, herdsman Rakhat handily wielded a meat knife, despite the absence of a finger. He had lost it when pacifying the violent temper of a steppe horse. Relatedly, the father of our "General" had a beautiful black horse, a restive mare in its herd. As such, she excited the young stallions, whilst her protector fought with endless pretenders. That is why this mare knew no peace and was kept away from the main herd. One night, she ran away with her chosen companion. Furiously, her partner rushed about looking for this traitor. Fully alerted, Rakhat heard about these fugitives and set out to search for them: taking food and water. A dozing dog with a worried look accompanied the investigators as they tried to trace the runaways. "Look, Actos!" - Ordered Rahat.

Around the spring, nature went wild. One hot day overwhelmed everyone by its heatwaves. The surrounding silky grass blinded as they shone. All meaning the horses were smothering in a soft, natural, carpet, while their manes tumbled down on golden locks. Similar to washed sheep wool - clouds lazily started off and sailed after the herder. At the same time, inquisitive ground squirrels, standing on their hind paws, stared at the uninvited travelers. They scratched and disappeared into cool burrows.

Oh, the wide spread of the steppe is like an open palm, which cherishes its inhabitants only to suddenly drop them as if from the edge of a flat table. For his part, Rakhat dismounted and released the reins. His dog had found fresh horse droppings and hoof prints. Below in the birch forest, there were anxious sounds from these runaways, in response to a babble of barking. Yet, it would be dangerous to go down straight down because of protruding roots and slippery grasses. Moreover, the roar of the river throwing stones about in its anger could also be heard. So, going down the gorge needed to be undertaken cautiously. Especially

when the granite cliff came into full view, since the
waters plummeted down a steep wall. He had heard,
however, that a small singing waterfall - shimmering
with iridescent plays of colour like a crystal necklace in
the sunshine - cascaded amid safer streams. Certainly,
springs flowed from under the cliff. Features helping
to form a dam swarming with crayfish.

My younger son, Erlan, and I, had been to this amazing
place, wherein they swam in the icy water along with
Sasha. Furthermore, Sasha, armed with flippers and
a snorkel, fearlessly swam among the beds of rushes
and water lilies - as huge catfish tried to escape the
underwater gun in his hands. But, having shot a fish,
he pulled out frightened crayfishes exposing them to
the light of day.

So, beyond doubt, a cold clear river flowed from this
natural dam. In which case, these horses would slowly
walk toward the river, often dropping their heads to
say "hello" to the life-giving waters and plunging into
their coolness.

Rakhat waited, therefore, until they had quenched
their thirsts. Then, he went to the river, drank, and
washed. He was in no hurry. Actos, on the other
hand, tired of barking, perched next to the shore,
before suddenly screeching and diving into the water -
dabbling and gamboling in it. On the mirrored surface
of the dam, viscous waves started to diverge because
of internal movements. A muskrat came up on the
other side of the cliff. Yet, the dog did not dare go
farther and returned to its master. Rakhat knew that
the fugitives were somewhere around, in the bushes

of barberry perhaps? Anyway, they will not run away and it is a good time to swim. He undressed, took off his sweaty clothes and plunged into the water. Cold jets, pierced his skin as fine metal needles. His legs felt a springy pressure. The flow of water enveloped and massaged his numb calves. Nevertheless, he was accustomed to the cold. Hence, Rakhat dived into the dam and started to swim. Immersing himself in the serene intrauterine fetal status he had enjoyed within his mother's womb. Indeed, he washed away all the years of fatigue and restraint until unwilled cries of joy and delight broke from his throat. His horse and dog watched him on the shore with amazement, nodding their heads and echoing the shouts of the herdsman.

Once out on the shore, Rakhat pressed himself against a warm horse crupper and limbered up. Afterwards, starting to get dressed hurriedly. He then perched himself in the shade of curly birch, he had a snack before beginning to prepare for the return path.

Picking up a long lasso, he went to the couple in love - helplessly waiting in a thicket of lush bushes.

"Well, guys, you got caught. It is time to go home". He threw a lasso around their necks, tied it with a single knot bound to the saddle of his horse, and went home. Steppe argamaks - native nomad companions, expanding the boundaries of their land plots and taking their travelers along mountain cliffs (to the pinnacle of fame), protected the peace of nomad camps and grazing flocks. Faithful and reliable friends: one of the treasures of the Kazakhs. In a sense, these nomads merged with their horses, becoming, thereby, a powerful centaur: a mythical creature terrifying biblical people.

For Rakhat, the herd became the meaning of his life. He was attached to these proud beauties, and he knew each horse and its habits.

They are free creatures and do not want to be saddled. It was the reason why the rebellious Tulpar has taken off the forefinger of the herdsman. Thus, Rakhat courageously endured this challenge. It is all in Allah's hands. He respected the horses, and they respected the man protecting them from wolves. Life cannot be without losses, but balances everything by giving the joy of love, friendship, new days, a starry sky, and the loving touch of the lips and hands.

Springtime Outing

We have been waiting for this day for all the long winter and the early cold spring. The Earth, as a raw recruit, looked through thawed snow and last year's brown foliage, exposing its shaved bald head "in Kotovsky style" - to the warm with gentle rays of the spring sun. In some places, fresh green grass had started to arise, as sticky leaves cropped up from turgid buds. Gradually spring started to take up the reins, after withstanding the whims and attacks of old-wife winter and drip-dropping went west. All amid the warbles and chirping of little birds as they started to get louder.

Thence, city was decorated with bright green foliage and red tulips. Multi-coloured flags waved in the breeze. It was May Day Eve. With songs, with bouquets of lilacs - under banners battling the deafening gusts from marching brass bands (with balloons), vivid vociferous streams of people drove through the main streets of towns and villages.

"We salute the glorious workers of the famous plant named after Kirov! Hurrah! We salute our dedicated health workers, safeguarding national wealth - the health of the Soviet people. Hurrah to our comrades, glorious doctors and nurses!" These cheers wafted from the horns over the jubilant crowds of demonstrators. Hurrah Hurrah! This human traffic jam growled like thunder and then calmed down and dispersed. May Day – it was like a solemn chord before a long-awaited moment.

Raushan Burkitbayeva - Nukenova

The next day - the second day of May, every year we would go to the mountains for an outing. "Well, kids, get ready!" – Father told us. – "Tomorrow we will go to the mountains" – "Yippee!" The bus with dad's co-workers and members of their families rolled up to our house. We loaded a large cauldron, water bottles, bags with food and moved off. Dinga, our shepherd-dog, feeling our excitement, also showed his impatience. He thrust his head out of the bus window, catching new and unfamiliar smells.

Leaving behind the city streets, the snorting bus climbed along a mountain road, then stopped in a gorge near a roaring river.

Each of the kids, like multicoloured butterflies, immediately jumped out of the stuffy cabin, and scattered along the mountain slopes. Dinga rushed from one group to another. However, he was afraid of his own bark (which wafted among the mountains), since he knew it would echo from slope to slope.

Unsurprisingly, both children and parents unloaded big bags, arranged tents, spread felt blankets, korpeshe. They additionally unfolded large dastarkhan, covering it with eatables prepared the day before: baursaks, pies, belyashes. Every housewife prepared in advance to give a good account of herself.

Men went to the nearby shepherds to buy some sheep and mare's milk. They bargained over the price and jollied the trader with a pint of vodka. After which they return as if from a successful hunt. Indeed, they dressed the sheep and cooked kuyrdak, surpa, pilaf. Their samovars were also getting ready. In general, these labours hummed along; all proving as noisy as a mountain river. The men, after finishing their jobs, reclined against a pile of blankets, pillows and korpeshe.

Afterwards, they shuffled cards. My father had always been lucky with cards. Undoubtedly, he was a recognized champion. All making his face enlighten with a smile, as his eyes moved gravely. Herein, his mathematical abilities were confirmed, at the same time as he encouraged his teammates to keep a sharp look out.

We, the children were like treasure hunters. As such, we went through nearby mountain slopes and picked flowers and mushrooms. Examining, as we went, every piece of land, every path. After going down to the adults, we also picked something yummy for ourselves and quenched our thirsts. In the manner of climbers, we explored new spaces. Once, holding back from the older children, I saw a snake on the path amid high dry grass. Frozen to death, I started to scream hysterically: "Mum, mum!" My dog Dinga and elder brother Mukhtar came running to my scream. Other boys dragged me to the adults, toward the river. Thereafter, washing my face, my mother allayed me with tea. Indeed, our parents told their children not to go too far away from them. Moreover, Dinga scampered around protecting and preventing every step. Overall, the older boys watched the younger ones then disappeared again. However, we played near our parents until the evening, Following this, we scampered around the slopes. All our mothers were busy with the dastarkhan, of course, and strolled near the river - while the fathers of our families, tired of playing cards, played football and ate cooked lamb.

I always felt sorry for these poor things. "Myaa, myaa" - they bleated plaintively; probably they all called for help from their mothers. I was attached to them, when, shockingly, dad brought one of them home. I fed it with grass and then was very worried when I found out what happened to them ….. and could not eat meat. After all, they were my wards: similar helpless children. I continually cried and got offended at grandfather and father, when they slaughtered a sheep. But Dinga was happy, she would have a feast.

My mum, that said, cooked a delicious kuyrdak and prepared whole pots of golden belyashes. Our family was big. Our grandparents lived with us. Overall, there were five children and a couple of students - dad's endless nephews. Some had finished their studies; others immediately came to replace them - so my mother cooked a lot in big pots - belyashes, jam, jelly. A springtime outing. All among emerald velvet mountains like humps of camels flesh before my eyes. They come from the caravan of memory. Indeed, the heartfelt songs of Shamshi were heard, the voices of our parents, the laughter of our brothers and girlfriends, the barking of our sweetheart Dinga. These were the music and sounds of my childhood. Later, when my own children had grown up, I began to learn the old songs. As if from the spring of my memory, they came up by themselves, probably because our parents often sang them: "You are my song", "On the shore of Arys", "In a boat". Sadly, through the river of time, our loved ones parted from this life. Their voices, their songs, coming back to us in a boat of dreams.

A springtime outing. We have been waiting for it every year, and then thought back to that day for a long time. Every outing was ended with a landing. Father would urge us to do something, such as cut brooms, or load some stones, or sand - it was necessary for the school. Every year he built something: a boarding school for children, a dining room, workshops. He rode on a truck, but the building materials were delivered in his car.

Men, relaxed from clean air and hearty food, started to tease my father. But, he stubbornly forced them to follow his example even though they protested. He was tall, athletic, with an open wide forehead, finely wrought features, delicate white hands and unafraid of menial work. In fact, he enjoyed physical labour and still does - in spite of his age, Nowadays, he is seventy years old, yet still does everything by himself. What tomatoes and grapes he has! Indeed, he grafts and intercrosses everything. All meaning, friends are always teasing him and calling "Our Michurin". I used to go to his school, even though it often appeared that he was not in his office. He would go outside, throw off his suit, change his clothes and go on top of the building to fix the roof.

Principal - workaholic. Unfairly, he was called an exploiter of child labour. After all, he made his own children work in the summerhouse and the children from the boarding school work in the fields; weeding beds, watering plants, etc. We were not really enthusiastic about that, but we followed his example, and when we saw the results of our work, we shared father's joy.

We usually returning home tired, sunburned, surrounded by these boons. Friends made fun of dad: "Oh, Asake, why do not you just relax and lay down, take some fresh air!" But knowing that it is useless to argue with him, every year they cautiously waited for the time he could be approached - some even refusing to go to the outing with him knowing that dad would make everybody work. In my opinion, this was great! Clearly, May Day is a day of solidarity for all workers. Peace, Labour, May! And my father celebrated this holiday the way his restless heart and hard-working hands directed him.

Shadow of the Rain

Epicrisis

To Professor M. Sh. Abdullayev

It is impossible to get used to it, but somehow I have to deal with this. Unfortunately, I am not God's son and cannot work marvels such as healing, or resurrection. Instead, I am just a doctor doing my job - and my capabilities are limited.

Over the years of medical practice, as a student, I used to boil the pot on shifts in an ambulance. Later, in intensive care and surgery, numerous times I had to fight for the life of a patient, be beside someone during their final days and minutes, and then reflect on this sad demise in terse phrases while consoling their loved ones.

I am not a writer to express the depth of human sufferings and tragic moments. Moreover, in real life, there are many more happy moments of victory over disease than there are amid problems. This is where the satisfaction of my work and my striving to improve medical science and art comes from. After all, the majority of surgeons are creators called to heal the body. However, when it comes to the soul, things are often more complicated.

Today, we are serious about concepts of personal and family karma, about fate, the preordination of encounters, diseases, miseries and joys: all forming a successive chain of life events, which we create ourselves.

Raushan Burkitbayeva - Nukenova

Curiously, there is a category of people who love to dwell upon their illnesses. They even delight in their hereditary diseases - such as aristocratic migraine, or gout. They will tell you about the unfortunate sufferings of their ancestors. In such cases, it often helps a doctor to make a diagnosis: especially in atypical malcontents. Although, sometimes, inside the specific symptoms of a particular family illness, a patient denies that his relative had it.

One such episode (from my own medical experience) is etched in my memory. It was in Moscow, where I was on medical residency in one of the clinical departments that determined my future specialization. Throughout days and nights, streams of faces of sick people flashed onwards. For my part, I had to assist in these operations in order to be ready for any surprises in my independent work. The training room, ward rounds, dressing rooms, operating rooms, night shifts – were like shooting out of a canon within a continuous conveyor.

Of course, only severe cases (the details of the operations stuck in my memory), have long since been are erased from memory. This work, after all, is constantly under high pressure; fifteen to twenty operations per week. So, medical cases were written automatically. They passed from the desk to the operating room etc.

Yet, it was during a night shift that one of the nurses asked me to attend the emergency room in order to examine a patient who came from Saratov. Tired from the daily bustle, I reluctantly went for the examination. A young man lay on a bed. Pale faced, framed by red hair and twisted through a grimace of pain and suffering, he lay still. Indeed, his piercing blue eyes, snub nose, along with red stains all over his body, caused involuntary sympathy and empathy within me. So, after examining the patient and gathering the necessary information, I filled out a medical case form. A typical case of severe hereditary disease, although this man denied his relatives had suffered it. Having made the necessary prescriptions and procedures, therefore, I went back to the staffroom.

The next day - during the overall ward round in one of the wards - again the freckled face of a patient with fiery hair caught my eye. This man was in his fifties, while my patient yesterday was 24. I asked his last name, place of residence, if he had a son. He was a Muscovite and he denied the existence of an heir. Yet, the resemblance was striking!

My curiosity washed away any night fatigue. Hence, I returned to the staffroom and looked up yesterday's records, then I asked the desk nurse in what ward the young patient had been placed and went to him.

Among hardened patients (making me wise from experience and knowledge of the intricacies of this disease, along with guidance given regarding departmental procedures), a frightened face of a new comer stood out. "How was your night, did you get settled?" - I asked, looking at the patient. The resemblance was undeniable. His ward neighbours, however, had already told him about it.

Yes, sometimes there are look-alikes or something of the sort. "Well, let's go" - I asked him to go to the dressing room. "Go ahead, be a man!" – his ward neighbours cheered him. The boy shyly hung behind me when, with a downcast look, he contextualized everything. In the twilight of the hall among the bare gray walls, his thin frail figure, dressed in faded pajamas, stood out amid a lush cap of golden hair.

At the door of this dressing room, we bumped into a man wiggling from pain. My mentee and he came face-to-face. Suddenly, both patients froze with surprise and fear. Then they silently and curiously stared at each other. After a long pause, the elder asked his surname, where he was from, after which they drifted apart - having run an eye over each other. The day passed as usual - very intensively when drawing to an end. I was going to the dormitory. "I cannot wait to go to bed, my legs are soar... ". Unexpectedly, someone knocked timidly at the staffroom door and the red-haired elder appeared in the doorway.

"Come in, sit down," - I said to him. With a troubled look on his face, he walked to the table, slowly sat down on the edge of a chair and began to ask about the newcomer and his illness.

Instead, I asked about the state of his health after the surgery. He seemed to be healing well.

Nervously gabling, this man told me a long story about his business trip adventures in a provincial town. All these years, little did he know that he had a son out there.

Ever since that time, he has not heard a peep from the woman with whom he had a torrid, but short, affair. Then he returned to Moscow, having plunged into a routine of life, whereby he forgot about her. He was young, passionate assertive and energetic, while she was fragile. Back then, he had promised to marry, even though he had a family in Moscow: a growing daughter. The name and surname of the boy's mother matched with the girl's that he seduced once.

I mollified the man: "Of course, the case is neglected; it will be a difficult operation, but let's hope for the best." All hunched over, with his head bowed, the man left the room.

Every day that followed, the attention of the medical staff and patients was drawn towards these patients. It all started to feel a little bit odd and I could not help empathizing with this man, or wishing for a good outcome in his operation. They often talked, the elder trying to cheer up his newly discovered kin. Clearly, father and son got close during these weeks in the hospital.

The operation went well. During the whole time of the operation, the lone figure of his father loomed in the hallway. Nurses understanding the delicacy of the moment, anxiously watched him. He, in turn, kept offering his blood in case it was needed. But, he refused to go back to his ward in spite of all possible remonstrance.

All this time he never left his son's bedside, taking care of him. He grew lean and old. There was fear and supplication in his eyes: "Oh, God! Punish me, a sinner, take my soul, but do not take away my child!" Yet, his only son, who, as a ray of sunshine with a smile enlightening the world in those gloomy hospital walls, faded before his eyes. You can endure any pain, but not a heart wound. All his previous pain and physical suffering were nothing compared with those torments lacerating his heart.

Complications developed, which even a young body could not defeat. The best doctors, counselors, struggled to save the young man. Father, frantic with grief, rushed about the hallway, begging professors to help his son. But, doctors are not Gods. They cannot control everything, and no matter how much effort they made, sometimes they are powerless. Sadly, the young man died from complications in the postoperative period.

There are no words to describe his father's torments, his meeting with the mother, who has come to take her son. And I cannot forget this family tragedy.

Every bad case in medical practice imposes on a doctor's special responsibility for their work, for their professionalism. This is a life exam. "Did I do everything I could to the end?"

It has been said that the way to truth and perfection is through suffering. A man pays with his own lifeblood for his mistakes, old debts, and the sins of youth. Yet, sooner, or later, there comes a moment of retribution – a retribution for our good and bad deeds.

Life is like a boomerang, what goes around comes around, good and evil, as the response to everything we have done before.

"Happily, those whose mouth causes them no grief are not stung by remorse for sin", - it is said in the Bible.

Oh, do not mess with love my friend,

Although all young girls are fine.

With our own blood,

We shall pay the debts of conscience.

Sip of Water

"Sister, give me some water"! – Moaned the soldier exhausted by pain and thirst – "Water"! With chapped lips, therefore, he eagerly clung to the damp cloth forwarded by a caring hand. "You cannot drink, be patient, my dear". The fever is followed by a shiver. However, thirst and cold plagued his wounded body. But, having recovered and then having left the hospital, he returned home to Siberia. Home. Yet, who was there waiting for him? There was nobody close to him anymore.

During each stop of the train, he got out of the crowded, smoky, car with a pot to fetch water. He swilled this water, as if remembering his recent painful thirst. Everywhere the taste of water was different. Sometimes it tasted a little bit bitter, almost salty, sometimes it had the taste of wormwood and a marsh smell. So, driving along the barren desert, passing majestic camels, through muddy rivers, he recalled mighty Siberian rivers: especially the Taiga, which generously endowed its fish and all living creatures.

On the third night, his train arrived on Kazakh land. The desert gave a way to the steppe and everything became greener outside. Here were mountains dressed in green velvet and edged with a silver blue fox collar. The faces of women and the elderly brought back to memory the features of his fellow villagers: all giving him a warm feeling within his heart. Nonetheless, he could not understand their language, although women treated soldiers returning from the war, with salty milky balls - Kurt, sweet dried grapes - raisins, camel and mare's milk. They showed them pictures of their sons and husbands in the hope of some news. Conversely, thanking them for this feast, many soldiers were dazed and confused: "I have not seen him, do not know where he is". However, the surrounding mountains stood in silent witness. It is warm in these parts ... In front, the Balkhash Lake stretched out like a blue ribbon.

At the next station, he again went to fetch water. "Please, a drink," – he stopped. A cup of cold water spread as balm in his dry throat. After washing, he drank and drank. It seemed that he had never tasted similar water.

The traveler looked at the girl's face, who gave him this refreshment. She stood before him with raven black hair - separated accurately into two halves - plaited in two thick tight braids. Her slightly slanting misty eyes looked at him deeply. Overall, her neat nose, plush lips, and crimson cheeks, were shaded by a matted skin colour. All features making him freeze as he watched her beauty. She laughed.

It seemed like a silver bell rung in his ears. The water ran out of the pot onto his shirt. But, he did not feel anything as he looking at those laughing eyes. "Do you want more water?" - "Yes, yes," - he repeated, choking with waves of joy that surged across him due to this steppe diva. "What is your name?" – "Makuch". - "You are meeting someone?" - "No" - she said. Indeed, other soldiers stayed on the station, but it seemed to him pointless to continue. The train left without him.

Shadow of the Rain

In these steppes of Kazakhstan, he found his happiness - the most delicious water, a tender wife, whereas milder climes had only offered cold trenches. Thus, he built a house with his hands and all the household outbuildings. In the village, he became one of their own, a respected man. He began to understand the Kazakh language, although smiled slyly when did not understood something. Here his children were born, on the shores of Lake Balkhash. An amazing Lake. One half of it is fresh, and the other - salty!

Some say water goes away from old shores the same way people do ..... and years. His Makuch also left. The taste of this water also changed, now it has become salty, mixed with bitter tears. Apparently, it is no coincidence that this lake has two parts – the salty and the fresh. The same happens in human life, there are two parts, one is sweet and another is bitter.

He planted a birch tree in the yard of his house in memory of his wife. It had a hard time taking root in these arid lands. However, watering it every day, he talks to her about something dear to his heart. Thin branches thoughtfully nodding at him. Ah, water disappears without a trace in the sandy soil. All living things have a rough time without warmth and water. "Do you want more water, little sister?"

Raushan Burkitbayeva - Nukenova

A Ball

The roar of water drowned the cheerful shouts of children playing volleyball near a mountain river. Moreover, the laughter of women sunbathing in the shade of a willow was hidden from prying eyes. Indeed, high thick grasses and caustic jokes mellowed the surrounding men playing cards. Yet, the smell of lamb shish-kebab mixed with a strong fragrance of wild herbs hung as a light cloud over the outdoor grill. The midday heat got drivers drowsy, snoozing in their cars.

The river roared furiously. Fiercely and constantly throwing silver streams on the boulders, as if trying to break them. Cool flying moisture from water splashes, infused with rays of the hot sun, gleamed with rainbow colours.

July - shilde – is the hottest time of the year. The city is attacked by an ardent heat. Even the nights do not bring relief, except in areas closer to the mountain gorges, wherein a heaven-sent cool breeze blows.

Here, at the foot of the emerald mountains, on the shores of the stubborn river, amid friends, a man seemed to have forgotten that his wife is threshing in feverous raving exhausted from serious illness – back in the city. Curiously, all the clocks have stopped in their house, as if charmed, pending the outcome of the disease. Only one small watch, "Dawn", given by her father, measured the march of time in their home. And the river kept furiously roaring, lifting cool clouds of water, appeasing the scorching sun.

Shadow of the Rain

So, not hearing the shouts of children playing volleyball, he was immersed in his thoughts, and suddenly rushed toward the river. Once there, he thought the waves seemed to be playing as they threw a ball (dropped by players), and carried it downstream. Without hesitation, the man jumped into the water. Unexpectedly, strong currents and slippery stones knocked him off his feet. Hence, the ball continued to be tossed in this turbulent maelstrom and flicked out of sight. The man himself nearly got taken down by this furious power. Indeed, he barely got to the shore. However, once he did he continued to chase it. So, jumping behind the wheel, he drove a few kilometers downstream, where the water calmed as if from exhaustion. Then, going into the water, he found the ball and gave it back to the children.

The men, who were playing cards, did not even notice his absence. For their part, the children were delighted by his courage. Meanwhile, women quietly drank wine to the health of their girlfriends. One of them suddenly thought to herself, not knowing what had happened: "If the ball floats away down the river, my girlfriend will not get better: we will lose her" – after which, she got afraid.

By the end of the picnic, the whole company gathered around a table near the boiling samovar. This is where the children told the story of the balls salvation. A woman sighed with relief after hearing the story of her kin: "Do not worry, she will recover, since you caught the ball". The men, on the other hand, looked at each other and, without getting what was she talking about, raised their glassed to toast the health of the hero's wife.

The heat slackened and the city came to life from on its anxious torpour. Returning late at night, the man only then felt pain in his toes. His wife stared at his happy face with astonishment. "You see, I got it, that ball. You will get on your feet. I need you. Our children need you!"

The balcony door opened from a sharp gust of wind, tulle curtains swelled like a sail. Storm clouds came down from the mountains to the city and heavy rainfall started bringing the long awaited coolness. Drooping, dusty foliage flushed with emerald colours. A loving, barefoot, couple was seen running away splashing through puddles.

Shadow of the Rain

Patchwork Quilt

Our reminiscences are islets of dry land. Similar, some say, to mountains of frozen bitter tears washed by an immense flow of time. Each one consisting of elusive, but irreversible seconds, minutes, and hours. They compose a shadowy colossus of stories consisting of a countless myriad of human destinies, events. All disappearing into an abyss inside an invisible whirlpool. So, the hands of a clock relentlessly outline these familiar circles: deepening the funnel, wherein our steps drown. As such, it is getting harder to walk – sinking, as we all do, into the quicksand of time. Each of us leaning over the years from the vantage point of a biting headwind. Go ahead toward the end, to that limit conceived by someone programmed roundabout, until the last exhalation occurs.

Allotted heartbeats are as a measured piece of cloth wrapped around our frail lives. Woven from our experiences, they will wear out over time: even smolder in some places, thereby becoming a sieve or network, which will catch only the most valuable crumbs of our life. Then, it will disappear without a trace, as a column of water through the net of time: evaporating as if one was not there – all this is at least disappointing, unfair, stupid and ridiculous.

Wisdom - is eternal, though often simple and ordinary, without claiming to be great and immortal. It can be the common heritage of humankind, as on stone slabs with intricate ancient texts, which scientists are trying to decode.

Raushan Burkitbayeva - Nukenova

The farther we go, the deeper we go into the past, while persistently trying to rebuild a new fragment of this endless historical mosaic. All in order to experience those exciting moments in the kaleidoscope of lives and achievements over and over again. And the most interesting thing is that the farther we move away from these initial shores, the more persistently and stubbornly we want to go back. How devotedly we feel a reverse loop in our memory by scrolling through this spiral - clockwise. Back to the Future…

The endless searches of inceptive origins regarding "the promised land" - "Zheruiik" - is as the search for truth. The further the crater of history throws stones aside, the harder we collect them and build a "Wailing Wall" against times unfulfilled plans. "Oh, if I could start all over again". Again, we start this way in the opposite direction, rejoicing at other findings as our birthright. Ultimately, any unity of life and matter, or past and present, only timid structures within our plans for the future remains mysterious. Indeed, all of us are superstitious - as the worm that gnawed the apple and, then saw the light of day, becoming frightened. Thence, he hurried back to take refuge in the womb of mother-history. Yes, there are some brave hearts, but this is another story.

Our household history is made by the hands of our mothers and foremothers. Recently, I was in a museum wherein there was an infinite delight at the art works by our great-grandmothers. Clearly, confident skillful hands embroidered wonderful pictures with pink corals, singing a melodious steppe song. This piece of art now breathes with proportionate rhythm, then flashes with bright poppies and tulips: all making the heart beat faster. Afterwards, it rings with the nightingale trill of silver chequered birds and laughs dimly as gray feather grass resounds in a spring breeze. Of course, these corals and turquoises were procured by a warrior raiding fabulous India. A man who fought with Tamerlaine's detachments. Following which, they got polished by a road bag due to a shaking path through the mountain ranges amid loose sand: each piece soaked in horse sweat. They were also warmed by the warmth of his hands on halts. When he touched them, remembering his beloved .....

Stars in the night - a reflection in those eyes,
And only the moon is guiding us.
I will sing a love song for your,
You cannot sleep with longing like me.
That distant fire will heat our Yurt.
I send gentle thoughts to you.
Wind brings the breathe of love,
Sing my song to her - nightingales.

Every stitch was awash with that song. Touching this image, one cannot help feeling the tenderness and awe of female hands, particularly those that had revived these emotions across distant years, like an eternal oath of loyalty and the undying beauty of our ancestors.

Nonetheless, relentless time was trying to turn us into tumbleweeds: a snarl of thorns having lost their roots. But with the help of Allah - and persistent archaeologists, we are not so hopelessly poor and rootless. Certainly, priceless discoveries connect us with distant and truly great times, as reflected in golden armour. Indeed, a royal leopard holds out its graceful paw and, as if from the golden horn of Amalthaea, the guesswork of scientists flows when they examine the curls of this mysterious Capricorn.

That distant world of the ancestors was spiritually more perfect and holistic; as a reflection of this harmony, the creations of forefathers still shine at us. Overall, this is their message and guidance to us - their lost arrogant offspring, immersed in our own trash and unbelief.

Speaking of gold, the recovered General's shoulder straps were embroidered with golden threads - twenty-seven grams each. That is what I found when my husband got them out of the hands of the President. Yes, it is truly not a rank, but happiness from the recognition of one's merits and persistence that count. After all, such things seems as far off as stars... And every stitch of gold in those shoulder straps is the pursuit of a dream: a triumph of justice.

These are not just buzzwords. Such things are gained in silence through courage, as well as days and nights of the endless searching for truth: of defending the weak. Yes, it is a duty. But a duty to the present and also the future. When all said and done, we moderns need to take an honest look into the eyes of our unborn grandchildren. Especially if we seek the right to a well-deserved pride in being their grandparents. Is not this the thing, which motivates us, being this centripetal force, outthrusting from the abyss of oblivion and non-existence?

Days of fate... like grains of sand in the desert under the scorching sun. May the lust for life be an untiring desire to get to the life-giving sources of joy - each gushing as an oil column. Transfiguring, thereby, everything around, which seemed dead and unnecessary until now. There is nothing unnecessary in the world: every why has a wherefore, one just needs to find a reason.

Tired of the supposedly pointless search for the essence of being and our endless worldly demands and needs, wounded and deceived from youthful hopes and ambitions, we remain essentially naked before Life. As such, one faces the strokes of misfortune with bitterness and humbling, falling from the ranks of loved ones.

From the terrible cold of emptiness, the bitterness of losses, we are sheltered by our precious memories. Each one warming us and healing our soul wounds. So, meeting close and loved ones in our ancestral home... in familiar walls, wherein all things are recognizable and speak for themselves in the language of our memory, is a vital experience. Those carpets, which are used to scrutinize or decipher the meaning of ancient drawings thence take on a new significance.

And those patchwork quilts sewed by our mother's hands are likewise. Oh, this is a whole encyclopedia of family heirlooms! Every shred - it is a different story. A whole topic for discussion at the table. These ruminations, of course, come from my father's gray hairs and mother's beige slickers - from the gabardine holiday suit renewed over for decades. Unquestionably, these warm sunny cells were from a poplin suit, while the insets were from coloured silk and satin. Moreover, these indelible bright rich colours are of crimplen and tricotine. Each remnant of which went with notes to warehouses in the Merken District Consumers Union. Thereafter, everyone got everything through connections. Here are patches from Bologna, whereas dad brought us raincoats from the Black Sea. Looking back, we rustled and showed off in front of our classmates.

Now, each piece of tissue was a particle of clothing from past years, which protected us from the heat or cold.

Furthermore, shreds from grandfather's coat and sleeveless jackets made by grandmother for our younger brother gave us additional memories. For instance, this pink piece of cloth was from mother's best woolen dress and knitted suit, while his was of a traditional fabric.

Patchwork quilts are a variation on the theme of nostalgia for the past, which involve the whole family including grandchildren and daughters-in-law. Certainly, the hands of our mothers and grandmother created a gallery of sketches from childhood: a veritable laboratory of our tastes and habits. What is more, similar patchwork quilts, mats, blankets were in every home. They were easy to make, albeit having an informative essence – an infinite source of memories. Thus, they save the flows of warmth, light,, and information, which are cherished in every home. These are the fragments of our lives in coloured picture of life's stages.

Tower over the steppe.

Ancient burial mounds.

An evil wind as a whip,

Shadow of the Rain

Frightened a snowstorm.
Our yurt is covered with snow,
No chance to see it.
A tractor is left by someone.
Is there a change to go through?
Look, smoke, a trace of hope,
A glimmer of duration through thin stream.
Thus, the traveler quickly dismounted,
Wrapping in clothes,
Shaking the tight braids.
Doors, like a book,
Opened abruptly.
Daughters-in-law bustle,
Not hiding their fear.
Guests from that era -
Warrior-aruah*.
Are sleeping in snow mounds.
Listen these prophetic parables,
Of an ancient Koran.

---

* Aruah - the spirit of the ancestors (Kaz.)

Raushan Burkitbayeva - Nukenova

Algorithms

The bus stops. It is a bracing morning with cringing, sleepy, people. Indeed, the long-awaited bus stuffed with passengers, deceitfully draws up and slowly presses forward amid an angry crowd ….. those left behind. Overall, a common situation. In the same manner, time is playing with us - it moves along an invisible path to an invisible expanse according to a schedule. So often, we are busy with our thoughts and deeds, that we do not hear our loved ones, especially the elderly or our parents. Afterwards, we deeply regret it when we lose them.

It turned out that I have not had a heart-to-heart talk with my father for many years too. Both of us did not have time. Study, work, family, distance... He lost his listener in the form of my mother. I remember him reading aloud new books to her, as well as newspapers in the kitchen, while she cooked something. After many years, however, I finally got a chance to talk with dad. He came to me in Almaty. The whole evening and following day, until we got to Sarkanda, I listened to him. He told me about the genealogy of our family (all the old men) whom he knew, He outlined his vision of history and religion. Overall, our traveling companion Khalyk was surprised by the extensive knowledge and agile mind of my father.

- I will keep telling my stories, so Igor will not fall asleep – my father joked.

In ancient times, a terrible governor called skilled jewelers to make an engraving on the rim of a precious ring. It needed to be succinct and concise. Yet, only one master came down to business. Indeed, having completed the engraving, he returned the ring to its owner with the words: "Do not open it. Read it only in exceptional cases".

Many years passed. The state began to weaken. Eventually, besieged by an enemy, the governor was forced to flee. Yet, the road forked. One led to a mountain cliff, whereby fugitives were forced to flee. Their enemy, however, gave chase. So, at the edge of a precipice, the governor reined in his horse and recalled the engraving. Opening the ring, he read: "All things must pass".

After waiting a while, they turned back. The persecutors thought that the governor and his entourage had rushed into the abyss out of fear, but they were mistaken. He returned, gathered his tribesmen and crushed his enemies.

- "All things must pass, we will get over it" – he comforted my mother-in-law with these words. Those who shed tears over your middle son are kind hearted, but you have other children and grandchildren.

He, having lost his eldest son fifteen years previously, like nobody else, understood and shared her feelings.

All things must pass ... but the memory will remain,
The pain will subside and the passions appease.
Only at night, these ghosts will rise.
And an olden time will be returned.
An inquiring finder will find,
The print of eras on the hills.
And a stubborn prospector,
Will find the starting point of a road...

Raushan Burkitbayeva - Nukenova

An earthly fatigue will veil,
The kilometers of worldly cares.
Exposing to the moon a little part of
Someone's joys, bitter adversity.
And again, plunging as if in an abyss,
In endless fated attempts,
Will moan over a precipice,
While waiting for the right path.

Our parents, aqsakals are truly the priceless treasure of every family and nation. Their hard lives, encounters with famous people of a bygone era, their memories – are an inexhaustible fount of wisdom and information. Rashat Shaymardan is among them, as a hero of the guerrilla movement and companion to the legendary Kovpak. They were heroes, combat pilots, feeling more comfortable in the sky than on the ground, Courageous people of high honour and boundless modesty - the legends of our time. Their children, too, have chosen the difficult path of the defenders of our Homeland.

Professor Shadybay Nurgazievich Abdullayev as student of Professor B.S. Rozanov - who went through the mill of Moscow's Botkin hospital with youthful enthusiasm - recalls his meetings with D.Oystrakh, P. Kogan, M. Tynyshbaev etc. Moreover, his children and grandchildren are continuing the family tradition. They have became doctors. Indeed, their son, Marat Shadybaevich, is a Doctor of Medicine. And although an exceedingly modest man, he, nonetheless, has healed hundreds of patients, while his wife, daughter, and brother, are also doctors.

How many deeds of high resolve and heroic actions were committed by our forefathers: our grandfathers? How often did the proud spirit, courage, and broad soul of our peaceful people provide enough spunk to preserve these immense territories?

Well, clearly, Moldakhmet Hanafevich Galimzhanov is among this rank. A military, Party secretary of Denisov District in the Kustanai region who in the past, and in recent years, headed the company "Kazakh tili". A Tatar by nationality, he - with all his heart – defended our Kazakh language: its state status.

Labyrinths of memory in every family keep their own legends, relics etc. All of which is transmitted from generation to generation.

Raushan Burkitbayeva - Nukenova

A Ladle

During the war, our grandfather Tleubay was an oddity in the cafeteria of our local train station "Lugovaya". A reasonably famous location where passengers and people from neighbouring villages would come to eat, or just get warm. As such, it was a landmark, wherein one could hear, firsthand, how things were going along the lines.

Obviously, the trains delivered food, warm clothes, weapons for the front, as well as bringing the wounded and demobilized back – not to mention providing news about the war and long-awaited letters.

It was the spring of 1945. Everybody was waiting for the end of the war. Then, finally, the day came. We had been waiting for this day for so many years and months, but now, "Victory! Victory! The end of the war!" - even Tleubayev shouted this news as he rushed into the kitchen. It goes without saying, of course, that this happy development was spread throughout the streets and excited villages. Thence, universal delirium startcd a great feast.

Suyinshi (a gift) is supposed to be given for good news and, curiously, he got one. He was given a ladle. Strangely, it took a place of honour by the fireplace in his house. Some saying gallons of milk, sorpa, koje were poured by this ladle. Indeed, the caring hands of our grandmothers polished it, making it sparkling clean as the Medal of the Order of Merit for the Motherland. Joyously, therefore, and in sorrow, this ladle was always filling to the brim with boiling broth, or foamy mares milk. As such, it was the family breadwinner.

After the death of grandmother, this ladle went to my elder sister Rose - who kept it as a cherished relic: a part of her dowry. Moreover, as the fable of this ladle passed by word of mouth, from her sister to her daughter Dinara, its fame grew.

Once, the shank of the ladle broke. All meaning, my sister got scared and felt sad - as if she had lost her role as a fostress. Yet, having repaired the ladle, my sister solemnly replanted it in a place of honour. In the kitchen, of course, as a symbol of plentitude, of dastarkhan, and traditions. Our sister also inherited skills in the culinary arts from grandmother Tynda. Along with a quick wit from grandfather. Again, this ladle can measure litres of milk, but equally dishes out time: the continuity of customs and traditions. Thus, may your own ladle be always full and dastarkhan!

Raushan Burkitbayeva - Nukenova

Night Platform

Nina Nikolaevna was awakened by the sharp shock of the carriage. The creaking sounds of wheels, the radio checks of dispatchers, the murmur of sleepy passengers had all filled her compartment. Unexpectedly, the train slowly stopped at an unknown station. Ominously, outside the window, a lone lantern enlightened the darkness. There was no one on the platform. These incidents, therefore, reminded her of those fears surrounding an empty night platform.

Look - the lean figure of Alexei Kalashnikov suddenly appeared in the light of that lantern ….. or so it seemed. He stood there, awkwardly, shifting from foot to foot and holding a bouquet of wildflowers in his hands. For her part, she had been on a visit to her eldest son in Orenburg. But, that week seemed like an eternity. How was her house doing without her? So, after a number of excuses, she finally wanted to return home. Ah, she secretly felt relieved when handing over baskets of goodies. Indeed, she pressed against her husband's bristly cheek. How are the kids, the grandchildren? Her heart started to beat smoothly again, She could sense that all was well.

They have been together for more than half a century. Nina was six years old, when her mother died. Father tried to marry twice, but none of those women could replace her mother. Recognised so, she lived three years in an orphanage, then at her grandmother's place. After all, there was a war going on. Happiness, however, smiled upon her through the blue eyes of

Alexeim when she was eighteen. Indeed, she eventually gave birth to eight children. Overall, living a difficult, but happy, life. Relatedly, Alyosha was a handsome man, Clearly, many girls had tried to hit on him! Yet, he appreciated order, cleanliness, and honesty. Hence, when the children organized a party in honour of their Golden wedding, these values came into their own. But fate had other plans. He should have lived to see another birthday, except for the fact a disease came out of the blue and depleted his strength. Sometimes he would complain about his helplessness. At others, he did not want give up, or seem weak to his wife. Nevertheless, he shriveled and life flickering out. In which case, feeling few worries (because the children were around to support his wife), Leshenka passed away.

Obviously, the children started to ask her over - to allay her grief. Nowadays, she goes to Almaty to see Galinka: to give her grandchildren some marvels from the capital. Curiously, ever since her husband died, she had become interested in everything. Hence, she spent entire nights thinking back to her previous life.

Their first date. Their small, but cheery, wedding. The birth of their first child. Each a vivid scene popping up one after another through the rhythmic rattle of wheels - like the sound of a pendulum – striking and profound.

Their granddaughter muttered something in her sleep. Yet, the train eventually shuddered and got under the way. Leaving, of course, a lone lantern and platform. Tears ran from her eyes. After all, a lone figure with a bouquet in his hands was somewhere out there. "You will wait for me. Someday I join you and we will be together again" she said to herself.

Currently, my grandchildren and our younger daughter are expecting me. A thought which cradled Nina Nikolayevna. She mused that we were all passengers and each has his own terminal station. Some will get there earlier, some later. Nonetheless, while the green light is given, everyone moves forward. These trains carry us into the unknown, to new meetings and partings. This is life is all about.

Shadow of the Rain

Aybar and Zholbars

Dedicated to my first-born – grandson Aybar

Another day flowed from the ocean of time. The morning of the spring equinox, when the length of a day is proportional to the night. Following which, the fiery igniting stellar body is overshadowed by the forces of darkness - until Nauryz comes.

Then, together with the first rays of the sun, a new year enters into every house: every corner of the earth, awakening life, renewing all living creatures. Indeed, the Great Steppe anticipated this wonder as a bride!

Meanwhile, among unscalable cliffs belonging to those Celestial Mountains of Tien Shan (in the lair of the snow leopard Irbis), a little kitten, Zholbars, was born like a spark from the morning star.

Now, a snow leopard is extremely rare, almost a mythical animal. A beast whose royal grandeur and dazzling beauty is similar to the glaciers of Khan-Tengri's peak. Indeed, such as event rivals sipping from the life-giving waters of a mountain spring.

Hence, the crystal tops of Trans-Ili Alatau, similar to a sparkling crown, obscured these mountain ranges and cliffs. Curiously, they hid behind the lush brilliancy, preserving the peace and quiet required by Gods and snow leopards.

Unsurprisingly, mum-snow leopard gently licked her peeping cub. All meaning, elastic waves of milk (in swollen nipples) burst with tenderness - as sticky buds on soft mammalian paws. Each awakened from a long pause after hibernation.

Also, age-old blue Tien-Shan spruces and birches welcomed the birth of this small leopard, cheerily rustling on revived slopes, while at the foot of these majestic mountains - in their sweltering polluted valleys below, the city of Almaty stretched in its construction fever: as colourful as a patchwork quilt.

A few festive white yurts, like small copies of those rocky peaks, unfolded their domes between the palms of squares and parks. The mountains, on the other hand, as well as the city, were awakened by the sounds of a many-voiced chorus of folk instruments and performers. Indeed, anyone following this rapid, heating, Kuis, felt incited by the suggested flavours wafted around. It seemed that they hovered over steaming cauldrons, with their gurgling hot fat, wherein golden baursaks swelled like tennis balls. All accompanied by welling and steamed pilaf puffing as in Saka baths.

Overall, rainbow tulips and irises shyly bowed lush blossoms, even though annoyed by excited bumblebees on the slopes. Additionally, energized spring winds gusted with a wedding veil of migratory birds. Perhaps they knew they were carrying southern warm currents of love and music to the very heart of the country - into its new capital, Astana.

Each mountain, therefore, echoed repeatedly with sounds resounding amid gorges. Every one of them a song of happiness at the birth of a young leopard.

Thusly, they flew over to new cities, to young families as heralds.

Truly, a secret flame of Life kindled under the heart of the future mother. So, from this spring of Light (nine months down the road), at the end of December, near Baiterek, the long-awaited baby was born: who was named Aybar.

"Oh, Tengri! Umai"!

You have heard our prayers! Bless our kids!

"Hello, Aybar"! – gnarled Zholbars welcoming him from the mountain heights through the steppes expanses.

Now, it was the year of the Rabbit and Cat according to the eastern calendar. Hence, the current year was coming to the end. In which case, young families celebrated the New Year with their sons in an unusually quiet and reverential manner.

No one, however, can speed time! In which case, the harsh winter had taken its toll - with its severe frosts exceeding 40 degrees, and snowdrifts retreating reluctantly. Each one acting like an aging diva ..... attracted back to whistling and hooting youths.

Again, the heavenly bodies heralded the coming of Nauryz.

Over the year, therefore, Zholbars witnessed this blind kitten turning into a beast with a strong, firm, body and a powerful tail. With a steadfast gaze (like a laser) he looked for a trophy. Indeed, he was already a "king of the skies and high mountains", whose warm silky fur was highly valued. Yet even this monarch used to decorate the clothes of khans and shamans.

Raushan Burkitbayeva - Nukenova

So, mother-snow leopard had taught him all the tricks of hunting roes and argali. Also, she had shown him how to blend in with the dappled shadows of dense juniper, hide among boulders, and pause with anticipation before attacking prey - all under the roar of falling streams. As such, laying in wait appeared to be the secret of rapidly overtaking a victim: one only needed to jump faster than a speeding bullet to knock it down. Thereafter, reveling in the hot blood gushing from its throat.

Indubitably, a snow leopard is always patient and careful! Above the clouds, or among the insurmountable steeps, this mysterious beast merged with both snow and clouds: becoming like a ghost, a legend. A tale retold by experienced hunters and shepherds.

Certainly, Zholbars fearlessly jump over bubbling waterfalls, flying, as they do, through chilled streams like a sonorous arrow. Yet, they are not afraid of any abyss, nor dizzying cliffs, or prolonged frosts and snowstorms. Hence, they called the beast celestial. A mammal who could be seen by only a few chosen people: angels and, perhaps, children in their fantasies. Eventually, Aybarchik turned three months. After which he wanted to visit his grandpa and grandma in Almaty. Their house was located at the foot of those same mountains, in the snowy mountain passes wherein the lair of the snow leopard was located and where the Zholbars were growing up.

But, in the yard (falling asleep in a stroller), their baby serenely smiled at these Zholbars, who appeared in his dreams and visions. Thereafter, he stared at the passing clouds and the distant snow-capped peaks. Every adult watching the eyes of the child, trying to figure what was he looking at.

"What a serious boy!" they commented. However, Aybar, bent his brows and turned away from the admiration of adults. "Why isn't he smiling?" The boy looked narrowly into the distance, drooling and laughing. This was the way he communicated with Zholbars. Nevertheless, they eagerly played with the baby. They said he was similar to a sunbeam – guarding him during his peaceful sleep. Indeed, they flew together over the mountains and valleys to the Sun and Moon. Meanwhile, wise eagles accompanied them in these flights, dreams, visions.

In his first dream, Aybar and Zholbars were the children of Light!

They did not like darkness. So, reflected by the multifaceted peaks of mountain ranges and the rays of the setting sun and the rising moon, these Zholbars found their sleep illumined within the caves. In his dreams, kid mingled with solar and lunar bunnies and glided through glittering glaciers, before being whirled up high in the sky - to the abode of spirits.

In his second dream, Aybar and Zholbars were born together with a song, a melody! "Nya Nya" – the cries of a newborn baby, or the mewing echoes of a kitten. Albeit, without shouting and crying kids seeking the attention of adults. All meaning, when Aybar was seven days old, he heard the song of his sister for the first time. Ah, she sang to him for more than an hour near his cradle. When she stopped, he insistently cried, trying to make her continue the melody. Interestingly, this song marathon lasted for an hour, while the baby was still awake!

When he turned three months, he gladly sang along to his grandmother. At the same time, Zholbars lamentably whimpered: asking for milk from his strict mother. However, he learned from her how to silently and patiently listen to his own breathing – until he became as invisible as a shadow. Waiting for prey, for the right moment to attack argali near the waterhole. Thereby, every dawn they became stronger and more mature - as if they were going to meet each other in real life.

In his third dream, Aybar and Zholbars were born for action and journeying!

All of them loved to swim. Water was their native element. Even in their mother's womb, they were splashing like fish. Predictably, Zholbars fearlessly crossed the untamed mountain river after his mama-snow leopard!

Simultaneously, when Aybarchik was three months, he could swim in the bath – rising like a float on an inflatable balloon to the admiring shouting of his relatives. Yet, bumping against the rubber ring with his flushed cheeks, while pushing off with his legs from the bottom of bath, he easily applied his little hands as a turtle. Unsurprisingly, Aybar and Zholbars in their dreams and fantasies raced to cosmic distances.

In his fourth dream, Aybar and Zholbars were inseparable friends!

Certainly, they became friends long before their appearance on God's earth; they chose their parents themselves, as well as their ways and destinies. Once the future parents of Aybar (on the eve of the wedding), came to the monument of the Golden Warrior. Indeed, they observed the tradition of urban newly-weds by crossed his hands in a ritual gesture and make a wish about things to come. While this was happening, the angels Zholbars and Aybar were watching them from their celestial heights, and at that very moment, Aybar chose this young couple to be his father and mother!

Fascinatingly, all newlyweds of the southern capital come to the foot of the monument, where they make their dearest wishes known before heaven.

What is more, the young man dressed in golden armour, who stands on a winged snow leopard, appeared in a dream to a famous sculptor, which he then depicted in the statue standing above the city of Almaty.

All implying, that the first year of Aybar's life was racing by. Thus, when he grew up and confidently walked alone, each of them would come to the square to thank the creator for a dream come true.

For his part, Aybarchik curiously looked at the sculpture of the Golden Warrior firmly standing on a winged snow leopard. A figure floating amid the vast expanse of the heavens, while amusedly recognizing himself and his old friend.

These legendary, mysterious, snow Zholbars will again hide in the tops of the sparkling mountains, while watching them will be his friend Aybar awaiting new flights among the discoveries of a fairy world! May the Great Tengri bless their way!

29.12.2011

Raushan Burkitbayeva - Nukenova

In the Southern Garden

(Fairy tale)

Blizzard and Frost had wonderful hard-working children, whose names were Blizzy and Frosty. They had fun together and danced in the surrounding snow, as it coated fluffy snowfields, roads, trees and houses with brilliancy. It was almost as if they were sheltering everything on the ground in a warm blanket - both frozen lakes and rivers of ice crystal.

Winter moved from North to South, where after the family of Blizzard and Frosty reached the southern mountains - at the foot of which there was a large orchard. Now, young agile Blizzy dropped into a garden enfolded with silence and became amazed by the slender brown-eyed Southerners – apples, apricots, cherries, plums. Indeed, they stood with their eyes locked on the ground, marveling at the generosity of the young rakes, who gallantly laid soft such fluffy carpets and threw light white coats on their shoulders: shimmering with the brilliant shine on the sun. Having finished work, therefore, the fervent and restless Blizzy remembered they both had slender big-eyed girlfriends: birches with whom they danced in the north and exchanged secrets.

In which case, vying with each other, they started to ask frightened these southerners for a dance, but each of them modestly refused. It seemed no warm lace scarves and shawls, nor high snowcaps and ermine collars (which they generously offered to these

463

dumbfounded prudes), could shake them up. Hence, they shouted, "We dance alone once a year, when we put on our wedding outfits, - yet, our protesting girlfriends became confused by the attention of young good lookers. Thus, we are free". Some replied, "Is this completely true"? Maybe, we can come over afterwards. Perhaps, we will dance with you then. Blizzy felt indignant. "Yes, yes" – he whispered to himself.

Now, an old apricot tree, groaning with gnarled branches, overheard this dialogue and began to grumble at these young beauties: "Silly girls! Do not you listen to them; do not tell them the flowering time. Their frosty kiss will kill your fruits".

But, having yielded to the charm of persistent, gentle, and caring boyfriends, the young silly trees revealed the secret of flowering time. "It will be in April, from new moon to full moon".

Nonetheless, winter retreated to the North. Having said its last goodbye. Hence, the last March frosts were leaving behind him.

The ice cracked, rivers came to life, floating blocks of ice started melting. Clearly, the gentle sun warmed up the earth: cheerfully drip dropping his jingles from the rooftops. Moreover, the first snowdrops bloomed in thawed patches wherein the green grass gleamed out from under the heavy snow slush.

Eventually, spring with its warm and gentle hands took up the reins. All meaning the family of Blizzards and Frost had gone. Yet, a matured Blizzy was in love with southerners and, kissing them goodbye, promised to return on a date at the appointed time.

Raushan Burkitbayeva - Nukenova

It was getting warmer every day. Trees woke up from hibernation. Tight buds swelled on the branches. Tender green leaves covered their shivering branches and paths in the southern garden were covered with emerald carpets. So, revived and improved in appearance, the darkies – trees of apples, apricots, cherries and plums prepared for the major event of the year - flowering.

Finally this long-awaited day came! Pink buds opened in the morning on thin flexible branches. Wedding dresses that charmed passersby with their splendour and beauty.

However, in the far north, Blizzy was still in love with the apricot and tore around, although his stern father would not let him go south.

"Wind, Wind! You should fly with rain to the South and give my greetings to my beloved. My friend, ask her for a wedding dance. Give her a kiss on my behalf!"

And a favourable wind sent these greetings to Blizzy's beloved, blossomed, apricot as she waited in the southern garden. Ah, tender spring rain also asked her for a dance and twirled her in its gentle embrace. Therefore, pink rain on quivering petals spread on the bright green grass as a train.

"Thank God, this fellow Blizzy did not come! We will have fruits this year", - rasped the old Apricot tree looking at her dancing with their young neighbours.

Of course, in the full moon, flowers blossomed on apple trees. But, cold crept from the north as a rebellious Blizzy came back to this southern garden. Thereafter,

465

the tender apple trees in their wedding clothes stood awkwardly waiting for their cavaliers.

"Oh, you are so gorgeous and stunning" - exclaimed Blizzy, asking his beloveds for a dance. At that moment, white snowflakes mixed with delicate petals. Indeed, a white-pink blizzard whirled around the garden, scattering the fragile flowers across green paths.

"Silly apple trees! This year you will not have any apples", - rasped the old apricot tree looking spitefully at the cold kisses of an enamored Blizzy dancing with enchanted apple trees.

The Spring Ball in the southern garden ended. Every day it got warmer. Soft fruits ripened on the branches of the apricot as it poured with the sweet juice of memories from its wedding dance. However, the sad apple could only recall her regrets. Next year, they will not tell their secrets and the exact date of flowering will be hidden.

Yet, life goes on. There will be more winters and springs...

Raushan Burkitbayeva - Nukenova

Tulpars

The whole caboodle gathered at the summer pasture near the Tolganai river toward the evening. We were lucky; we were met by Tazhgali in Kandyagash. The rest of the guys traveled half a day on the steppe in jeeps that are off-roaders. These vehicles can only furrow the blooming steppe when it was painted by bright colors, soft and fluffy, like a bride's dowry.

If this heat remains, within two weeks all the ground will burn and will be as ugly as a large bald area amid once lush hair.

Curiously, the whole steppe was pitted by sharp ground squirrels, which stood on their hind legs and keenly surveyed any intruders driving their terrible machines. Some were so bold they refused to run away.

By the evening, near the trailer of herdsmen, iron tulpars of friends gathered. Each flashing with silver bumpers and farsighted headlights.

After thirsts had been quenched with fresh mare's milk, the travelers exchanged the latest news and discussed the advantages and benefits of every vehicle imaginable –especially regarding their bells and whistles. Meanwhile, in the city, an ominous car was the calling card of a man. The plate and make of the car determining the status of its owner.

Therefore, the attention of all the owners of these iron tulpars - vehicles attracted to clouds of dust became diverted. Indeed, like a team of horses coming from the horizon, they seemed like a dark spot, which blurs and takes on its own shape, Each of these machines speaking mechanical volumes. This may be why their paints are becoming more distinctive – ranging from spotted, to piebald, and flame-colored. In a sense, the entire team went to a watering hole. All meaning, Asaukul's golden vehicle led the team, with its mares and foals -by teaching them to trot obediently after their mummies.

A silver-gray stallion named "General" led his monstrosity sideways, jealously looking around at another "white horse" and goading his family.

Herein, the whole team of about a thousand heads entered the lake and quenched their thirsts - choosing clean ducts.

Meanwhile, on the other side of the lake, men were standing mesmerized by this picture. Afterwards, they skirted the lake and climbed the dam, before beginning to approach the team. Two of the most courageous town folks, Victor and Rakhmet, made a move in a middle of the team. Therein, these horses quietly passed people: parting to one side - and making it seem they did not notice either the vehicles, or stallions, surrounding them. So, keenly guarded by their families and taking advantage of the oversights of neighbours, they advanced. All causing a merciless fight, which whipped huge waves of indignation among overly peaceful spectators. Clearly, two young mothers who had just foaled that day tried to stay with their newborn foals. After all, they could barely stand on their thin legs.

Each horse has its own vice, character, equivalent vehicle, and patron. Thus, near each stallion stood its beloved and the foals they had bred together.

Moreover, each team had its own hierarchy and laws. A fact determining the number of conquered beauties. As fiery leader, Asaukul stood in the middle of the team. His neck being gently pinched by the red mare proudly glancing at the other attendants.

Cautiously, therefore, General stood away from crowd. It was quieter and safer this way. Although, when the time came, he would be in the centre of the team with all the best mares near him.

Nowadays, seasoned men, as boys, discussed the habits of horses. Never forgetting, of course, about their iron tulpars. Furthermore, each of them imagined himself to be the leader of this team, and, as in children's fantasy, reincarnated in these horses to show off in front of a large number of mares. Predictably, each saw himself as the fastest racer: "I am the most worthy, the most powerful and fast!"

Every one of them had his own distance, his own victory, his own top and his own conquered women.

As the clouds are reflected on the surface of a lake, in the same way men are reflected in these vehicles: these horses. All of them being unique, free, and as proud as centaurs.

Night Fairy

The hottest days of summer came. Draining, sultry, midday was exhausting. The body and head becoming heavy and numb. Overall, it would be good to lie down on a cool floor and crawl away somewhere from the stinging and merciless rays of the Sun. Indeed, turtles and snails are so lucky to have their own heaven sent homes. They can bury themselves in the coolness and freeze for a while. However, when the ruthless heavenly body leaves its throne, only a soft pink sunset offers anyone hope: fanned, as this is, by a long awaited freshness. Nonetheless, all living things were beginning to return to active life. With renewed vigor, everybody was getting down to their usual business, as if in afterthought. The world was reviving. Although, the night was filled with mysterious sounds and rustles. Ah, the starry nights of July. Those stars, unable to withstand stress, fall into an abyss like a dotted line in the sky. Therein, night beauties open their beautiful eyes. In recognition of this, the surrounding crickets burst into sonorous crick-crack, while graceful Roe Deers rush to their watering. Interestingly, garrulous cool brooks bring back vigour and strength to these exhausted animals.

After taking a shower and washing away the daily fatigue, therefore, in a light sundress (like a night fairy), Irina froze in front of her canvas. Mysterious sounds wafted from the open window, as a round-faced Moon let her silver curls down. The breath of a nocturnal breeze bringing fever to inflamed clay-walled cottages.

Indeed, she knew the narrow streets of Khiva would find flesh in her memory at these surroundings, while the invocatory cries of the muezzin resounded from the dome of a minaret. Each of these events like an antenna. Now inspired, she allowed confident strokes to paint their first marks.

Oh, the sweet-veiled Orient - these plaintively stringy sounds of songs. Ah, the narrow streets wandering like thoughts. Ooh, mud walls twisted on the ground as a maze, even though everything was hidden from prying eyes in the Mahalia*. All is monotonous and colourless. Yet, these are only its trappings.

Let's take a look inside this kingdom, she mused. Inside its windows opening onto secret courtyards. Into the shadow gardens mantled by vineyards and flowerbeds: as though a wonderful angel sank into a pile of silk blankets and pillows on a trestle-bed. Certainly, green tea quenches thirst, but not the thirst of her hot heart. Thus, throwing a dark veil across her head, she glided like a light shadow over these serpentine streets. The silver of her jewelry jingling in the excitement. Yet, as if spellbound, she hurried to meet her fate. Neither the laughter, nor whispering of the neighbouring old ladies able to restrain her. So, she glided to a date as a gentle ray. Although, near the ancient plane trees, her beloved perpetually waited for her on the shore of a noisy river.

A silent companion-moon illuminated this thorny path. Oh, poor girl, She broke into perspiration, while her heart was anxiously beating. Why, why ... Night will cover one's secrets with a starry blanket. This is it.

The painting is ready. She will live her own mysterious life inside it.

Letting her hands down, Irina moved away from the canvas. She examined her creation. Putting aside the brush and quietly walking out of the studio, she again sat on the ground and become a woman. Tomorrow, I will go to the market to buy vegetables. Children will come for lunch. The rhythmical snoring of my husband will happily echo in our bedroom. Hence, perching nearby, she fell asleep to the familiar sounds of home. The poor man was tired; he spent all day in the Summer House. What should I cook for lunch? God, what a stuffy heat... I want to go to the Carpathian Mountains...

---

* Mahalya - district in Uzbekistan

Raushan Burkitbayeva - Nukenova

Bouquet of Daisies

How naive and arrogant are people when considering themselves to be the kings of nature! How noisy and fussy! What vanity. Obviously, a bouquet of field daisies is elegant, beautiful and meaningful in its graceful silence. Clearly, the wind shakes tender stems. Everything is simple and brilliant. Indeed, every room is illuminated by their appearance. Moreover, at this moment, a field of daisies is the queen. All eyes would be on her. Silently, therefore, they would strike through the soil reaching for the sun. Then, having opened the umbrellas of their flowers, they would look at the world around them without asking for anything - and so on every year. They come just to please our eyes, decorate our fields, our meadows and roadsides. Poppies, bells, dandelions - all of this close-knit crew arises century by century without complaining - even if there is only a little rain. How much wisdom nature has! Just to live and offer enjoyment is enough. And we little people, are ridiculous compared to them. Asking for things all the time. Why cannot we just bring joy in silence? Ah, we scream and cry when being born, demanding attention. Indeed, we invent things to get away from our natural being. Yet, is not it easier and wiser - to be oneself? How many of us make this world better?

Field Daisies

Ah, field daisies. They have so much tenderness, natural beauty, and purity: a 'touching innocence! Today young girls have very little of such natural beauty. How much needless make-up and disastrous bad taste do they need? Nowadays, they walk around almost naked. Yes, I am old-fashioned. The less an enamored boy sees, the more fantasies he has. Permissiveness kills the romance of teenage years. Where are those tresses, cheeks, veils, fishnet gloves, fans, letters, notes? All is simplified and vulgarized.

I feel sorry for our young folks. Life is devoid of old-time vibes. Apparently, it is more likely to be felt by that famous couturier. Indeed, they are increasingly returning to the silhouettes of the past. Corsets, hats, multi-layered transparent garments and mystery. Returning to our young creatures their original charm and mystique of magical hands.

The less a woman is available, the more she is respected. There is a place for everything, and everything has its place. The same includes dressing. Maybe I am conservative. I just want my children and grandchildren not to be deprived of romanticism, adolescence, and first love. Women, do not hurry to reveal your mysteries. Take a look at men - they are wiser than we are. In traditional English suits - elegant and full of dignity. That is something to think about.

Raushan Burkitbayeva - Nukenova

Rose of Winds

My Alma-Ata. This city is like a garden at the foot of the Alatau. It is like a patchwork quilt made of pieces, squares and neighbourhoods, with houses separated by asphalt roads. All the seams (after a winter muddy season) that get thinner in pits and potholes. However, each time someone gets into those pits, dashing riders remember our "city father". Now, this is not horse-drawn transport, which disappeared from the streets of our city long ago, but something other.

Hence, this velvet patchwork is an area in the centre - around the Academy of Sciences, whereby the famous writer, actor, laureate and statesman lived and worked... Ah, blue spruces and mighty oaks line up in a guard of honour along these sidewalks. Moreover, laid back gray-haired old men and tidy honourable old ladies solemnly sit on benches, while their grandchildren romp around. Here, under a rank of jasmine bushes, flock stylish boys and girls. All dressed in leather coats, jeans, caps and bandanas: rollerblading, and chewing on "Sugar-free Orbit". Hence, the "new" Kazakhs replace old-timers in this area. Furthermore, they stealthily approach the entrance hall on Mercedes as they boldly look around such gloomy doorways. Thereafter, the rattles and sounds of saws are heard from the windows of their apartments. They want to have a major overhaul and redevelopment, while older residents (used to polite manners) look at these nouveau riche settlers with confusion. God, what an outrage and impertinence. What if these ceilings cannot stand firm and we find ourselves in our beds, but on the floor below. Oh, reckless youth. They do not respect anyone! They intend to hide the elderly in historical museums. Who would have thought that Dzerzhinsky and Lenin would not a find a place in the squares? They used to be leaders and idols, not to mention immortals. Yes, mellow seasons for pensioners are over. Instead, inhabitants of the lower floors are being resettled in other neighborhoods. Here, however, they open beauty salons, restaurants, and offices.

In other neighbourhoods of workers and intellectuals, numerous flea markets, as well as special stock markets are being opened. It is like a rabbit-warren. However, ordinary folks need to subsist and to survive. This is a cotton patch soaked in fuel oil and sweat.

Yes, the "fathers of the people" and children are different now - independent and stupid. Furthermore, the outskirts of typical neighbourhoods are full of atypical buildings - palaces for "business" folks. In other words, a "Fantasy World" for architects - like Luxembourg, although without paved roads. Oh, the city is growing and changing.

A wind rose – with winds blowing in different directions at the same time. How can this be represented graphically? Maybe, it can be seen at the direction of flying leaves across the trees? Perhaps, it can be imagined as a paper kite? Ah, the wind rose as a whirlwind of airflow, a cheerful carousel with horses running in Gorky Park. Ah, the wind will blow in the desert and hide around the corner. Only beautiful roses will stay in our cozy and warm city. Then, the wind will scatter the citizens throughout the city as petals who will settle in different areas - velvet, silk, cotton...

Ah, this wind rose in the Rose City with its fountains and beds of roses. Certainly, a rose is the favourite flower of Almaty.

Rose, my elder sister is vulnerable. There is nothing unusual in her appearance, but she is very sensitive, kind, although full of fantasies. I would have given her a yellow rose.

Aunt Rose Komratova. A velvet black and maroon beauty similar to a fatal love. Oh, the intoxicating aroma, mysterious smells, dazzling appearance. Spikes shield her from treacherous men and unwanted girlfriends. She - a queen from birth. Clever, witty, graceful. She is a true rose.

Aunt Rose Kabylbekova. She is a white rose. Sometimes cold, sometimes tender. She would always offer something to eat and drink. An excellent hostess. Very neat. Yet, as stains are visible on a white cloth, in the same way weak spots appeared on our aunts body. Now, she endures them and erases them from life. I wish you strength and courage, dear snow-white rose.

All roses from Karaganda are blue roses. They are rare and amazing. Each one similar to a wonderful doctor, housewife, or restless mother. One is very gentle. The other impulsive. Ah, Akimzhanova Rose taught us histology after defending her dissertation. On the other hand, Zamanova Rose was busy with patients with infectious jaundice at the Department of Infectious Diseases. Sadly, they both burned out as candles: melted within a blue haze. But, our niece was one of them - little Sophie. As a fellow student, she also became my friend during my happy college years. "Do not be a bluestocking" – she taught me. "Do not forget to offer thanks - even for a little thing" – she taught.

Ah ha, the lilac rose. A flower known for its tenderness, aroma, fragility, beauty and mystique, it easily reminded us of our beloved aunt Raisa Urazalievna Dzhandosova. Overall, a mysterious stranger, she descended from a dizzying patriarchal reality. A milky, reverent, and sweet Duchess.

A simple red rose. This is my friend Rose Rakishevna. She was a doctor and an obstetrician-gynecologist. Moreover, she worked in the maternity clinic now associated with women's secrets. Indeed, Rose was a funny, but serious person: a responsible and amazing mistress, not to mention a mum. Indeed, she loved red dresses and red lipstick. All of which suited her well - because men went crazy about her. Thus, a red rose is the symbol of passionate love. It is equally a torch of Friendship. Overall, our crimson rosette will warm and cheer.

A penultimate pink rose. She was a square rose. This was our Rosa Malikovna. Some said the shades of all colours were blended in her. Certainly, she was very cheerful and tender. Fragile, truly, but resistant and wise at the same time. A wonderful and good advisor. The top of all roses.

Lastly, it needs recalling that the yellow, burgundy, white, blue, purple, pink and scarlet roses form a rainbow bouquet of gorgeous colours. They decorate our lives, the city, the Earth. May rose beds be planted in their honour. After all, flowers and women are the soul and face of our cities. Hence, these seven roses must never fly away with seven winds, Scattering, thereby, the seeds of life and beauty.

Shadow of the Rain

Half Asleep

The wind... it can take different forms. After all, the long-awaited coolness following hot evenings in the south of Kazakhstan is a friend. Moreover, mountains guard refreshing and bracing winds. Indeed, sometimes, strong hurricanes blow in the south. Yet, on the steppe, a number of winds blow across these open spaces at any time of year. Occasionally, they rage with such ferocious force, that they make everyone shiver. They may even enters homes: no matter how thick one's walls. Also, they can keep howling at night. Showing, thereby, who is the real owner of a place.

At one time, we lived in Semipalatinsk. It was there, that we met these winds. One night, covered with two blankets, I could not warm myself. So, I tossed and turned until I finally fell asleep. However, my blanket had slipped to one side, and I felt cold again. Suddenly, I felt someone's warm and soft hands sheltered me, pushing me under the blanket. It was such a miracle of warmth. In the morning, I thought of those hands. Apparently, it was mum. Only she had such hands. It has been two years now since she passed away, but she will be with me forever...

Raushan Burkitbayeva - Nukenova

Stones

Since my childhood, I love collecting stones. Probably I got this from my mother. One day she brought stones from the south, worn away by the waves. They even smelled in a special way. She then sang a quiet song about the land swell: sometimes even the song: "Rula te rula te rula... la la". When we went to Talas to swim with dad, all these beautiful stones were more than our eyes could take in! Indeed, they had sparkling rainbow colours. Some, of course, were veined with mysterious signs, which only became visible once dipped into water. For their part, my brothers chose flat round stones and let them skip on the surface of a river. They were competing as to who could throw it further.

Certainly, wherever I was, I would always take some stone as a memory. They carry the energy of a place – unlike Alakol, Borovoy, Turkestan, Zhidebay ... each a place in the north where the soil is loamy with no stones.

Stones can talk, foretell, and heal. In my collection, there are also stones from my home yard. When I am homesick and feel sad, I hold those stone in my hand. This relieves my sadness. Undoubtedly, when touching this treasure numerous precious and vivid pictures flash into my eyes. They give me power. It is beyond doubt that days pass by as river water, while these stones remain as memories bearing the traces of bygone stories. Oh, how impressively they keep silence...

Shadow of the Rain

Green Branch

The Kazakhs have some very expressive names. For example, Talshybyk means the branch of a tree. Yet, such name tended to be given to a favourite daughter, who then grew up thin and flexible as a reed. Hence a green branch, or young shoot, was flexible and soft (there is such a saying in traumatology).

Our fathers have special feelings toward their daughters, a very tender and reverent feeling. They do not kiss them. They just sniff their foreheads, like flowers. Nevertheless, they protect them from hardships. After all, who knows what the lives of their sweethearts will be like? Indeed, my dad still pokes his nose into my forehead whenever I come home. "Eeeee" – is a short word for Kazakhs.

In early childhood, I once came down with a sickness. Every day my dad would come to the hospital and stay with me. However, the doctors could not help and I got worse every day. Oddly, my sickness lasted for a long time. All meaning, both parents grew lean and exhausted. My ward mate, seeing all this, told my father to hand him a green maple branch. "Break it in half and the child will be done with sufferings. You are young, you will have other kids".

Obviously, dad backed off from her with a glare. He then took me and mum from the hospital and drove us home. Following our journey, an old women who lived near our apartment was consulted. It was common knowledge that she knew about folk remedies and incantations. So, my father told my mother: "Go see her - maybe it will help." Now, that old woman cured me, although I grew fragile and delicate. Thereafter, my father spoiled me most out of all his five children. Even now, I am the first to eat strawberries from his garden. "Let Raushan eat it", - he would say out of habit. All causing my elder sister Rose to laugh, "Again she gets all".

They claim every tree, every bush in the yard, was planted by my father's hands. His vines form a hedge along the house. Thenceforth, I learned to look at these green flexible branches of grapes (which grasped iron pipes with spiry tendrils stretching up to the sky), and the heavy emerald clusters hanging from them as souces of inspiration.

Grape leaves hanging over us,
The four of us sit at the table.
And around are the flowers like our mother's eyes,
Without her, our ancestral house emptied.
A precious machine stands in silence,
You sewed clothes for children on it.
And it was a coveted forbidden lure,
Of playful reckless undertakings.
We have grown up; we are in our forties,
Our children are growing up.
The island of happiness - our dear homes.
Our close ones are waiting for us impatiently.
Grape leaves, as mother's hands -
Will hide from rain and sun.
Fidgets frolic around - your grandchildren,
And weave wreaths from daisies.

Neighbour

Loaded with bags, tired after work, I am slowly walking upstairs towards home. Another stairwell... a neighbour's cat Manya waits for me at the front door - curled up in a fluffy ball. While I am trying to unlock the door, she gently rubs against my legs. "Well, come in". She pompously crosses the threshold of the apartment and goes to the children room, and then she goes to the hall and lies down on the windowsill to bask in the sun. The apartment of her owner is on the north side, so she comes to us to lay on the sunny side and sunbathe, chew some green leaves from home plants, and take a nap before the arrival of children from school.

Its transparent tender ears remind me of rolled white calla flowers. "Manya, where are you, come help yourself" – I call her. She slowly approaches the saucer, eats, gratefully rubs against me and purrs. Again, she pompously goes to the hall to her favourite place: a chair to take another nap. Hearing the doorbell, she runs first to meet our children. The cheerful romp of twins wafts from the children's room - of the son *Kuanysh and daughter with Manya. "Mum! – my daughter Nurgul* runs to the kitchen - I have composed a poem about Manya".

A little cat,
Sits by the window –
This is Manechka.
She wants a spice cake,
And she plays with us.
A little cat,

Raushan Burkitbayeva - Nukenova

Sits by the window,
Narrows her eyes,
She loves fairy tail.
She plays in the splashes of sunlight.
Come over here, shouts everyone.

Manya seems to be flattered. Having done this courtesy call, she scratches the door of our house and leaves the apartment "Murr", - she hums - "Well, buy, see you tomorrow."

"Hope she will not forget to grab something tasty on the way home - I think to myself - and she will be waiting for me. She is also a living soul, requiring attention and care".

----

* Kuanysh - joy (Kaz.)
* Nurgul - shining flower (Kaz.)

Shadow of the Rain

Everything should be where it belongs

She had nimble and subtle hands. She always completed everything in time. "Never put off till tomorrow what can be done today", - she told us. Indeed, she managed to take care of 10 people. All between classes and her infinite plans and checking tests. Additionally, she had to take care of us and the garden. Hence, she got very irritated whenever something was not in its right place, especially scissors. "Everything has its own place". Tangentially, Marigolds swayed along the ditch with yellow brushes of inflorescences. Mum used to pick and dry it. She bathed children and grandchildren in its petals to prevent allergies and prickly heat. Moreover, she grew aloe and celandine in pots. She collected peach pits, using them as an astringent. Clearly, she had plenty of such secret recipes. Picking seeds was also one of the rites. Each being gathered, packaged and marked. They were a whole pharmacy - and are still used by us today. "You forgot grandmother's cure for thrush in Almaty" – rages my son.

In the summer, I often went to my father's in Jambul. As usual, my nephews were gamboling in the yard, playing with toys, then piling them in boxes. Yet, Alshees* should be put in a bag, but sewn by a Apashka*. Equally, "Scissors need to put into their place: otherwise apashka will be mad" – said my nephew Bakhyt to the new owner of an old house. Dad and I looked at each other, and our eyes were filled with tears of sadness and tenderness. Everything remained in its original location, although mum was no longer with us.

Raushan Burkitbayeva - Nukenova

Now, Bakhyt* - mother's favourite daughter, looked at us with a sternly familiar look, while quickly piling scattered toys in a box, Thereafter, she climbed on the fence and began to survey the familiar quiet street: stuffing herself with juicy ripe berries under the shade of a cherry tree.

A high lush rose bush planted by mum, still languidly sways and emits sweet fragrances. As if its bright petals, cheeks, and lips were those of our ruffian. Furthermore, our whole family sits at the table under the vines, drinking tea, Dad sits at the head - Tor* since its vine leaves protect him from the hot sun. Overall, it feels so good to be at home, when we are all together. A place for everything and everything in its place.

---

* Alshees - dice (Kaz.)
*Apashka – grandmother (Kaz.)
* Bakhyt - happiness (Kaz.)
* Tor - a place of honor (Kaz.)

Maryam's Song

The hall was buzzing like a beehive. All making the delegates cheerfully greet each other. Moreover, the best representatives of Kaskelen region were gathered in the building of the district Cultural Centre for the report-election conference.

As such, delegates' registration and the issuance of working papers was in the lobby. All meaning, lovers of bibliographic novelties crowded in the bookstalls. Hence, trays of sandwiches with red and black caviar, sprats, cakes and piles of pastries were lined up in a makeshift buffet – while each of their glasses reflected the bright light of surrounding chandeliers. Indeed, young graceful waitresses in starched apparel seemed to freeze with anticipation, as delegates from remote farms hastily drank mineral water at high tables.

Bravura marches resounded in the hall. The rings of duty men were sounded. After which participants took their seats according to the plan. Overall, the room was filled with a festive atmosphere. Employees from every organizational department were bustling: alerted, as they were, to the significance of every speaker. So, under the applause of attendees, their President took his place. The anthem of the Soviet Union then played. The Party Conference was opened. Everything was going strictly according to the rules.

Gradually, the festive excitement gave way to a business mindset. Thus, criticisms were voiced and retorts arise from across the room.

Making myself comfortable, therefore, in the last row near the column, I watched the others. Certainly, an article about this event should land on the desk of my editor tomorrow. As such, I had planned an interview the brightest representatives of the district, although it was difficult to remain unimpressed by each individual's speech. Generally, of course, this is a common assignment: a portrait by a contemporary - the first service test of a young journalist.

From the very beginning, however, my attention was caught by a vivid personality. A tall statuesque woman in a simple, elegant suit. Overall, her movements were full of grandeur, while her proud bearing, piercing eyes, and confident voice, were the traits of a clearly outstanding persona. Without question, her whole appearance asked to be captured by a portrait with a golden frame. Unsurprisingly, perhaps, she had a type of Kustodiev beauty, even though her mature femininity was veiled by a business-like manner.

Since I was a newcomer to the district, I asked who this beautiful stranger was. "Are you serious, came the reply? That is the secretary from our district committee, Maryam Bespaevna Zhuyriktaeva!" Still uncertain, I learned more about this fascinating woman until my curiosity was satiated. "Oh, what an exceptional woman - and the way she sings!" – Additionally, I found out at the same conference that she should have been born a man, what a batyr she could be! It turned out that she actually was a direct descendant of Batyr Nauryzba, about which I learned much thereafter.

Astoundingly, she proved a harmoniously blend of beauty, strength, spirit, femininity and charm. Her character attracting people like a magnet through charging them with a powerful energy. I thought the legendary Tomiris would be similar to her - the one who managed to decapitate the King Cyrus. A woman-warrior: a fearless amazon, but still remaining vulnerable to treachery and the meanness of men. Nevertheless, gossip had it that our representative was a caring mother and grandmother, not to mention a loving sister. Indeed, when talking about her loved ones, her eyes moistened with emotion.

Strangely, if I compared my first impressions with my more recent vision of her as a state officer (a member of the supreme authority), she equally shone. Except that her eyes grew sad, while her look became wiser.

In the years since, I continued to watch this woman. Furthermore, the more I got to know her, the more I admired her. Yet, can these kinds of amazing women ever find a decent man? Probably only in their dreams...

As the sedate speaker's voice buzzed softly in this stuffy room, I unintentionally fell into a doze. My endless travels having a narcotizing effect. Suddenly, noises, cries and shouts awoke me to a different scenario. Now, it was dark with troubled voices around. "What a mess, where is the Director of the Electric Service, where is the phone?" – people shouted. It turned out that the lighting had gone. The fact this had happened during a party conference seemed like some kind of sabotage. The noise surged up. This situation lasted for quite a long time. Nevertheless, in this uncertain environment, a confident female voice thrilled from the presidium. "Comrade Delegates! Calm down, stay in your seats. The problem with the electricity will be resolved soon; people are already busy with it. Thence, I ask all of you to support me". Unexpectedly, she started singing – the Secretary of the District Committee Maryam Bespaevna. Her deep voice with its nice timbre drowning the waves of excitement ….. since the familiar melody was recognised by all the delegates. Peace returned to the hall. But, having finished one song, she started another. Her heartfelt melodies calming the dark room. In some corners, the light from surrounding fireplaces shimmered within each singer's eyes - forging a mysterious unity of spirit directed by the confident voice the Secretary.

Soon the light went on, but the song did not stop. Everybody sang standing like a well-orchestrated choir, albeit under the direction of Maryam Bespaevna. Obviously, the actions of their leader received well-deserved applause. After all, this was the most remarkable event of the conference.

In a dark room
Your voice is flying.
It will shatter our confusion.
A magic fairy,
Is leading us -
Here is the unity of spirit and feelings.
Through the dark shadows
We make our way to the light.
In one impulse.
We all smile at you,
Bright-eyed beauty,

Shadow of the Rain

All fears were groundless!
Often in the wear and tear of life, in dark days and sleepless nights, I see my singing Maryam. It chases away the gloom of the night and gives me confident hope in a better future.
Or all of them are stuck in the last century.
Let one of them break out from the library a book
To overcome this river of time:
Poets, glorify this woman!

---

* Takyr - bare ground (Kaz.)

Raushan Burkitbayeva - Nukenova

Eternal Flame

A passion for fire is set in our genes. "As if a bright light, I direct my eyes to you ..." Each baby stretches its little hands to bright things. Over time, it will gain more experience with fire through pain and tears, but the magic of living flame will magnetize its entire life. Of course, matches, lighters, et al, are essential attributes inside the pockets of all boys. Moreover, fires in kitchens and the playroom, or on balconies and in the yard (when forgetting about danger), demonstrate that lighting a fire is a primeval instinct, Indeed, subduing and taming this element is always more than boyish mischief.

Bonfires on dzhaylau in a night gorge, wherein roar the mountain rivers opposed cold and involuntary fears: clothing the fragile bodies of sentinels as they cling to the warmth and smell baked potatoes. Moreover, they scare invisible evil spirits hiding in the darkness. The light of the bonfires even sends signals to distant bright stars, which stand their guard in space.

Additionally, every new capital is richly decorated with garlands of lights at night. They cheerily wink to tardy passers-by as the latter hurry home fully enamoured. But, these lights also become exhausted, while the electrifying of our lives during busy days adds an artificial acceleration to events.

A motorcade stopped on the road near a fire by this river. Someone had forgotten to extinguish it. As for the fire, it seemed to be pleased to see the traveler. Its flames danced with joy - flying up into the night sky: reviving each interrupted conversation across time.

A cheerful flame sparkles in the dark,
An ancient memory awakens in the soul.
And it seems someone is dancing with a torch,
While painting a picture with a fiery brush.

Blurred signs merge into the image -
A familiar face...
Cheeks as poppies...
Walking almost touching each other,
Eyes igniting with the fire of youth...

The traveler knew this magic of fire was fascinating. It allowed warm thoughts and memories to merge before dissolving into the hushed river. Strangely, through this sonorous and clear silence, the nearby rivers deafening roar resounded as a machine with the noises of steam and gas. It seemed similar to a revived fire-breathing Aydahar – a dragon from ancient tales, which tried to swallow stubborn young men entering its hellish inferno. Some deftly wielding a crowbar like a spear of Batyr.

Thereafter, a fierce battle was fought. "... I will die here, get burned, but I will never let people bad mouth me!" Occasionally, these warriors even won this ordeal. But there were still more hardships ahead.

It is hard to always be ahead of the game. So, glancing from the fire to the sleepy river, the traveler saw the outline of a new capital - a city in a new era on the shore of this resurrected stream. At that moment, fire sparks echoed as fireworks: each scattering like a luminous bead. "Be careful, you can get burned!" -

A warning shout brought the traveler back to reality. "You scared the hell out of an old metallurgist!" – grinned the traveler.

Yet, the bonfire (as if in a dream), silently burnt out and vanished into the night fog. For their part, the vehicles continued toward the suburban residence of the President.

Oh, an eternal flame is burning. It was first kindled by a firm hand in an ancient Promised Land - in Jerusalem in memory of the victims of the Second World War. May it become the personification of an inner fire: the heat of people's hearts as they open to each other.

Shadow of the Rain

Water of the Memory

Carnival, the beaches of Baradero ... a fabulous world festival sailed away in the waters of history, while legends arose near guitar sounds as a sparkling fountain of fireworks flared and faded. All is like a mirage left behind by our ship. Around us now, an endless expanse of blue water. The emerald outline of Cuba, fading as a misty apparition into the distance. Indeed, our XI World Festival of Youth and Students sailed into history. We are coming home.

Initially, we needed to find our sea legs. We felt dizzy from sleepless nights and exhausting bumpiness. Only cheerful dolphins (an honourary escort) accompanied the ship "Georgia." A ship similar to a cheerful town - the hostel of the Soviet delegation setting off on the road homeward.

An overflow of multilingual talks wafted around the decks. Indeed, young people from Georgia, Armenia, the Baltic States, Central Asian republics and Kazakhstan are returning back.

Our group is a melting pot – including Marina Lomidze from Tbilisi, Fatima Batieva from Tskhinvali, Muazama Khodjieva from Tajikistan, Eugene Ilyin from Chuvashia, Lena Kobakhia from Sukhumi, Augusta Pinigina from Yakutia, Nurlash Zurbaeva from Aktyubinsk, Gulnar Syzdykova from Tselinograd and Raimondas Buzyalis from Lithuania.

Assuredly, our whole life was planned after the festival; each hour of the day being scheduled. For example: August 10, 1978. Sports day.

10:00-11:00 - Discussion Club "Youth of the planet is tempered by struggle".

11:00 – boat drill.

12:00 – sports tournament.

15:00 – volleyball team competition.

21:00 –sports and gaming evening.

22:00 – movie "Draw Game".

August 11, 1978. "Dear October". A club with interesting meetings. "We remember those who are steeped in legend".

August 12, 1978. 60 years of Lenin Komsomol. A meeting with delegates of XVIII Congress of the Young Communist League. Themed night "Time, Homeland, Us".

Indeed, we live in a busy rhythm as our ship moves along its given route. Today we are passing across the Bermuda Triangle. Having heard intriguing stories about this mysterious place, we all fell silent - anticipating some kind of incident, but everything proved normal. Everything except for photos from the stands, which had gone missing; apparently, the delegates had something to do with it. Yet, the ocean exhibited its power! Everybody then recalling the sad fate of the "Titanic". Unarguably, despite all the advances in technology, people remained vulnerable to natural elements. Yet, thank God this danger was minimal, even though there were still hundreds, even thousands, of miles to the Soviet Union.

August 15 – an "Invitation to the table". Talks covered etiquette governing the setting of a table, recipes etc.

17:00 - competition "Miss Young Lady". Followed by a meeting with notable cruise participants.

August 16, 1978. 18:00 - arrival to the port of Ponta Delgada, Azores (Portugal).

An excursion to the island. Indeed, we heard that the port was founded in the fifteenth century by King, Don Pedro Nastroyan. Also, we learned the population of the island was 30 thousand people and the name of the island means "green island". Overall, the terrain is mountainous; corn and tobacco are grown on the slopes. Streets in the city are narrow and stone-paved. Buildings have inscriptions, slogans, a Nazi Swastika. Assuredly, soldiers with machine guns and malevolent faces are around the port. Truly, this is a corner of paradise, but we do not feel any warmth from local residents. After all, we are young communists for them - their enemies. Hence, we are in a hurry to leave the islet.

So, we climbed the stairway and swept through the town with sadness. But what is this? A motorcycle roars: there are shouts by police officers. A tanned young man approaches our delegation. His face illuminated by a big smile framed by long locks. He excitedly says something to our children - who have not yet ascended the stairway. Then he gets out a trumpet and begins to play a familiar melody ... I cannot believe it - it is our "Katyusha!" How is it even possible? Now, all delegates are curiously watching from the boat. The boy, now performing tricks on his motorcycle, has tried to play our "Katyusha". Thus, our hearts were gladdened, while the delegates found their understandable stress removed. Unarguably, over two thousand Soviet citizens - the passengers of the ship "Georgia" were pleasantly surprised and gladdened by the warmth of a local boy who had arranged the entire performance in this port. Thereafter, each of us was no longer in a hurry to leave. Instead, everyone was fascinated by this daredevil, since it seemed we had a genuine friend here with a fearless heart. Thus, we started to sing along to the sounds of "Katyusha" - "apples and pears were blossoming, mist glided over the river ..."

Of course, the ship eventually sailed away from the port of Ponta Delgada, albeit to a dear song, "So long, our brave friend. May God give you happiness, come see us in the Soviet Union!" What will happen to him? We anxiously peered into the contours of the fortress-prison on a high mountain. Yet, the song of this lone trumpeter cheered us up and brought us together, because we are all children of one mother - and our Motherland is waiting for us.

A festival of the Union Republics started on August 17. Days for Georgia and Armenia. That evening "I love you, my native land".

August 21 - the day of the republics of Central Asia and Kazakhstan. We prepared beshbarmak and baursaks. We sang native songs, danced, told stories about our lands. Only our stops and tours in Barcelona and Istanbul were particularly interesting after these exchanges.

August 25, 1978 20:00. The ship "Georgia" moored in the port of Odessa. Hooray, we are back in the Union. We are home!

P.S. On the first days of the festival, I lodged in "Leonid Sobinov" a motor ship. I shared the cabin with a young, graceful violinist from Alma-Ata - Ayman Musakhodzhayeva, a student of the Moscow Conservatory. Nowadays, we live and work in the new capital of Kazakhstan, Astana. She – the People's Artist of the Republic, World Artist, and Rector of the National Academy of Music. How small and interesting our world is...

Raushan Burkitbayeva - Nukenova

Nagashy

Betpak Dala. An uninhabited wilderness. Its soil cracked from the heat, charred by scorching dehydration and drought. A land of defeated hopes. Oh, Betpak is brazenfaced and stubborn. As such, it is easy to get lost and stray from the road on the bleak steppe. After all, there are no guides here. But what is this, a mirage? A lone tree (like a silent guardian) reminds its surrounding there is life and shelter somewhere. Each observer dragged to this spectacle, since it stands with outstretched gnarled branches as if in supplication to the sky. Its bark turned bronze from wind, heat, cold, and crisscrossed streams of bitterness.

Of course, Saxaul is the sacred tree of the desert. Ribbons from various fabrics hang from its wiry branches instead of leaves. Each traveler having tied a ribbon there as a notch. A method by which the spirits are addressed. They are physical hopes and prayers – ways of asking them to send people water.

Mukhtar, my older brother (a drillmaster), knew the harsh character of the desert. His crew dug wells and paved channels: thereby giving a future to villagers. Clearly, they were greeted with respect and joy everywhere. So, when the current route passed through the Bostandyk village, we instantly realized Nagashy lived there: a fellow Parimbek, the brother of our grandmother.

Walking waist high through the dust, Mukhtar got to the house of his Nagashy. Mynasyp apa and met him in the yard. The latter was fussing over a samovar, although her bright emerald eyes lit up with joy on seeing a companion: - "Amansynba, Zhanym!" – "Hello my dear!"

Interestingly, in the cool room on a pile of blankets, sat Parimbek ata. He had a giant stature, an aquiline nose, piercing eyes, as well as a proud bearing and stiff mustache and beard. It was said strangers were afraid of our stern grandfather, but to us - the grandchildren of his sister - he showered nothing apart from tender care.

However, when he came to our city, our grandmother started to act strangely – giving a hard time to our grandfather Burkutbay. Yet, we were allowed to ask for anything, because Gien (the children's sister), should be indulged in every pleasure. It is a Kazakh tradition – nagashys are the most kind and caring fellows. Having compassion for their sisters, they spoil their nephews.

When I used to study in Karaganda, grandfather came to visit me. He appeared in the lobby of the new building of the institute as Batyr, wearing a wide velvet coat with a fox backing. Indeed, he had a fox malakhai with a handmade bag and a stick in his hands. Obviously, my grandfather was a very flamboyant man. So, when he saw my picture on the board of honour, he started to poke it with his stick: - This is my granddaughter, where can I find her he asked those around? As for myself, I was just walking out of the lecture room. Fellow students called me: - "Come quickly, a formidable old man is looking for you out there"!

– "Nagashy, how did you get here"?

– "I came here to see you. I brought some goodies from the village".

"Sudyn kasieti sagasynda. Adamnyn kasieti nagashysynda" he crooned. "The value of water – is at the mouth of the river. Thus, the dignity of man is in his wife's relatives". Continuing, he stated, "Agashtyn kasieti sayasynda" – "The worth of the tree is its shade", whilst whispering "Yydin zhaksy bolu agashynan. Zhigittin zhaksy bolu nagashydan", or in other words, "a house is good when made of wood. All the good traits of a dzhigit coming from a mother's relatives". Truly, scholars have observed that subtle creative elements are passed through the maternal side. At least according to Kazakhs. Meanwhile, each mother encourages these traits in their children: whether singing, or a gift for versification, eloquence, wisdom, or wit.

Nagashy's voice was hoarse like the voice of a manaschy, a Manas narrator. Moreover, he was very strict with his kith. Alternatively, my nasyp apa was a white-faced women with personal secrets. How she managed to keep her skin white under the burning sun no one knew. Either way, she was sedate in manner. But our grandmother, Dildakul was noisy. Undoubtedly, mum had a hard time with her. She was quarrelsome and fractious.

Mukhtar held a magazine, "Women of Kazakhstan", with my photo on the front page. I had been a Delegate of XI World Youth and Students Festival in Havana. He showed it to his grandfather: - "Oh, my darling"! - Grandfather wept. "Hey, kempir*, bring some karakul furs here. This is for our daughter-in-law, and that one is for our granddaughter, so she will not freeze in Karaganda". He also gave a gift to his nephew after hearing this good news. Without question, Zhaksylyk would kill a sheep to celebrate. Hence, he ordered his son to perform the deed. So, at the home of nagashy, the whole crew of drillers rejoiced with pride along with grandfather.

My grandparents are the life-giving oasis of my childhood. They gave me strength for my future life. The warmth and tenderness emanating from these old men melting my heart and giving me peace of mind amid life's troubles. Looking back, their love proved a reliable shield against enviers. In which case, their departure from this world was analogous to the withering of a sacred tree on the edges of Betpak Dala. Particularly when it stands on the border between life and death, between truth and lies, hope and disappointment, love and hate, between past and future.

---

* *Kempir - old woman (Kaz.)*

Raushan Burkitbayeva - Nukenova

Patriarch

Dedicated to Abdizhamil Karimovich Nurpeisov

Under the cone of a reading lamp and growing blind from fatigue (among yellowing stains on the paper sheets scattered across the desk. Each one of them flecked with fine patterns of letters like granulation and watermarks), lies the motionless shadow of a griffin.

Phrased differently, the gray-haired word painter-zerger* in a greasy quilted Chapan* with some kind of old scarf, or molded handkerchief, rolled around his head like a turban, could be seen bent over his manuscripts. Here, under a narrow circle of light his two offspring found space: the novel "Blood and Sweat" and "There was a day...".

"The snow", he penned, "dry and scratchy, kept lashing from a shadowy sky. It whipped and burned faces, making eyes watery when someone tried to get into a collar".

Yet, an August evening, as warm as fresh milk was drawing on the district: each of its moments making its way into the office of the writer. Here stars (unable to withstand the heat), fell down from their boundless orbits and drew up a black screen with fiery strokes ..... before going out into an unknown abyss.

"Look what we have here! I think it sounds very well". So, tracing with a ballpoint pen as if it was a pointer to the text of the printed book, he cogitated. Indeed, the latest draft (when its sounds were compared by ear, by touch, by colour and subtle flavour) allowed this tutor to strictly look into my eyes, and begin, slowly, to sort out words and phrases. Again and again, re-reading them aloud, he enticed me like a jeweler, or a venerable Swiss watchmaker, to make full sense: with every gesture fit for purpose. Indeed, each syntactical point g]needed to grind every word, comma, interjection, emphasized or eased emotions - not to mention incentive accents – all making the melody of murmuring speech.

-"Do not look at your watch". He caught my sidelong glance: my fidgeting – he chastened me. "Listen carefully"!

– "Abe! I think it would be better to replace the phrase God knows... with gracious God. It is a succinct and historically meaningful phrase".

– "Write it down, you have found the right one. Write it directly in the book".

– "How? Can I" ?

– "Write, he said"!

– "Do you like the verse translation of this song – its appeals to the Mullah*"?

Having read the text, I overcame fear and shyness in front of this great writer and wrote my own version of these transcriptions from Kazakh into Russian. All of them full of sarcasm and bitterness: each a fragment recording (albeit in an ugly form), the moments of our existence.

Slowly, cruising around, that golden eagle circled an immense cloud before widely spreading its powerful wings. Catching dense streams of wind, it then dived into the problem without losing from its sight the issue at hand.

Unarguably, looking at the venerable old man from the side, with his beak nose, deep-set eyes and grasping crooked fingers, I felt like a featherless yellow-beaked youngling in an eagle's nest: nestled on the edge of a granite cliff.

At that moment, uncaught words couched on a dusty thicket of tired wormwood. Knowing the temper of my patron, however, to be similar to a sharp blade mercilessly cutting entire sections from a novel, I anxiously waited for a response.

Confessedly, my thoughts flew beyond his office. I recalled my family was waiting for me to have dinner with them. Yet, how could I interrupt my teacher?

In himself, the writer was immersed in inaccessible spaces like an oceanographer. Over and over, he lived the fate of his heroes. Similarly, perhaps, to a hauler fisherman pulling a leaky net across the seas wherein every living word flapped like a fish until it fell back into the abyss of a silent ocean.

Oh, the music of the skies as it overturned the Aral Sea. His novels made it tangible to us.

Nowadays, he is like the wiry, petrified, saxaul. A tree keeping the warmth of the earth and the heat of the scorching, merciless, sun in its bark. Nonetheless, wise traditions rigidly stand as a shield against every lifeless desert: sizzling, as they do, amid quicksand and yellow vipers.

I was afraid to voice my teacher's age. Til, këz - Tasca! Afterall, both word and look can be reductive.

Yet, he is in his 90's. So, may God bless him with longevity and health. His nation is immortal and alive, as long as our elders, aksakals, and the creators of words are among us. They are like minarets ….. beacons of light in this troubled world and thoughtless ocean.

---

* *Zerger - jeweler (Kaz.)*
* *Chapan - outerwear in Asia*
* *Mullah - a Muslim priest (Kaz.)*

HERTFORDSHIRE PRESS

Title List

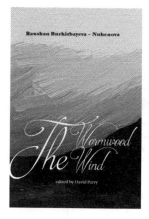

The Wormwood Wind
Raushan
Burkitbayeva- Nukenova (2015)

A single unstated assertion runs throughout The Wormwood Wind, arguing, amid its lyrical nooks and crannies, we are only fully human when our imaginations are free. Possibly this is the primary glittering insight behind Nukenova's collaboration with hidden Restorative Powers above her pen. No one would doubt, for example, when she hints that the moment schoolchildren read about their surrounding environment they are acting in a healthy and developmental manner. Likewise, when she implies any adult who has the courage to think "outside the box" quickly gains a reputation for adaptability in their private affairs – hardly anyone would doubt her. General affirmations demonstrating this sublime and liberating contribution to Global Text will prove dangerous to unwary readers, while its intoxicating rhythms and rhymes will lead a grateful few to elative revolutions inside their own souls. Thus, I unreservedly recommend this ingenious work to Western readers.

HARD BACK
ISBN: **978-1-910886-12-0**
RRP: **£14.95**

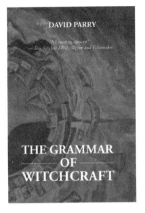

The Grammar of Witchcraft
David Parry
(2016)

In this collection of Mini-Sagas and poems, Parry narrates the final journey taken by his alter ego Caliban from the surreal delights of a lesbian wedding in Liverpool, all the way back to a non-existent city of London. In himself, the author is aiming to resolve lyrical contradictions existing between different levels of consciousness: betwixt reality and the dreaming state. And as such, unnervingly illogical scenarios emerge out of a stream of consciousness wherein bewildering theatrical landscapes actively compete with notions of Anglo-Saxon witchcraft, Radical Traditionalism, and a lack of British authenticity. Each analysis pointing towards those Jungian Spirits haunting an endlessly benevolent Archetypal world.

LANGUAGES ENG
PAPERBACK
ISBN: **978-1-910886-25-0**
RRP: **£9.95**

The City Where Dreams Come True
Gulsifat Shahidi
(2016)

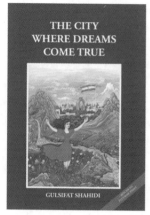

Viewed from the perspective of three generations, Shahidi presents a rare and poignant insight into the impact which Tajikistan'sterrible civil war had on its people and its culture during the early '90s. Informed partly by her own experiences as a journalist, these beautifully interwoven stories are imbued with both her affection for her native land and her hopes for its future.

The narrators – Horosho, his granddaughter Nekbaht ,her husband Ali and his cousin Shernazar – each endure harrowing episodes of loss, injustice and violence but against all odds, remain driven by a will to survive, and restore peace, prosperity and new opportunities for themselves and fellow citizens.

LANGUAGES ENG / RUS
PAPERBACK
ISBN: **978-1-910886-20-5**
RRP: **£12.50**

Crane
Abu-Sufyan
(2016)

In this remarkable collection of prose poems, author Abu Sufyan takes readers through a series of fairy tale scenarios, wherein are hidden a number of sour existential truths. Indeed, from the bewilderment felt by anthropomorphised cranes, to the self-sacrifice of mares gallop-ing towards their (potential) salvation, all the way to the bittersweet biographies experienced by a girl and her frustrated mother, this book weaves darkly enchanted frame stories into highly illustrative fables. Structured, as they are, in the style of unfolding dialogues, Sufyan's haunting literary technique serves to unveil a story within a storyline. An almost Postmodern strategy, whereby an introductory, or main narrative, is presented (at least in part), for the sole purpose of sharing uncomfortable anecdotes. As such, critics have observed that empha-sized secondary yarns allow readers to find themselves - so to speak - stepping from one theme into another - while simultaneously being carried into ever-smaller plots. Certainly, as adventures take place be-tween named and memorable characters, each exchange is saturated with wit, practical jokes, and life lessons contributing to an overall Central Asian literary mosaic. All in all, this tiny volume is both a de-light and a warning to its admirers.

LANGUAGES ENG
PAPERBACK
ISBN: **978-1-910886-23-6**
RRP: **£12.50**

My Homeland, Oh My Crimea
by Lenifer Mambetova
(2015)

Mambetova's delightful poems, exploring the hopes and fates of Crimean Tartars, are a timely and evocative reminder of how deep a people's roots can be, but also how adaptable and embracing foreigners can be of their adopted country, its people and its traditions.

LANGUAGES ENG / RUS
HARDBACK
ISBN: **978-1-910886-04-5**

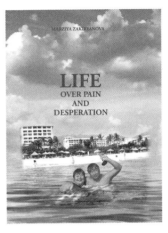

Life over pain and desperation
by Marziya Zakiryanova (2014)

This book was written by someone on the fringe of death. Her life had been split in two: before and after the first day of August 1991 when she, a mother of two small children and full of hopes and plans for the future, became disabled in a single twist of fate. Narrating her tale of self-conquest, the author speaks about how she managed to hold her family together, win the respect and recognition of people around her and above all, protect the fragile concept of 'love' from fortune's cruel turns. By the time the book was submitted to print, Marziya Zakiryanova had passed away. She died after making the last correction to her script. We bid farewell to this remarkable and powerfully creative woman.

HARD BACK
ISBN: **978-0-99278733-2**
RRP: **£14.95**
AVAILABLE ON **KINDLE**

Chants of Dark Fire
(Песни темного огня)
by Zhulduz Baizakova
Russian edition (2012)

This contemporary work of poetry contains the deep and inspirational rhythms of the ancient Steppe. It combines the nomad, modern, postmodern influences in Kazakhstani culture in the early 21st century, and reveals the hidden depths of contrasts, darkness, and longing for light that breathes both ice and fire to inspire a rich form of poetry worthy of reading and contemplating. It is also distinguished by the uniqueness of its style and substance. Simply sublime, it has to be read and felt for real.

ISBN: 978-0957480711
RRP: £10.00

SERAGLIO'55
**Georgy Pryakhin
(2016)**

This is a wonderful publication, full of Georgy Pryakhin's personal recollections of a lifetime spent not only as one of the most revered Russian writers but as a political supremo in the inner circle of the Gorbachev government during the last years of the USSR. It will enchant readers with a thirst to learn more of the inner workings of those who lived through the USSR, Glasnost and Perestroika. Pryakhin's vivid recollections of real events, idealistic dreams and his way of seeing life, tell stories that go much deeper than the words printed on the page. Born in 1947 to mixed Uzbek and Russian parents exiled and killed by Stalin's brutal regime, he grew up in a Stalin orphanage to see the very worst of life in Russia and its internal conflicts, which moulded his desire to tell the world through his writing about what he had seen, heard and felt, which he later translated into how he could help others through working in politics to change the life of Russians for the better, forever. Pryakhin's stories, told in the present tense, give the reader every feeling of what it was like to be there at this most important of times in Russia's recent history and are a rare insight into the workings and machinations of life at the top during colossal societal changes. I am delighted to be able to introduce and recommend this worthy publication

LANGUAGES ENG
PAPERBACK
ISBN: 978-1-910886-28-1
RRP: £14.50

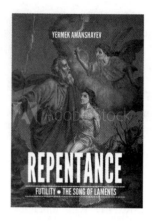

REPENTANCE
Yermek Amanshaev
(2016)

One of the rare stories you would wish never end. A story which mirrors reality and makes us question social cause and effect, and shows the small differences and the small similarities between people today.

Johan Alstad, writer, Norway

I highly recommend "Repentance". From the beginning I was hooked wanting to know what was this book was about. The authors take you on a journey of discovery. At first glance it appears to be about a father wanting to find his grown up son after years of neglect on his part. It turns out to be a realization that we are all accountable for our actions. I found myself questioning my life, not that it is in anyway the same as this father. The story is gripping, entertaining and thought provoking. A brilliant read.

Alan Cox, Radio broadcaster, United Kingdom

LANGUAGES ENG
PAPERBACK
ISBN: 978-1-910886-33-5
RRP:£14.50